BLOOD REVENGE

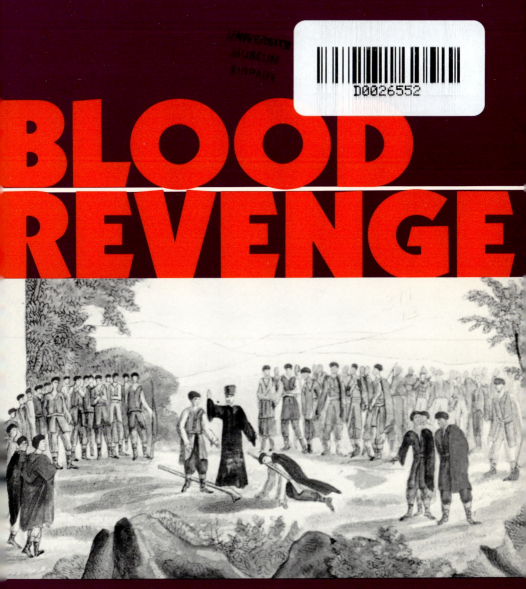

THE ENACTMENT AND MANAGEMENT OF CONFLICT IN MONTENEGRO AND OTHER TRIBAL SOCIETIES

CHRISTOPHER BOEHM

BLOOD REVENGE

THE UNIVERSITY OF PENNSYLVANIA PRESS

Publications in Ethnohistory

A series edited by
ANTHONY F. C. WALLACE AND LEE V. CASSANELLI

LEE V. CASSANELLI, *The Shaping of Somali Society: Reconstructing the History of a Pastoral People, 1600–1900*

LAWRENCE J. TAYLOR, *Dutchmen on the Bay: The Ethnohistory of a Contractual Community*

DEREK NURSE AND THOMAS SPEAR, *The Swahili: Reconstructing the History and Language of an African Society, 800–1500*

JAMES MCCANN, *From Poverty to Famine in Northeast Ethiopia: A Rural History, 1900–1935*

CHRISTOPHER BOEHM, *Blood Revenge: The Enactment and Management of Conflict in Montenegro and Other Tribal Societies*

Blood Revenge

The Enactment and Management of Conflict in Montenegro and Other Tribal Societies

Christopher Boehm

upp

UNIVERSITY OF PENNSYLVANIA PRESS

First published by the University Press of Kansas in 1984. Second paperback edition, with an expanded Preface, published by the University of Pennsylvania Press in 1987.

Library of Congress Cataloging-in-Publication Data

Boehm, Christopher.
  Blood revenge.

  (The University of Pennsylvania Press publications
  in ethnohistory)
  Reprint. Originally published: Lawrence, Kan. : Uni-
  versity Press of Kansas, c1984.
  Bibliography: p.
  Includes index.
  1. Montenegro—Social life and customs. 2. Vendetta.
I. Title. II. Series.
DR1822.B63 1987   949.7′45   86-24904
ISBN 0-8122-1241-X (pbk.)

Printed in the United States of America

TO

MOTHER AND DWIGHT

Contents

List of Illustrations and Maps

Preface

When travelers from well-regulated complex societies journey to tribal areas and encounter the indigenous custom of vengeance killing, they are inclined to interpret the feuds that they observe as murder running rampant throughout the society. That is, the level of strife strikes them as being anarchic compared to what they are accustomed to at home. This was the case with most of the Europeans who traveled to observe and write about the politically autonomous Montenegrin tribesmen who, during the eighteenth and nineteenth centuries, lived near the Adriatic Sea and remained unsubjugated by the mighty Ottoman Turkish Empire that all but surrounded them. By contrast, more-careful observers who learn to interpret tribal behavior in the light of indigenous beliefs usually portray feuding more accurately, as a customary social activity of great violence but as one that involves, nevertheless, the careful following of culturally prescribed rules.

In writing about the feuding of these nineteenth-century Balkan warriors, I shall carry the analysis farther. I shall emphasize that Montenegrins did not merely act out their own cultural tradition by obediently following cultural rules for revenge killing; rather, they understood their own feuding behavior quite well, from certain perspectives that were very important to them. They seem to have put such understandings to good use, and by their own standards, at least, they usually were able to keep the vicious feuds in their midst reasonably well under control. In my interpretation of their behavior, I shall emphasize that this was not simply a case of having a political system automatically find an equilibrium point; rather, the equilibrium that prevailed within and between the tribes was, to a significant degree, the result of carefully calculated actions on the parts of the tribesmen and their leaders. Some anthropologists might disagree with this emphasis, but a detailed analysis of feuding in Montenegro will demonstrate that nonliterate people at times can be active and astute as social engineers who understand some of the larger workings of their own social systems.

This book employs techniques of ethnohistory, commonly used by anthropologists, to reconstruct not only the feuding behavior of traditional Montenegrin tribesmen but also the wider social milieu in which blood feuds took place. Given the emphasis that I have placed upon psychological variables in explaining the feud, I believe that the limited nature of historical accounts by visitors to Montenegro and of preserved archival documents could have presented a serious disadvantage. But fortunately I have been able to combine information from both the present and the past in order to portray as accurately as possible the values and beliefs of Montenegrins who lived more than one hundred and fifty years ago.

My own knowledge of contemporary Montenegro is based on a three years' stay in Yugoslavia, extending from the summer of 1963 to the summer of 1966, most of which was spent living in one Montenegrin tribe. In writing this book I have relied upon this personal experience and upon data collected from people living today in order to interpret a traditional period that in some ways is strikingly different from the present but in other ways is extremely similar. Because this information from the present has been important for interpreting the past, I shall give an introductory account of my fieldwork among the Montenegrins and introduce the reader to their present-day perspective on feuding; then I shall turn to the fully tribal period before 1851, which is the direct concern of the book.

After the introduction to today's tribal Montenegrins and my stay among them, a short background chapter will explain how the Montenegrins obtained a living from their rugged mountain environment and will portray their social, political, and military life. This will make it easier to understand the Montenegrin blood feud as an expression of the tribesmen's noblest concepts of ethics and honor, which became manifest through deeds that we ourselves might view as cold-blooded murder conducted in a cowardly fashion.

The book then turns to the details of feuding, since this activity was rich in its cultural manifestations and took a number of shapes. For example, some feuds were very brief, while others continued for as long as a century. Some feuds were limited to just one or two killings, while others cost scores of lives, sometimes in just a few years. Feuds never occurred within a clan, but bloody conflicts sometimes did take place between two clans that had lived in the same tribe as good neighbors. And if two feuding clans were situated in different tribes, the killing back and forth occasionally would escalate to include all the clans of both tribes, involving thousands of people as potential targets.

To provide a broader perspective, in the final chapters the feuds of Montenegrins are compared closely with feuding in several other societies, including the Bedouin Arabs of the Middle East, whose feuds were studied by Peters. There I shall explain why it is that feuding societies all over the world seem to survive very well socially and biologically in spite of the disruption that feuding brings. This analysis will prove useful in trying to understand what it is in human nature that makes feuding possible, how such a curious way of life may have originated, how feuding systems are maintained over many centuries without destroying themselves, and why it is that feuding societies are able to compete effectively with more-tranquil social groups that are never torn apart by homicidal violence in their own midst.

I should emphasize that in addition to writing a historical ethnographic description of feuding in traditional Montenegro, I have also provided a general model of the feud and have tentatively tested this model against data from societies outside the Mediterranean area. However, while certain chapters are addressed directly to professional anthropologists interested in the feud, the entire book is written to be easily comprehensible to beginning students and to scholars from other fields who have never studied anthropology. It is my sincere hope that by avoiding needless jargon and by trying to make clear the anthropological techniques and concepts that I have employed, I shall succeed in serving all of these audiences.

This book was written originally as an ethnography to be used in introductory courses in anthropology, and as such was written in as engaging a manner as possible. In that endeavor, Drs. L. L. Langness and Robert B. Edgerton provided excellent literary advice as co-editors of the now defunct Mayfield Series, advice for which I remain deeply appreciative. Subsequently, on the way to publication with the University Press of Kansas, the manuscript has profited from readings by my son, Michael Boehm, James A. Clifton, Arnold Green, Keith Otterbein, Edward Shorter, and Andrei Simić, and in the process has been made into not only a descriptive work but one with some formal theory as well. Others who have commented stylistically on the manuscript include my daughter, Jennifer Boehm, and my mother, the late Verna Boehm, along with my good friend Nancy Jordan. In addition, Milovan Djilas, whose personal autobiography figures prominently in this work, took the time to read and comment upon the original manuscript. To all of these readers I am very grateful, even though sometimes I have failed to implement their suggestions.

For assistance in preparing the manuscript I am indebted to Mary Ann Maggard, Brenda Nix, and Carolyn Scheben, while photographic assistance was given by Joseph Ruh and Christina Link. I also wish to express to the editorial staff at the University Press of Kansas my appreciation of the excellent support they provide to their authors.

In addition, I must express gratitude to the Ford Foundation and to the National Institute of Mental Health, which funded my doctoral field research; to Northwestern University, which funded a summer's research in Yugoslavia during which I investigated archival sources for ethnohistory; to Northern Kentucky University, which funded a library research project on feuding; and to the H. F. Guggenheim Foundation, which funded the recent research project on egalitarian politics that enabled me to add a theoretical chapter on ethological aspects of feuding.

The Guggenheim grant and a 1984 conference on Ostracism funded by the Gruter Foundation enabled me to conduct some further research on feuding, the results of which have been published elsewhere since 1983, when the present work was written. These two articles deal with a pattern found in Montenegro and in many other feuding societies, by which a clan member, whose aggressive behavior reaches a point that is indigenously defined as being reckless, can be stripped of clan membership. The clan acts collectively as a group that otherwise would be liable for his behavior and, in effect, ostracizes him. Once this formal decision has been reached, his clansmen will no longer retaliate if he is killed, so he loses their protection. In Montenegro and in a few other tribal societies, sometimes his clan brothers themselves put him to death. One obvious implication of such formal use of coercive force within the community is that nonliterate people such as the tribal Montenegrins may well have invented the Law, as it currently is defined by many scholars.

The first article, entitled "Execution Within the Clan as an Extreme Form of Ostracism," provides the ethnographic details. It was published in *Social Science Information* in 1985. The second, entitled "Clan Execution in Montenegro: Implications for Social Control, Biology, and Law," was published in *Ethology and Sociobiology* in 1986. It compares the Montenegrin pattern with that of other tribal societies, explores clan execution as a protolegal form of behavior, and examines the long-term demographic consequences of clan execution. Because the two articles are readily available, these more recent analyses have not been incorporated into this new edition of *Blood Revenge*.

Note on the Serbo-Croatian Language

The predominant language of today's Yugoslavia is Serbo-Croatian, one of several South Slavic tongues. The Montenegrins speak the *ijekavski* dialect and out in the country usually refer to it as Serbian, a usage that I have often followed in this book. When giving the Serbo-Croatian form of a noun that appears in English in the text, that word appears in parentheses in the nominative case singular. Otherwise, Serbo-Croatian words that appear in the text are kept in the nominative singular but are pluralized as though they were English words, to avoid confusion.

PRONUNCIATION

Written Serbo-Croatian is based on an alphabet that is all but phonemic. For most letters, the logical English phonetic equivalents will work, with these exceptions:

r   may serve as a vowel (trilled)
h   *ch* as in German *"ach!"* but softer
c   *ts* as in "cats"
č   *ch* as in "chop"
ć   *ch* as in "which," only softer (retroflexed)
š   *sh* as in "shop"
ž   *z* as in "azure"
j   *y* as in "young"
dj   *j* as in "Jim," only softer
dž   *j* as in "Jim," only harder

The accent is normally on the first syllable of a word in Serbo-Croatian.

Glossary

barjak: battle flag
baša: a woman who dressed like a man and bore arms
bijeli obraz: honor; literally, white cheek
bitka: battle
Bog: God
brastvo/bratstvo: clan
brat: brother
čast: honor
četa: raid; raiding party
četovanje: raiding
čibuk: a long pipe
čojstvo: manly virtue
crni obraz: dishonor; literally, black cheek
crno vino: red wine
dobar glas: a good reputation; literally, a good voice
dobri ljudi: judges; literally, good men
dužan krvi: to owe blood
dvoboj: a duel
gazda: landlord
glas: voice
gusle: a bowed stringed instrument
gužva: turmoil; a mixup
ijekavski: a dialect spoken in Montenegro
junak: good warrior; hero
junaštvo: bravery
kajanje: the way one feels for committing a deed that afterwards one wishes one
hadn't committed

kaludjer: monk
katun: mountain habitation
kmet: judge; good man
knez: political leader of a village or clan
kolo: a dance
kopiljan: bastard child
krv: blood
krvna osveta: blood revenge
krvnik: blood-revenge enemy
krvni umir: pacification of blood revenge
kuća: house
kukavica: coward
kuluk: blood-feud court set up by Vladika Petar
kumstvo: godfatherhood
kurva: slut
lijen: lazy
loš glas: a bad reputation; literally, bad voice
lukav: shrewd
lupeštvo: stealing
mek: mild
miriti krvi: to pacify the blood
moba: a group that helps a neighbor with his work
obraz: honor; literally, the cheek on one's face
odličen: ostracized
okideni nos: dishonor; literally, cut-off nose
oro: eagle
osvetnik: vengeance taker
platiti krvi: to pay blood money
pleme: tribe
pobratimstvo: blood brotherhood
pop: an illiterate lay priest
prebačeno mjesto: out-of-the-way place
prijateljstvo: the in-law relationship
radna: hard-working (f.)
rakija: plum brandy
rat: war; mobilization of tribal armies
ratovanje: warfare
riječi: words; angry words
rječnik: dictionary
selo zna: the village knows
sentencija: sentence
skup: a large gathering of people
slava: feast of patron saint
sloboda: political autonomy
sloga: social harmony

sramota: shame
starješina: household head
streljenje: execution
struka: blanket carried by warriors
sud: court
sud dobrih ljude: court of good men
svadja: quarrel
svadjalica: quarreler
ubistvo: killing; murder
u krvi: engaged in a feud; literally, in blood
umir: pacification
veselje: a happy social gathering
vjera: truce
vještica: witch
vladika: bishop
vojvoda: tribal chieftain
zakrvljeni: engaged in a feud; literally, in blood
zbog krvi: because of feuding; literally, because of blood

BLOOD REVENGE

Map 1　　Modern Yugoslavia and Its Federal Republics

1

Introduction

During the early 1960s I set off for the field as a graduate student in cultural anthropology, to spend three years of my life with a group of people who for many centuries lived in what anthropologists technically refer to as a tribe. When the Western world discovered the tribal Montenegrins two centuries ago, these giant warriors lived in large territorial groups, regulated their own political affairs, and were organized to fight fiercely and effectively to defend their tribal lands. The tribesmen spent much of their energy in warfare, headhunting, and raiding against external enemies; but they also carried on vicious blood feuds among themselves in which the males of one clan had free license to kill any male in an enemy clan, and vice versa. In short, the Montenegrins were warrior tribesmen of a type to be found all over the world.

Had the destination been South America, New Guinea, or Africa, my intention to live in a tribe would hardly have been surprising. But I was planning to go to Europe. It is well known that many centuries ago, Europe's original peoples lost their political freedom and their tribal identities as well, either to the conquering Romans or when they were incorporated into the various feudal systems which arose in the Middle Ages. Today that portion of the world is well known for its modern peasants, many of whom continue to farm in traditional ways; but peasants live in nations, not in tribes. The question necessarily arises: How could a locally autonomous tribal people possibly have survived in Europe throughout all those centuries?

3

Map 2   Montenegro in the Balkans

I chose to study the Montenegrins of Yugoslavia (see map 1) precisely because of their persistence as a tribal people who for a long time had managed to live quite independently of the nation states and empires that surrounded them. Along with fierce neighbors living in the northern mountains of Albania, the Slavic-speaking Montenegrins are among the few "tribal" peoples surviving today in Europe. The reason these Balkan segmentary tribes still exist is partly due to their geography, which locks them into isolated mountain valleys. This holds a tribe together in modern times, even though it is no longer completely self-governing and of course no longer fights its own wars to defend its territory.

Today the Montenegrins are no longer politically independent, but in their own minds the tribesmen still feel strongly the presence of their tribal social life and tribal identity. This deep ethnic self-awareness continues through an intense appreciation of the local history each tribe possesses and of the common history proudly shared by all the tribes. In addition the tribes today still have important economic functions, in that some of them continue to dispose of their own communal pasture lands.

The peninsula that these tribes inhabit (see map 2) lay for over four hundred years within a mighty Islamic empire, that of the Ottoman Turks. During the late fifteenth century, other Balkan Slavic Christian peoples submitted quickly to the warlike and politically well organized Turks. These people watched their own tribal or feudal systems disappear. But the tribesmen in Montenegro had already resisted the domination of their own Christian brothers, the feudal Serbs, throughout the Middle Ages. Being in the habit of fighting for their local autonomy, they never fully submitted to the Islamic Turkish conquerors, and after the end of the sixteenth century they began to intensify their resistance to the point of occasionally engaging in armed rebellion.

The keys to this stubborn independence were the very effective tribal military and political organization and a code of values that placed merit upon maintaining the honor of a true warrior. This code also focused strongly on the notion of political equality for every man in the tribe and on political autonomy for the tribe itself. With these assets, the warlike Montenegrins were able to hang on to much of their basic autonomy for a number of centuries. In the mid 1800s they amazed the Western world by forming a free Christian nation-state right in the midst of a powerful Moslem empire which, in earlier times, had actually threatened to conquer Christian Europe.

While studying up on Yugoslavia in preparation for my fieldwork, I took a special interest in the Montenegrin tribesmen as I read the accounts of western Europeans who had "discovered" Montenegro

An old man threshes wheat in the tribe of Gornja Morača. Behind him is the valley of the Morača River while the highway lies out of sight behind the mountains. In the foreground, the author's son examines kernels of wheat that have fallen to the ground as wind blows the chaff away.

between 1750 and 1840, before the tribal state was formed. These travelers (or spies) tended to romanticize the tribesmen as wild and woolly Christian crusaders fighting against Islam; but as amateur ethnographers, some of them did quite a good job of documenting the Montenegrin way of life before it was changed radically by the formation of a state.

The tribe in which I settled was a far cry from the fully autonomous tribes of the old days. It was more like the semi-independent tribes that continued to exist in the tiny Montenegrin kingdom that persisted from 1851 to 1914, before the multi-ethnic nation of Yugoslavia began to form. As part of a modern Socialist nation, my chosen tribe had no right to make its own laws and govern itself, and many other things had changed as well. As one might imagine, headhunting had ceased long ago, well before World War I, although a few isolated incidents were reported then. Still earlier, blood feuding and raiding had been curtailed

Another threshing scene. In the background below lies the valley of the Morača River. On top of the mountains, most of the tribesmen are still pasturing their sheep for the summer.

by the rather sudden formation of a Montenegrin tribal state in 1851. But in spite of these radical changes, the tribe of Upper Morača, in which I lived from 1964 to 1966, still existed strongly in the minds of its members. As an isolated territorial and social unit that had a strong ethnic identity, Upper Morača was always referred to as a tribe (*pleme* in the Serbian language) by its members, who still communally owned and regulated forests and certain summer pasture lands that belonged to the pleme. Furthermore, there were times when the entire tribe gathered for an important event, either to attend a funeral or to celebrate a religious or national holiday by singing, dancing, joyously firing off pistols into the air, and drinking plum brandy in large, cordial social groups. At these times, as an honored foreign guest, I was able to sense the presence of tribal unity very directly.

In 1964 the isolated tribe of Upper Morača was still four and a half hours by foot or horseback from the nearest road. I had to reach Morača by following a sometimes very narrow trail, which curved back and forth along one side of a canyon and which enabled me, in places, to look straight down over the edge of a sheer precipice at the intensely blue-green waters of the Morača River as they rushed below me. As I approached the tribal territory, the canyon widened into a rugged mountain valley, and along the steep sides of the valley lay the seven or eight scattered settlements that made up Upper Morača. The particular tribe I selected was too isolated to justify the spending of scarce governmental money for public utilities, so there was still no electricity, running water, or plumbing. But there were already a small general store, a post office, an administrative office, and a beautiful modern school; and a road was being constructed (very slowly) up the canyon. At that time, the several thousand members of Upper Morača Tribe were surely the most isolated large group of people in Montenegro, and probably in Yugoslavia.

In spite of the absence of modern technological improvements, the men and women of Upper Morača lived quite well, partly from small gardens but mainly from the livestock they herded. In addition, they still produced their own woolen bedding, some of their clothes, and most of their tools. In many ways, in spite of the large modern school building which sat in the tribal center at the bottom of the valley, taking this long walk along the edge of the steep Morača Canyon enabled me to enter a world very different from that of modern Socialist Yugoslavia and Europe. For over two years, I joined the people of Upper Morača in this very unmodern European setting. I was viewed by them as an oddity, visiting from a faraway country that was rich enough (and, some thought, foolish enough) to pay someone just to live with them and write down their customs.

In going to live with the Montenegrins in one of their stone houses built on a mountainside with a cattle stall underneath, my interest was focused equally upon their old tribal ways and upon their present style of life, which was peaceful. As a cultural "antiquarian," I was particularly fascinated to discover that there were still a number of men in the tribe who played the mournful, Middle-Eastern-sounding instrument called the *gusle*.[1] This was used for accompaniment as they improvised or recited from memory long and vivid heroic epics about their own local tribal heroes. They also sang about the Eastern Orthodox Serbian ethnic group to which Montenegrins belong and which speaks the same Slavic language.

Because I had decided to study Montenegrin ethics, I paid close attention to the manner in which the tribesmen and women behaved, to the arguments that they employed to justify their actions, and to the

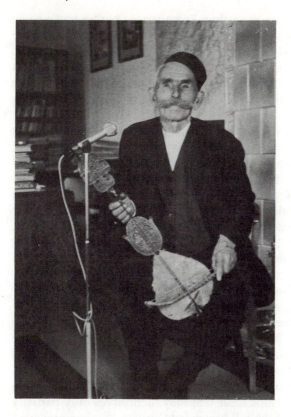

This old tribesman, wearing the traditional Montenegrin cap and long mustache, came into the Ethnographic Museum in Cetinje, historical capital of Montenegro, to record a heroic-epic song that he composed extemporaneously. In Upper Morača tribe, gifted singers like Radoš Baošić, Periša Krušić, and Gavrilo Todorović carried on this same tradition brilliantly, playing more simply fashioned versions of the gusle, a single-stringed bowed instrument that is used to accompany the voice of the singer.

gossip through which they evaluated one another's "morals." My particular research interest was in explaining the effects that many centuries of continual warfare and feuding had had on their moral viewpoint. When I finally tore myself away from my adoptive tribe and came home to complete a doctoral thesis at Harvard University after three years in Montenegro, I wrote mainly about the contemporary tribesmen I had lived with, their current and past views of moral life in their tribe, and my own perception of their moral system.

However, after my stay in Upper Morača the same image of an earlier, fully tribal Montenegro, which I had taken to the field with me, lived on even more intensely in my imagination. The original picture provided by visiting Austrians, Frenchmen, Serbs, Russians, Englishmen, and later a spirited Englishwoman named Mary Edith Durham became more vivid in my own mind because, in many ways, the Montenegrins I stayed with still lived very much in that same past. They talked about it constantly, because they knew it was heroic and unique and because their life was still quite isolated from that of modern Yugoslavia. I became caught up in that history as I listened to their heroic epic poems and to their endless stories of heroes, of battles against seemingly hopeless odds, of brilliant sheep-stealing and headhunting expeditions, and of a world in which, as they told me repeatedly, honor counted for everything.

Yet, there was one behavior that fascinated me more than anything else in the written acounts of the earlier, fully tribal Montenegrin way of life. This was mentioned so rarely that I sometimes thought the topic was being avoided deliberately by a people who normally loved to talk about the past. The topic was blood feud, a part of Montenegrin life that I had experienced great difficulty in understanding when I had read the historical accounts of Montenegrin life in 1851. From travelers' reports, it seemed as though the traditional Montenegrins were doing almost nothing else but sneaking up on one another and firing from ambush. But my training as a cultural anthropologist made it difficult to imagine any kind of normal life functions going on if such a pervasive and uncontrolled level of disruption and disorganization really prevailed.

Once I was out in the field, no one seemed to be able to explain feuding to me very well in its finer details. The notion of killing for revenge was still very prominent in the minds of the Montenegrins I lived with, and people who knew tribal oral history sometimes did mention feuds. But on the rare occasions when I could get a lively conversation going on this subject, it became clear that they themselves only partially understood all the details of the full blood-feud system that had prevailed until 1851, when the formation of a state suddenly curtailed the practice of feuding.

This book is the result of a determination to satisfy my own curiosity by conducting research on Montenegrin blood feuds as they flourished before a state was formed in this tribal refuge area. In deciding to become an ethnohistorian, I have been fortunate in having had access to some of the best historical materials that exist anywhere for a nonliterate tribal group. Most of the world's tribal peoples have been studied anthropologically some time after they had been pacified by the more ''advanced'' nations that arrived to conquer or control them and that then chose to sponsor the study of their customs, even as these were being severely disturbed. In the case of the Montenegrins, however, Europeans making brief visits as guests or political envoys had already been describing the tribesmen for nearly a century before the independent tribes finally lost their full political autonomy to one of their own leaders and their way of life began to change radically. Thus, these foreign visitors actually observed the warrior way of life in full swing, complete with meetings of entire tribes to make their political decisions, frequent raiding at short and long distance, occasional desperate warfare, head-hunting, and continual blood feuding. Because no one of these accounts approaches being complete, I have synthesized them all into a general ethnohistory (Boehm 1983), a historical re-creation of the entire life of a nonliterate people. The present book treats only the blood feud in traditional Montenegro and such other information as is needed in order to understand feuding.

The first mission of this book is to explain how the Montenegrins were able to engage constantly in lethal feuds between clans and even between tribes and at the same time were able to maintain a moral order that allowed people to do the normal things necessary to subsist and to live together socially. I shall also explain how the Montenegrins, in spite of their divisive feuds, were able to stay well enough unified politically so that they could resist the constant menace of domination from the outside. Most often, this came from an alien and powerful Turkish enemy, a mighty empire that repeatedly attempted to wipe out this small tribal trouble spot through truly genocidal attacks. I am very happy to say that the Montenegrins always survived, in spite of several very close calls along the way.

The main purpose of this book is simply to explain how the Montenegrins' blood feuds work. But as an ethnographer who has come to know Montenegrin culture very well, I also feel it is incumbent upon me to assist the reader in understanding sympathetically a way of life that is by its nature very foreign. Details of feuding will be shocking to any American other than someone in a violent street gang or perhaps a member of the Mafia. Even a member of one of those violent organizations might find it difficult to understand how it can be perfectly ''right,'' from a moral standpoint, to kill a young male fourteen to fifteen years of age simply because one wishes to avenge a member of one's own clan who was killed years ago by some member of the clan to which the youth belonged. I shall not attempt to convince the reader that this is right by our own standards, since obviously it is not. But I shall try to show how, under certain circumstances, such an act may be entirely logical and morally acceptable in the Montenegrin way of looking at things. An important second mission of the book, then, is to lead the reader through an exotic and alien moral world in such a way that his own values are set aside as much as possible and a very different way of life is appreciated on its own terms.

I shall not do this simply by preaching the doctrine of ''cultural relativism'' or ''cultural appreciation,'' but rather by involving the reader vicariously in the moral and practical decisions made by traditional Montenegrins with respect to feuding. In particular, we shall focus upon the rather difficult decisions that in a warrior society confront men, and sometimes women as well, as they enter into the inevitable quarrels that such a society breeds. We shall follow these people as they navigate the perilous course of their interpersonal conflicts and make their decisions along the way. By examining the alternatives that they perceive and by looking at criteria that they apply to making these risky choices, we will gain a full appreciation for their lives and values.

2

Doing Research on European Tribesmen

Cultural anthropologists, working in the field, must combine the art of living out a high adventure with the sober task of making a valid scientific description, under circumstances that at best are usually trying. Acquiring the understandings that are necessary in order to describe an exotic culture is necessarily difficult: it takes a long time and a great variety of experience before an adult can learn the culture of a foreign society. The more exotic the culture under study, and the newer it is to the anthropologist, the greater an investment is required in the form of participation in the activities of everyday life.

As every anthropologist knows, this protracted and intense experience is what makes anthropological fieldwork a profound personal adventure. In my own case, my first major field study was conducted on an isolated mountain tribe named Gornja Morača (Upper Morača) in the Republic of Montenegro, Yugoslavia. The topic I chose to explore in my doctoral dissertation was the moral beliefs and moral behavior of the tribesmen there.

LEARNING A NEW CULTURE

One learns one's own culture at a tender age, when cultural rules and beliefs are internalized so thoroughly and unconsciously that they become like a second nature. As an adult, socialization to a new culture can never again be so rapid, so thorough, or so unselfconscious. An anthropologist may learn a new language well and may learn the beliefs and rules of an exotic culture adeptly, so that he or she understands how to behave under most circumstances. But there will always be major points that are misinterpreted and important nuances that are missed. In particular, there will be ways of feeling that can never be fully understood, because the anthropologist is too well formed as an adult to learn culturally patterned emotions in the same way that a native, who has been born and raised in that culture, does. This means that the adventure of being an anthropologist in the field can be a lonely one; indeed, as an anthropologist, one always remains something of an outsider. But the field experience is also exciting and fulfilling, because one is continually learning and growing in one's competency as a sort of cultural apprentice.

In the development of my own career as a cultural "participant," I remember certain high points very well. The more-obvious break-throughs were advances in my ability to speak the Serbian language,[1] since these usually came on quite suddenly, after long, discouraging plateaus. But I was affected more profoundly by the series of doors that opened as I became better accepted as a special member of the tribal community that I lived in. Progressively, these opening doors enabled me to approach a thorough understanding of Montenegrin culture, and one of them, which I shall relate presently, provided me with insights that were important to my interpretation of blood feuding as this had been practiced more than a century before.

Let me begin, however, with a different example. After fourteen months in the field, an important door opened for me. I had made many unseccessful attempts to find out how much survived of the earlier strong beliefs in witches *(vještica)*. I remember vividly the night that a very old lady finally told me how things really were. A good friend of mine, she was bedridden; and I had offered to spend the night taking care of her while her family was away. After the kerosene lantern was put out to conserve fuel, we talked late into the night. Suddenly, without my even asking, she began to tell me about all the people in the settlement who were suspected of eating the souls of children in their own clans. I was astonished to realize that if I had left Upper Morača the day before, after more than a year's residence, I might have made the statement in print, as a behavioral scientist, that earlier reports concerning the widespread existence of beliefs in witchcraft in Montenegro no longer applied at all. For many people in the tribe, that statement would have been highly incorrect.

When that door opened to me, it was opened in terms of trust. Suspected witches were spoken of only to someone whom a Montenegrin fully trusted to realize that such conversations must never be quoted to other people. This was because people in Upper Morača were prone to conflict, and as they themselves put it, "words" *(riječi)* were usually the source of such trouble. That was why they were extremely cautious in deciding what to say and to whom. Thus, even good friends who trusted my intentions toward them personally sometimes would not take a chance on a foreigner's incomplete understanding, when it came to the danger of gossiping about things like suspected witches. Old Milena finally did tell me about them. But she opened up only because she had come to feel that I not only was a trusted friend but also was competent enough in my knowledge of her culture to handle this information with the total discretion that it required.

Another door that opened pertained, not to my acquiring information or gaining cultural understanding through the development of trust, but to how I was able to put actively into practice my growing ability to "be a Montenegrin." In any culture one of the last things a person is able to do, even when approaching fluency in the native language, is to make jokes the way natives do. In Montenegro I deliberately went along very slowly in this respect, even after I had become quite proficient in normal conversation. Very often, Montenegrin joking involves people's moral reputations, and this area is so sensitive that normally aggressive joking sometimes results in serious conflicts between individuals. Having been caught in the middle of one such incident and having obtained detailed notes on similar incidents as a result of my investigations into behavior involving morality, I remained cautious when people joked with me. This caution persisted even after my linguistic ability had become quite good. As the end of my stay in the field approached, I would constantly come up with rapierlike repartees afterwards, in the privacy of my own mind; thus in a sense, I was getting some practice. But I did not dare utter these retorts in public, brilliant as they seemed in my fantasies.

One day I passed the central spring of my settlement, where a large group of women had gathered to enjoy one another's society while they either washed clothes by the spring or worked with the heavy wooden water barrels that they carried home on their backs. A very aggressive middle-aged widow named Milanka taunted me with the predictable joke: Was the American "sneaking around the village," now that his wife had returned to America? Usually, I had simply smiled and said no or maybe as a way of acknowledging this inevitable joke, without attempting the usual aggressive riposte. But in this case I must have sensed that my cultural competency had reached the point that I need not take such a ribbing passively. Scarcely realizing myself what I was up to, I shot back

This spring provides water for everyone living in the scattered settlement of Starče, part of which is visible in the background, with its houses, fields, pastures, and woodlots. This settlement has about one hundred houses and five hundred people in all.

at Milanka: "Yes, indeed, I *am* 'going about the village,' and in fact I don't need to go very far, because there is a beautiful widow who lives just a little way above this spring." As I said this with an entirely serious expression, I pointed down the hill toward the sturdy Milanka's own house. The entire group of women and girls burst into gales of laughter. This merriment was intense, because Milanka was merciless in her unusually aggressive teasing of other people and was of such a violent disposition that most people, men and women alike, tended to absorb her jibes rather than to retaliate. Perhaps their fear was well grounded, since she had once laid open her brother-in-law's back "from the neck to the waist" in the course of a verbal dispute that ended in knife play, or so I had been told.

I was somewhat amazed at myself that I had chosen this particular person as a partner in trying my wings at serious joking Montenegrin style. But in fact, my cultural intuitions were sound. Public opinion was with me, since everyone knew that Milanka always used her jokes very aggressively with everyone and that she enjoyed picking on me in particular. In addition, I myself sensed the rules of the joking game. One should retaliate aggressively enough to be respected, but one should not overdo it and start an unnecessary conflict, which might even become physical. It was doubtful that Milanka would have let her anger get seriously out of control in front of such a large group, but this held only as long as my insult did not greatly exceed hers.

I was aware that Milanka had a pretty good moral reputation aside from her general overaggressiveness, so I felt I could safely joke about her sexual probity. This reckoning was all correct. But Milanka did turn very red in the face when I cast the same slur on her moral reputation as she had cast on mine. For a few moments she was quite angry, visibly very disturbed over losing out in public to a victim who usually behaved rather meekly. Then she managed a smile of sorts, and I sighed with relief.

Afterwards I was congratulated in private by several people, who told me that I had chosen just the right way to return her insult. In Montenegro this means that one has carried the insult close to the point of provoking a violent response without actually doing so. They also suggested, with knowing looks, that it was just as well that there had been a large group of people present. In thinking about the incident later, I was surprised that I had allowed myself to be a participant in this particular aspect of Montenegrin culture, since I knew from careful observation that even native Montenegrins, who of course knew their own culture, had to tread gingerly in this area. After gloating briefly over my newly found competency at being a Montenegrin, I closed that particular door almost as soon as I had opened it, resolving never to play the joking game that hard again.

What I learned, in this vivid personal experience, was that verbal dueling in Montenegro was a very delicate art, an art that in its practice held many dangers. There was danger to one's personal reputation if one responded too weakly, while there was a potential danger to life and limb if one responded too strongly. Both kinds of danger were still to be reckoned with in 1965, but in traditional Montenegro, when blood feuding was in full swing over a century ago, both kinds of danger were far greater. Just this small taste that I had of verbal dueling in 1965 provided me with much-needed insights into the more traditional process.

I have briefly acquainted the reader with my own scientific adventure in tribal Montenegro because the conclusions reached in this book about the earlier tribal period depend rather heavily upon the cultural intuitions that I developed from 1963 to 1966. This active field research continued for nearly three years, with only minor interruptions. Research was resumed for three months in 1975, but at that time I turned from today's tribesmen and their moral behavior to historical reports and archives, in order to understand traditional Montenegrin blood feuds.

This young woman is herding the sheep of her household. Herds range from a dozen or so sheep to over a hundred, depending on how many people there are to herd them and on the availability of winter fodder. In Montenegro, sheep are milked to provide very rich dairy products; their meat is eaten mainly on festive occasions such as weddings.

DECIDING ON A TRIBE TO STUDY

In 1963 I arrived in the historical town of Cetinje, the old capital of Montenegro. First I visited outlying tribal areas in the company of helpful Montenegrin colleagues who worked in the Ethnographic Museum there. Then I spent several months carefully evaluating a number of tribes in order to select one that would be suitable for the research I had in mind. I wished to live in a tribe that had not been very affected by urbanization, since my research was aimed at understanding the traditional moral system that had stemmed from a tribal way of life.

Of course, all present-day Montenegrin tribesmen live under the modern legal system of Yugoslavia when it comes to the payment of taxes and to serious crimes such as homicide or a major theft. But during the 1960s, for many other forms of social deviance, the tribesmen still depended upon less-formal traditional modes of detection or sanctioning. My search was directed toward locating a tribe in which such local traditions still persisted strongly.

Two criteria were used in narrowing down the field of some thirty tribes. First, I knew I would have to find a tribe that had not been very directly affected by the economic and cultural possibilities offered by urban life. Tribes near factory towns were changing radically, with most of the young people moving away to take jobs for wages while the traditional subsistence economy was left to older people. Second, I decided with some regret that the heroic tribes down in Old Montenegro, which had been the earliest to win their full freedom from the Turks,[2] were unsuitable even when isolated from urban influences. This was because goats had been outlawed some years before because of the ecological damage produced by their tendency to overgraze and to destroy young trees. This law depleted the subsistence economy of people living in the karstic limestone mountains near the Adriatic Sea, since they could keep goats so much more easily than sheep. As a result, even when there was no urban influence nearby, only a few of the younger people remained in these tribes.

Once I realized this, I turned my attention to a more mountainous district further to the North called the Brda, or Hill Tribes District, where geographic conditions favored the raising of sheep rather than goats. Since sheep were perfectly legal, the more isolated tribes of the Montenegrin Brda seemed most suitable for my purpose. After spending extended periods of time visiting Rovca tribe, Kuči tribe, and finally Upper Morača tribe, I selected Upper Morača. As a measure of its isolation, until just a year before I arrived, it had taken seven hours by horse to reach the nearest main road or the market town to the north. Isolation was increased because this particular tribe lacked electricity and therefore was relatively cut off from communication with the outside. The people themselves called it a *prebačeno mjesto,* an out-of-the-way place. As a result of the adequate subsistence possibilities and the isolation, making a living from a small herd of livestock continued to attract the younger people, at least the majority who did not move to town to pursue their careers beyond the eighth-grade education offered at the local school. The brand-new highway, four and a half hours away by foot, still did not decrease the isolation very much, although it had made the marketing of surplus products easier.

While Montenegrins living in this isolated valley felt removed from modernizing Yugoslavia all around them, they were keenly aware of the changes that were taking place. Even old grandmothers who had never had a day of schooling understood what I meant when I told them that I was working on my doctorate. And people were aware of world political events, through reading the few newspapers that were delivered by the

My former wife, our two children, and I visited this katun, where we were given lavish hospitality by the lady next to my wife. My daughter, Jenny, faces her mother, while my son, Michael, rides a horse for the first time. The Montenegrins build their cabins in clusters so as to have company. The cool mountaintop provides an excellent environment for processing and storing the dairy products—cheese and salted butter—upon which Montenegrins subsist in the winter.

courier who brought the mail up on horseback twice a week and through the few battery-operated radios that people could afford in those days.

My first contact with a member of this tribe had come by chance earlier on, when I had met a highly accomplished Montenegrin scientist who offered to take me up to the *katun* (mountain habitation) where his mother was herding her sheep for the summer. After an arduous trek up a mountain that had rocks strewn everywhere on its surface, we came to a small settlement of summer cabins. There, people of Upper Morača pastured their sheep on tribally owned lands in order to profit from the excellent high-altitude grass. That evening, in honor of our visit, the old woman slaughtered one of the dozen or so sheep that she kept. When an older neighbor came over to join the feast, he was given the shoulder blade of the sheep, so that he might make predictions from it. After studying the bone and tissue carefully, he announced that he saw much blood, and therefore a big war was coming. Then, with a significant look in my direction, he said that it was the Russians who were going to win the war. He knew, of course, that I was an American.

The prediction was not surprising to me. I knew that in spite of their isolation over the centuries, the Montenegrins always had attended to external politics very carefully. In traditional times they had needed to do this, in order to make the best possible decisions when deliberating as to whether to attack the Turks, resist their taxation, or temporarily submit (see Boehm 1983). More recently, having been through a bitter experience during World War II, when Yugoslavia was divided in a civil war, the tribesmen were continually worried that the United States and Russia might open hostilities and that they would be caught in the middle. Thus, an intense interest in the external political world continued, even though the tribes no longer made their own political decisions as they had done before 1851, when they were completely autonomous.

To emphasize the degree of isolation, I should mention that in 1963 I was told that I was only the third foreigner to have been in Upper Morača in the twenty years since World War II had ended. Some years before my visit, two German alpine hikers, presumably innocent tourists, had wandered into the territory of Upper Morača tribe. Their cameras had promptly been confiscated by concerned tribesmen who had spent four years fighting Germans during the war. I was told that they had suspected these tourists of being spies, scouting the terrain in anticipation of yet another war.

It was because of this isolation that I decided to visit a medium-sized tribe of nearly two thousand people, thinking that I probably would want to settle down there if they would receive me. Having in my hand a piece of paper from the government stating that I had official permission to spend some time in Upper Morača, I first arrived at the tribal center after an unexpected piece of good fortune. Having parked my automobile by the highway, where it was joined by the trail that led up the Morača River canyon, I was about to set off with my rucksack on my back when I suddenly I was greeted by a young woman who was leading a pack horse. She remembered me from my visit to the mountaintop some months before, and she immediately offered to sling my rucksack over the pack saddle on which her horse was carrying provisions from the store located three hours further down the valley. I accepted this hospitality gratefully, and for the next four hours my imperfect conversational ability in Serbo-Croatian received one of its most demanding workouts. Every bend in the trail brought up a new subject. A man had been killed and robbed at one point; somewhere else a man had fallen down the mountainside. No one knew how it had happened, but it might have been "someone from a different tribe." At another point, a soldier on horseback had fallen straight down the cliff to his death. This tribal world seemed to be full of dangers.

Between disaster stories we spent a great deal of time discussing certain people who could handle snakes and relate to them in a friendly way. Montenegro has a great number of poisonous vipers, and one man whom she knew carried them around on his person. He even could whistle to make them come out of the rocks and approach him. We talked on and on, and suddenly four hours and more had passed, and I was presenting myelf to the tribal administrator, a young man named Bajo Juškovic. Like many other Montenegrins, Bajo had a strong, well-chiseled face, and his manner was tough but good-natured. He took me home with him that evening, after I had explained my mission. We sat in the kitchen while his wife brought out cheese, smoked ham, and other Montenegrin delicacies. Bajo, like a true Montengrin host, urged his foreign guest to eat until he could eat no more. The same applied to the plum brandy *(rakija)* that I was urged to "try" over and over again.

This zealous Montenegrin hospitality had unfortunate results. As Bajo's first foreign guest in twenty years or more, I ate and drank beyond my capacity in an effort to show appreciation. It was a more than tipsy ethnographer who was shown to the only bedroom, while members of the host family relegated themselves to the kitchen. I had already learned that Montenegrins judge manhood by severe standards and that a true man does not drink too much. My growing queasiness, therefore, made me more than a little anxious as I contemplated how I would be disgraced. Yet my tortured stomach overcame professional resolve, and an open window was reached just in the nick of time. My trepidation was dispelled in the morning when I awoke to find that barnyard fowls had removed the evidence of wasted Montenegrin hospitality. Thus buoyed by feelings of relief, I began my first day in Upper Morača tribe. A few days later, after visiting other hospitable households, I told Bajo that his tribe seemed ideal for my study. I said that I would like to reside there for a long period of time in order to study the customary way of social life and to make recordings of heroic epics and other songs. I also mentioned that I would like to live in one of the more densely settled areas and that I needed a house if someone might wish to rent one to me.

SETTLING IN UPPER MORAČA TRIBE

It was decided I should live in Starče, the largest settlement, of about a hundred houses and five hundred people, which was spread over a mile of the southern slope of the Morača valley. As for a house, I was to

In 1966, this was the only means of transportation to Upper Morača tribe. My daughter, Jenny, proudly leads one of the pack horses. By 1975, when I returned for a visit, a road that was wide enough for truck traffic had been completed.

share one with my *gazda* (landlord) Radivoje Marković, who was the senior political man in the tribe. Radivoje visited his house only occasionally, since he spent a great deal of time with his only son, who lived in town. But he proved to be an excellent landlord, a good friend, and one of my wisest consultants when I needed to understand something about Montenegrin culture.

A few weeks later my first neighbor, Milisav, sent his horses down to the highway to carry up equipment and household furnishings. This private caravan moved slowly up the trail to the cultural world of Upper Morača tribe, with our two small children, Michael and Jenny, proudly leading two of the pack horses. Since our half of Radivoje's house would be scantly furnished, I brought along two kerosene lanterns, a primus stove and pressure cooker, some plastic cans to carry water from the spring, a folding table for my typewriter, and two tape recorders with batteries. This move was accomplished in the summer, with my wife and

I occupied half of this Montenegrin stone house for two years. The house is typical in construction but is rather large. Limestone rocks, used to build houses, are always easy to find in Montenegro, while crushed limestone is heated in giant kilns to make the mortar used in construction. In the old days, windows were kept very small, and loopholes were built into the walls, so that houses might serve also as fortresses in case of a blood feud or Turkish attacks.

children coming along to stay until the isolation of winter closed in the Morača valley. The caravan of four horses carried, in addition to the equipment mentioned above, camping gear and clothing for four people, a large medicine kit, and some dried foods.

The house itself had thick stone walls, small windows with shutters, floors made of heavy planks, and a fine view of the Morača River valley. Neighbors soon came by to see if they could help us, bringing gifts such as eggs, milk, or cheese; and arrangements were soon made to purchase the necessary daily provisions. My son Michael, aged five and a half, walked straight up the hill every morning with his younger sister, Jenny, to obtain milk from a neighbor who had decided to keep a cow down in the valley over the summer. These expeditions always took a very long time, even though it was only a ten minute walk, because people enjoyed

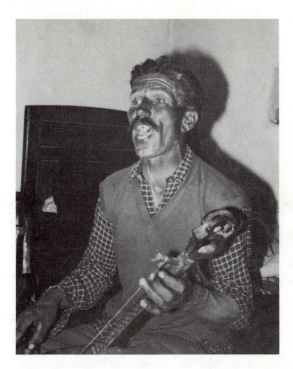

Radoš Baošić, of Upper Morača tribe, improvises a heroic epic. He knew a number of songs about Serbian heroes of old, which he had learned either by listening to other singers or from published collections. The gusle that he is playing is simply carved in the traditional manner, with a goat's head above the peg that provides tension to the horse-hair strings.

speaking with the American children. At the end of six weeks, the word started to go around the settlement: "The American's son now speaks better Serbian than the American himself, even though when they arrived, the American already spoke the language fairly well, and his son didn't know a word." When this rumor reached my ears, I was both delighted and discouraged, since I had studied the Serbo-Croatian language for a year in the United States and for three months in Belgrade when I had first arrived in Yugoslavia. It also brought home to me how difficult it was going to be for me, as an adult, to learn both the language and the culture of these hospitable people as well as I wished to.

My lack of cultural expertise soon presented a problem. Brand new in the community, I was told that I must begin right away to get in my wood supply for the winter. My first neighbor, Milisav, did not have time to take on the job, and he seemed to be reluctant to give me advice as to whom I should approach. Thinking in terms of my own values, I very nobly asked him who was the neediest man in the area. He told me the man's name without any further comment, and this was the person I originally hired to lay in my supply of wood. I expected, of course, to be

Traditional and modern holidays are celebrated in Upper Morača and elsewhere in Montenegro by having the entire tribe take a day off work. All members of the tribe gather at the traditional central meeting place to sing and dance the kolo, to meet with friends, to promenade back and forth, to sit in sociable groups that sing and drink plum brandy, and to have a good time in general. The name for such a meeting is either skup, which means a gathering, or simply veselje, which means a happy event. This one took place in early spring.

praised by all for my altruistic behavior in giving the work to a needy man with a large family. Instead, I found out much later, to my chagrin, that people had been busy criticizing my foolish business sense: the American had gone out of his way to hire a man who would not work even for himself.

Once I had seen my error, I hired instead a young woman who had come by to visit very early and obviously wanted to be friends. She was a rather special kind of person in her own culture, because she took unusual pride in doing heavier kinds of work swiftly and well. Ignorant of this, I hired her simply because we were becoming good friends, and I hoped she would do a good job. But again, I operated in ignorance of how Montenegrins think. The word went around now that the American did indeed have a shrewd head for business. He had hired a woman who liked to prove herself continually as a good worker and would therefore

This summertime skup is just beginning. Any person who is dancing in the large circle, or kolo, can go into the center and cut in on a person of the same sex who is dancing. As in America, this behavior can express either a desire to dance or a special message of preference for that particular partner.

work harder than many men. He had done so because he was *lukav,* which means "cunning" and is often a word of praise in Upper Morača.

In these earliest stages of fieldwork I truly bumbled along. I often defined the social situations that I had to cope with very differently from my neighbors, even though I usually managed to solve the practical problems that arose in spite of my ignorance of their way of thinking. But as time went along, I understood more. Friendly visits with neighbors were supplemented by formal interviews in which I sat down with people who liked to talk and took down notes on what they had to say. I spent one entire day simply writing down all the things that my good friend the woodcutter had to tell me about different kinds of wood and about how they were used in the construction of houses, corrals, fences, tools, and furniture or as a fuel for cooking, heating, distilling plum brandy, making limestone mortar, and so on. In the summer, people were so busy working that most of my early interviews were with people who were too ill or too old to work. Whenever I asked when I would get to hear the singing of heroic epics, I was told that nights were too short in the summer and that there was too much work to do. When winter came,

A man joyously fires an automatic pistol as he dances. This expression of
sociability and personal happiness is difficult for foreigners to understand,
especially because Montenegrins usually have a rather solemn look on their
faces when they fire their guns in the air. After particularly happy weddings,
there are likely to be bullet holes in the ceiling of the room in which the
feast was held; and when a son is born to a family, explosions of dynamite
boom across the Morača valley.

however, the nights would be long, and there would be little else to do
but sit around in the evening and sing.

As winter closed in, I left Morača to put my family on a plane back
to the States. After I returned, I began to participate more fully in the life
of the Upper Moračan tribesmen. I split my own firewood, helped to split
the wood of the neighbors who sometimes fed me, and attended social
gatherings which took place much more frequently in the early winter. I
carefully recorded on tape the efforts of the better heroic epic singers,
particularly those who still improvised their own songs and sometimes
sang local songs that had never been collected by folklorists or had never
been published. My days were spent partly in casual visiting, learning
about the Montenegrin way of thinking about things as this emerged in a
wholly natural setting. But partly they were devoted to conducting
careful, detailed interviews during which I took notes. Every evening I
would light both of my kerosene lanterns in order to have bright light.
Then I would type up these notes, making additions and comments as I
went along. Montenegrin culture was a great puzzle, and I was beginning
to solve some of its more obvious riddles.

These women are singing as they dance the kolo. In the background is
Upper Morača tribe's beautiful new school, the graveyard, and a group of
men and women who are sitting down and taking life easy on this day of
enjoyment.

When spring came, I began to move about with my neighbors, going up
to the mountains for badly needed hay or watching them spread the
manure, saved over the winter, on certain fields before they ploughed. I
noticed that other fields were kept as pasture while the soil reconstituted
itself.

As the days became longer and the work load increased, the gusles
were put away, and evening socials became a winter memory. As a
cultural participant, I helped to hoe potatoes and corn, to repair houses,
and even a few times to herd sheep. Once the sheep had been taken up
onto the mountain in the early summer, I visited a large extended family
there and observed how dairying was done. This was explained to me by
a justice of Montenegro's Supreme Court, who came every summer to
take his vacation up on the mountain, where it was cool. He herded sheep
and worked like everyone else, except when I was there to pester him
with my interminable questions. He was a wise man who explained to me
much more of his traditional culture than the methods of dairying that I
had hiked up the mountain to observe.

As a busy anthropologist, I simultaneously took the picture and recorded the singing of this group of men and women. (The object in the lower left-hand corner is a hand-held microphone.) The flashily dressed person who is ostentatiously firing a pistol is a man who has returned from the city to attend this skup. As a means of augmenting his income, he takes photographs of the tribesmen for a fee. In the background are houses of Dragovića Polje, the centrally located settlement of Upper Morača tribe.

Always one to avoid large social events in my own culture, I contrived to go to all the weddings in the tribe, though I scarcely enjoyed myself because of the need to operate simultaneously the tape recorder and cameras when I was not taking notes. I also attended all of the funerals and the holiday meetings of the entire tribe down by the tribal center. At these events, people who lived many hours apart on different sides of the valley were able to sit down and socialize, drink, and be happy. At the holiday meetings they also sang and fired off their pistols into the air.

This very active life was healthy enough, but I had contracted a severe case of bacillary dysentery during my earlier stay in Cetinje, which had extensive aftereffects. In Upper Morača for weeks on end I would be laid up in bed, gathering strength to go back to work, hoping each time that my stomach would right itself permanently. It was at these low points that I would become lonely for my own culture, where I knew perfectly the meaning of every word. There, without any effort, I could accurately comprehend the meaning of a social situation the instant I

Young unmarried women promenade in their finest clothes. At a skup, rural Montenegrins generally wear their best citified clothes. However, the young woman in the white skirt is wearing a traditional brocaded jacket. Homespun woolen garments are almost never seen at a skup, although some people still prefer them for everyday use because of their warmth and resistance to rain.

encountered it, without having to wonder for hours afterwards whether I really had understood what was going on. At other times, this cultural homesickness would strike when I was healthy and happy, and on a momentary impulse I would pack up my rucksack and set off down the trail that led to the highway, where my Land Rover was parked. Firing up its diesel engine, I would drive rapidly down the wild Morača canyon highway to Titograd, the present capital of Montenegro, and head straight for the Grand Hotel. Sitting with white linen and silver before me, I would order a steak, cooked rare, then finish off the meal with ice cream, topped with frozen whipped cream, for dessert. Once, truly desperate, instead of driving south for half an hour to Titograd I drove north for seven hours to Belgrade. When I arrived, I headed straight for the restaurant in the United States embassy and ordered an ice-cold Coca Cola.

At the end of two years in Upper Morača, I was ready to complete the final phase of my fieldwork. I had assembled a group of several hundred words in the Serbian language, which I felt were highly

This was the main Eastern Orthodox monastery in Cetinje, where the bishop
lived. The monks who also lived here and who served him were the only
literate people in traditional Montenegro. Note the lack of vegetation, which
is typical of Old Montenegro, the area that was most resolute in resisting
Turkish domination. This drawing is based on observations made by
Wilkinson in the 1830s.

important if one wished to understand the tribal conception of social life
and morality. Although my cultural intuitions were becoming fairly
accurate as I began to select these words, I checked my choices with
indigenous consultants and received a great deal of good advice. During
the last month I took one of my tape recorders and gave the other to an
assistant, and we began to record definitions for the list of two hundred
and fifty words. These definitions were obtained from forty members of
my tribe, while the American, for a change, offered his hospitality to
Montenegrin guests. I hosted them with the finest aged American
whiskey that money could buy at the United States embassy's commis-
sary and was told that it was almost as good as the local chokecherry or
plum brandy, which they distilled themselves and drank when it was
between one minute and twelve months old. By the end of the month, we
had recorded the ten thousand definitions that provided the key to my
understanding Montenegrin morality in its more subtle aspects. Along
with voluminous field notes describing moral behavior, these definitions
became the basic data upon which my doctoral dissertation was based.

This is Bishop Rade of Montenegro, whose title was vladika. Vladika Rade Petrović led the tribal confederation, and in the 1840s he tried very hard to form a political state there. He was nearly seven feet tall, and he personally led his tribal army in time of war. He is still one of Yugoslavia's most famous poets. His major work, "Gorski Vijenac," has been translated and published in all of the world's major languages under the pen name of Njegoš.

LATER RESEARCH ON BLOOD FEUD

When I returned to Montenegro nine years later to resume field-work, I visited my adoptive tribe for a short time as a tourist. But by then it had become very difficult to obtain permission to do fieldwork on one's own in Yugoslavia. Instead, I turned to the libraries and delved into the past. In investigating the nature of Montenegrin feuding as it persisted until a century and a quarter ago, I was no longer an ethnographer, strictly speaking, but was an ethnohistorian, an "ethnographer of the past."

As a historical anthropologist interested in the cultural life of nonliterate people rather than that of so-called civilized nations, I had to observe the same rules as regular historians. Sources had to be evaluated

The tower behind the monastery. In traditional warfare, both Montenegrins and
Turks cut off the heads of slain enemies as evidence of heroic accomplishment.
When the Montenegrins, with some Russian naval help, fought and defeated
one of Napoleon's armies nearby at Herceg Novi, this practice had significant
value as a shock tactic that helped to demoralize the French soldiers. But from
the Montenegrin perspective, the practice of capturing heads was strictly a
matter of individual honor, and if a Montenegrin warrior had been severely
wounded, his own blood brother might cut off his head to keep it from falling
into the hands of an infidel.

for authenticity and checked against one another for contradictions. As I
began to examine the documents that related to blood feuding, I very
quickly came to see that my own cultural intuitions were absolutely
critical for this evaluation process. For example, a French colonel who
went to Montenegro as a spy for Napoleon in about 1800 wrote the first
book ever to be written about these tribal warriors (Vialla de Sommières

A warrior tribesman at home in the early nineteenth century. The man's and the women's costumes are ones worn for special occasions, such as being buried. A warrior normally carried a sword and pistols in addition to his musket, and he always carried on his shoulder a long woolen blanket, or struka, similar to the one worn by the woman in the center. This served as his bed and as his tent during warfare. The sandals, fashioned of strips of hide, are still worn today for everyday use. This sketch was made by Sir Gardner Wilkinson, who visited Montenegro in the first half of the nineteenth century.

1820). Because Colonel Vialla de Sommières worked through an interpreter, he misunderstood key terms and thereby misinterpreted native customs in ways that were obvious to me. In fact, he even stated that Montenegrins spoke a Greek language, rather than Slavic! Other visitors were more accurate. For example, there was Sir Gardner Wilkinson, a British historian who visited Montenegro in the 1830s and sized up the tribesmen very well in some respects. However, in a state of ethnocentric shock, he personally tried to persuade the bishop of Montenegro to stop encouraging the tribesmen to take Turkish heads in battle and to desist from proudly displaying these trophies on a tower just behind his main monastery in Cetinje. Had Sir Gardner understood the tribal view of the world better, he might have saved his efforts. But his accounts (Wilkinson 1848) of Montenegrin daily life, raiding parties, and other military forays are far more accurate than those of Colonel Vialla de Sommières.

About the same time, a Serbian folklorist named Vuk Karadžić visited Montenegro. Knowing the language already, Vuk added many Montenegrin local terms to a kind of encyclopedia he was preparing (Karadžić 1935). He recorded heroic epics, and he also wrote a thin

The fortified monastery at Upper Ostrog, in the land of the White-Paul tribe of the Brda. This ancient structure is built into the walls of a cliff, and it contains the bones of one of Montenegro's most famous saints. In one cell there is a spring and a pool in which trout were once kept. With this certain supply of water and food, a handful of warriors could hold out for months, even against a Turkish army, protecting Montenegro's supply of gunpowder, which was stored here.

volume on the culture of the Montenegrins in which he outlined some of the basic rules and procedures of blood feuding. While Vuk did not approve of certain Montenegrin customs, his quick ethnographic portrait, as far as it goes, is accurate and well balanced. Half a century later, an energetic British traveler named Mary Edith Durham came to the Balkans and stayed to write several very informative books on Albania, Montenegro, and Serbia. Though she was never trained as an anthropologist, Miss Durham returned to the Balkans several times and later became a member of the Royal Anthropological Institute in London. She finally published an ethnography (Durham 1928) of the tribal people of Montenegro and Northern Albania, a valuable work which nevertheless bears the touch of a gifted amateur.

In these works it was usually easy for me to sort out the effects of ethnocentric bias, since, like myself, the authors had been members of the educated Western world. All remarked with obvious distaste on the blood feuds that raged in the tribal areas and described these feuds only to a limited extent, very anecdotally and with more of an emphasis placed upon condemning such a bizarre tribal custom than upon careful and detailed description and analysis. As a result, it was more difficult to understand the traditional blood-feuding system through their descriptions than it was by trying to rely upon the memories of present-day tribesmen, who have experienced feuding only in a very limited way.

Fortunately, I found other sources that were more useful. Several Montenegrins have published books on their own culture beginning in the mid 1800s, and one by Vuk Vrčević (1890) contains verbatim accounts of blood-feud settlements in which blood money was paid according to carefully agreed upon terms. B. M. G. Medaković (1860) also dealt with the feud, and V. Bogišić (1874) conducted an extensive questionnaire on social life in Montenegro and other regions, which touched upon feuding. In addition, Yugoslav historians recently have published many archival holdings relating to the tribal period before a state was formed. This meant that I was spared the toil of locating these documents in archives and reading them in their original handwritten and timeworn condition.

It was in interpreting these indigenous depositions and proclamations, written down by monks who were the only literate men in the entire tribal society, that my cultural intuitions were put to the most severe test. It was necessary to read between the lines most of the time, since these writings were not intended to be used for purposes of research. Very frequently, things that would be obvious to someone who knew Montenengrin culture were simply omitted in order to save effort. As an ethnohistorian, I possessed a great advantage by being at the same time an anthropologist who had lived with a traditional tribe for over two years. I believe it would have been quite difficult for someone without that experience to try to re-create an entire cultural phenomenon from such bits and shreds of evidence.

In writing this book, I have had very little trouble in sketching the general way of life that prevailed during the fully tribal period, because the evidence is abundant and unambiguous and because I already have synthesized it elsewhere (Boehm 1983). In dealing with the blood feud, however, I have been more careful in letting the reader know the nature of my sources and in making suggestions (where necessary) as to how far they may be trusted. This is because I have not been able to find anywhere a complete description of the traditional blood-feud system in Montenegro for that period, even though the Montenegrin lawyer Ilija M. Jelić's (1926) book on feuding among Serbs, Albanians, and Montenegrins has been very useful and draws upon obscure popular articles published in the late 1880s as well as upon many of the earlier sources that I have used.

While the present book has been written in a nontechnical style of writing congenial to a person who is not familiar with anthropology, I have tried to make it interesting as well to historians who are studying this corner of the world and useful to other anthropologists interested in Montenegrin blood feuding or in the special theoretical interpretations I have developed.

As the reader will see in the later chapters, I do not simply provide a catalogue of cultural institutions and behavioral patterns or limit the analysis to a neat functionalist interpretation of blood feuding as part of the social system. Rather, I try to make it clear how traditional Montenegrins collectively perceived and shaped their own feuding system, and how individual men and women made their own personal decisions as to when to begin killing and when to stop. In taking this more dynamic psychological perspective, I have had to lean very heavily upon my own field experience, putting to use the knowledge that I possess about how Montenegrins think and feel in general and about how they relate to the issue of blood revenge as one that still remains salient in their culture.

3

Traditional Montenegro: A Refuge-Area Warrior Society

Hundreds of the world's smaller-scale societies exhibit some form of vengeance killing, although in many others such behavior is absent. Since feuding societies vary greatly in the way that they gain a living, in their belief systems and values, in their art styles, and in their social and political life, there appears to be no single, inevitable cause for the development of homicidal retaliation as a well-developed cultural pattern. However, in spite of this diversity, feuding societies usually share one political feature in common: feuding occurs mainly in societies where there is not a great deal of centralized political control (Otterbein and Otterbein 1965).

This political status is particularly true of Eskimos, who have virtually no political leadership at all. As nomadic hunters, Eskimos live in nuclear families or in clusters of such families, which temporarily congregate when hunting conditions permit. Eskimos do not practice raiding or warfare; indeed, generally they tend to disapprove of expressions of violence among people (Briggs 1970). But certain Eskimo groups do carry on "feuds" in a rather restrained way. Later, I shall describe how the Netsilik Eskimos retaliate when a member is killed by another group, as an example of limited blood vengeance.

By contrast, many pastoral or agricultural societies are structured into permanent territorial political units of different sizes (usually households, clans, or villages and tribes, but sometimes tribal confederations) and are well versed in the violent arts of warfare and raiding. Among such segmental societies, entire segments sometimes retaliate for a slain member by killing any member of the segment that has inflicted this harm on them. We shall see that the Montenegrins' manner of feuding fits more with this tribal pattern than with the limited mode of retaliation that is characteristic of most Eskimos.

REFUGE-AREA WARRIOR ADAPTATIONS

Nonliterate people who are organized into segmentary tribes come in many different versions ecologically speaking (Sahlins 1968), and such people often practice feuding in some form or other. They may be pastoral nomads who live in temporary camps. They may be forest agricultural tribes who cultivate in one place until the soil is exhausted and then move on. They may be equestrian hunters or irrigation agriculturalists or fishermen. But in each case the natural environment and whatever economic life this environment allows play a very large part in shaping their social and political life (Sahlins 1968; see also Steward 1955).

There is one type of adaptation, however, in which politics perhaps plays an even greater role than subsistence. Sometimes, when a predatory kingdom or empire expands at the expense of less politically organized peoples, it meets with an unusual case of resistance. If they are to resist, a tribal people must either be able to stand their ground and fight for their local autonomy, or else they must flee to an isolated area where pursuit becomes either impossible or too expensive to make any sense. Many people have tried to save their autonomy by using either or both of these strategies, and in various parts of the world a few have succeeded here and there. But more often they have been exterminated, or they have been conquered and either exploited or absorbed into the dominant culture.

Such political success depends on a combination of factors. First, the territory that the tribesmen occupy must be of marginal economic and strategic value to the predatory power, so that this power will limit its investments in trying to subjugate the tribesmen. Rugged mountains and deserts tend to be marginal in these ways; they also provide special advantages for self-defense or flight. Second, a highly effective military technology must be developed, one that will allow the tribesmen flexibility in selecting group sizes and military strategies that will be appropriate to their rather desperate situations but that will enable them to coordinate themselves in large numbers if necessary. Third, a segmentary political system works perfectly to enhance such military flexibility, since both decisions and military action can be taken in units ranging from small household groups or clans to well-coordinated confederations of many tribes numbering in the tens of thousands. Fourth, such segmentary tribesmen must be motivated to continue what may become a very difficult struggle. The value that they place on local autonomy and on honor befitting a true warrior is always great, and such warriors tend to sharply limit the power of their own chiefs, except on the battlefield, where authority is needed. Fifth, warriors who live in their refuge areas obviously must have some means of supporting themselves economically. However, their subsistence patterns vary a great deal. Some are pastoral nomads living in deserts, some are sedentary pastoralists who also practice some agriculture, some are exclusively agriculturalists, and some practice agriculture with irrigation. But whatever their means of taking care of material needs, such tribal rebels have a mechanism in reserve that helps them out when their economically marginal environment fails them or when their means of livelihood is damaged in battle: they all tend to go raiding.

I have called this means of survival a "refuge area warrior adaptation" (Boehm 1983), since the ecological adaptation seems to be more political than economic. Some famous historical examples were the various pastoral nomads who once lived autonomously in Central Asia (Sahlins 1968), while even today one reads about the Afghani tribesmen and the Kurds of Turkey, Iran, and Iraq. In their own day—that is, until 1850—the Montenegrins were still another example of this remarkable adaptive type. They chose to defend their territory and to continue their local autonomy in the face of a numerically superior and predatory political system that was far better organized. Indeed, for five centuries the Ottoman Empire dominated much of the Middle East and the Balkans, and at one time the Sultan actually threatened to invade Western Europe, laying seige to the city of Vienna.

MONTENEGRIN POLITICAL LIFE

In the traditional period dealt with in this book, the largest permanent territorial unit in Montenegro was the pleme. A typical pleme was composed of various clans, a few of which were descended from the ancient Illyrians who originally populated the Adriatic coast. The great majority were descended from the ancient Slavs, who migrated from Russia before A.D. 1000 and conquered the Illyrians except in Albania. In traditional Montenegro a few clan names remained from this Illyrian heritage, but all tribesmen spoke the Serbian language.

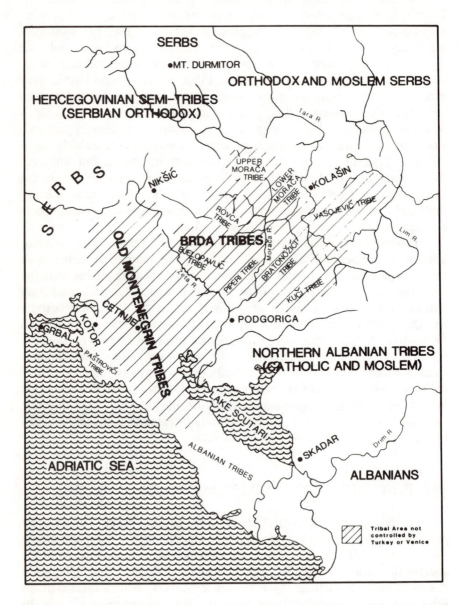

Map 3　　Old Montenegrin Tribal Confederation and Free Tribes of the Brda in the Early Nineteenth Century

In addition to these very old Illyrian or Serbian clans, the majority of a typical tribe was composed of more-recent immigrant Serbian clans, patrilineal kin groups that had been founded by men who had fled to Montenegro from adjacent Serbian regions for political reasons. There were chiefly two sets of circumstances that made people relocate in this way. One was feuding, since in an unequal blood feud the only means of clan survival might be to flee quickly and to resettle elsewhere anonymously. The other derived from problems with the Ottoman lords who subjugated the Christian Serbs and Albanians all around Montenegro. When a particularly headstrong Serb could no longer stand Islamic insults directed at his faith (or at his women or at his honor), he might kill his tormentor and quickly flee with his family to Montenegro. Since some tribe was always ready to crowd in one more warrior so as to increase its fighting strength, Montenegro became known far and wide as a hospitable refuge area. The prices that one paid for settling there were the rocky, mountainous terrain and the risky life of a refuge-area warrior.

The tribal area that first became autonomous was Old Montenegro, near the Adriatic coastline. By 1820, most of the tribes of the Brda had also become independent. Map 3 shows these tribal districts and the Turkish-controlled territories that surrounded the Montenegrins on three sides. A coastal strip was controlled by Venice.

Earlier, it is likely that the Montenegrins maintained an unusual degree of local autonomy as Serbian mountain pastoralists living under the medieval Serbian lords. The latter controlled their area for centuries before the Ottoman Turks invaded and subjugated the Serbs (Jovanović 1948). Very little is known about the tribesmen before the seventeenth century, but it does appear that for more than a century after the Ottoman occupation in the 1500s these mountaineers played the role of a political buffer between the Venetian and Ottoman empires (Jovanović 1948) and paid taxes regularly to the Turks, even though they were not obliged to serve in the Ottoman army like other Christian serfs (Djurdjev 1953). By 1600, Montenegrins under the military leadership of their Eastern Orthodox bishops *(vladikas)* had begun to resist Ottoman taxation by force of arms (Jovanović 1948), and by the late 1600s, major Ottoman military expeditions were being sent periodically to subjugate Montenegro, with varying degrees of success.

For the next one hundred and fifty years a pattern was repeated: Montenegrin tribes paid token taxes when Ottoman forces nearby were strong, but if local Moslem lords were called away to fight for their empire or if they developed rivalries among themselves, the aggressive tribesmen quickly took advantage. They stopped paying taxes; intensified their raiding for livestock, heads, and women; and sometimes tried to

Men cutting hay with scythes. When one household has a problem with its labor force, it invites its neighbors, relatives, and in-laws to exchange a day's hard work for a feast given by the host and his wife. This donation of work is called a moba.

prod their passive Serbian or Albanian neighbors into rising up and throwing off the Moslem yoke. When Ottoman power in the area was reconsolidated and when the empire's other problems were not too distracting, local Ottoman lords would gather large armies and threaten to devastate Montenegro unless tribute was paid.

Over a period of one hundred and fifty years many such campaigns were mounted. A handful resulted in severe devastation, with a goodly portion of the tribal population being killed or led off to be sold into slavery and with ensuing famines and epidemics (Jovanović 1948). However, after a major military defeat the tribesmen simply operated in small guerilla bands, making it impossible for their territory to be occupied for more than a few weeks. By burning crops and hiding away livestock and by cutting off the enemy's supply lines, they made certain that their rugged natural fortress could not be occupied permanently except at an exorbitantly high cost. As a result, this tribal thorn in the side

I learn to use a recently sharpened scythe while its owner looks on. The
owner is Radoš Baošić, one of Upper Morača tribe's leading singers of
heroic epics. Hay that is harvested here in the winter settlement is stacked to
be used in wintering the livestock when they are brought down from the
mountain. Snowfall in Montenegro can be extremely heavy.

of one of the world's mightiest empires persevered for a number of
centuries: the Montenegrins lived a locally autonomous life while their
neighbors remained in bondage.

MAKING A LIVING

Montenegrins were primarily pastoralists, although they also depended heavily on agriculture for grains and vegetables. Once a year they
made transhumant moves from their winter villages, which lay at lower
altitudes, to their katuns up in the mountains. There, even a short

summer produced very fine pasturage and also a cool climate, one suitable for processing the dairy products upon which Montenegrins depended as a source of protein. This pattern of adaptation forced individual Montenegrins to be quite mobile, since they not only had to move their herds around to utilize limited pasturage but also had to divide their time between agricultural work down in the village and pastoral pursuits up on the mountain. In addition, men from the age of sixteen on up frequently went raiding. This activity was crucial to survival after a Turkish devastation or during a bad year caused by drought, since the tribal population was large compared to the available means of subsistence. But raiding was pursued also as a kind of sport or test of manhood; and after a raid on Moslems, many a Montenegrin youth brought home his first human head to his mother, as a proud mark of manly accomplishment.

In addition to selling surplus products raised at home, Montenegrins used their own and Turkish or Venetian markets to dispose of plunder gained on raids. Crucial imports were firearms, swords, munitions, and the coffee and sugar that they viewed to be indispensable for hospitality.

SOCIAL AND MORAL LIFE

From the available ethnohistorical materials, the traditional Montenegrins of the eighteenth and nineteenth century give the impression of having been an intensely moral people. In the next chapter I shall explain the extreme preoccupation they had with their personal reputations, also a characteristic of other tribal peoples all around the Mediterranean area (see Péristiany 1966). But even in 1966, when I left Montenegro, the tribe, rather than the village or settlement or even the Yugoslav national legal system, remained the chief moral reference point, the social unit within which a man's or a woman's reputation as a good person was maintained or lost.

For traditional Montenegrins the most salient values were those that pertained to continuation of the male line, to bravery (junaštvo) and honor (čast), and to personal and tribal political autonomy (sloboda, or freedom). While the Montenegrins valued hospitality, aggressiveness, and bravery in males, females were judged more in terms of industriousness and sexual virtue. As we shall see in analyzing feuds, there was very much of a sexual double standard which simultaneously proscribed all nonmarital sexual self-expression for girls and women and encouraged young men to ruin any maiden who was foolish enough to believe in their promises of marriage. This will be discussed in more detail in the next chapter.

It must be mentioned that while Montenegrin women were exempt from the warrior's obligations that every male faced, and were exempt from blood-feud obligations as well, a woman did have to supply the men of her household with food and munitions at the front; and she was greatly esteemed if she overcame what was considered to be her natural weakness and decided to fight as a man. Such rare events are celebrated in Montenegrin heroic epic poetry. Furthermore, a woman never was obliged to take vengeance for a slain son, brother, or husband; but if she chose to do so, she was given more respect than a man who did this out of obligation.

For nearly ten centuries the traditional Montenegrins had been Eastern Orthodox Christians, but many elements of earlier pagan Slavic belief systems persisted in Christian guise. Furthermore, the tribal and military nature of Montenegrin life had dramatic effects on Christian practices. For example, the Orthodox confessional was seldom available to males because they killed people so frequently (Karadžić 1922); nevertheless, both *pops* (illiterate "priests" appointed by the tribes) and *vladikas* (Eastern Orthodox bishops), as well as *kaludjers* (monks), went to war like anyone else. Pops were allowed to marry only once, while a kaludjer or a vladika remained celibate.

THE COLLECTIVE NATURE OF MONTENEGRIN LIFE

If Montenegrin moral life was highly focused on individual male accomplishments involving heroism or honor, these criteria for maintaining a reputation in the tribe did not apply to individuals alone. A Montenegrin clan was composed of all the males who were descended from the same male ancestor, and to a significant extent an individual's reputation was shared with the clan. This meant that a true hero could enhance the reputation of everyone who shared the same surname, while a coward or a scoundrel degraded the reputations of all his clan brothers. Clan solidarity was particularly apparent in warfare, where large clans served as the nuclei of military units (Ranke 1853), and in feuding, where the entire clan was concerned with its reputation in avoiding any sign of undue submissiveness. All members of a clan shared the same last name and called one another *brat* (brother), while rivalry between clans was a salient feature of traditional tribal life that continues even today.

The household in Montenegro was usually a joint one composed of several brothers or the sons of several brothers and their in-marrying wives and children. The cultural ideal was that a house should never divide—that is, that closely related males should stay together and cooperate so as to live better than they could live in separate nuclear families. In practice, if a household did not expand too much, then its descendants could stay together for generations. But if they grew too numerous, two problems wre likely to arise. First, it was difficult to expand land holdings and to keep these contiguous, because arable land was at such a premium in this overcrowded refuge area. Second, while all the males were closely related, their wives married in from other clans and sometimes from other tribes. Quarrels among the women of a household were frequently cited as a cause of division.

The household (*kuća;* the people living under one roof; literally, a house) provided the basis for economic cooperation, and the clan *(brastvo)* provided a semilocalized group of social and political solidarity; but the pleme, or tribe, was the basic territorial unit. The pleme, which was composed of many unrelated brastvos, collectively protected the commonly held mountain pastures from other tribes, tried to keep the peace among its own clans, and made decisions about war or peace or other accommodations with external political groups, be they Montenegrin tribes, Albanian tribesmen, or state societies. The plemes also confederated at times under the leadership of their vladika to cope with major external political threats or opportunities.

Problems of social deviance were taken care of by the house or the clan (Boehm 1983) if they affected no one else, but the entire tribe might gather to sentence a traitor to death or exile (Jovanović 1948). The tribe was particularly active in trying to resolve blood feuds between clans if both clans were members of the same tribe. A tribal *sud dobrih ljude* (court of good men) was called together whenever the two parties were ready to call a truce and to try to reach a settlement, and such courts were indispensable in the pacification of feuds.

A SEGMENTARY TRIBAL POLITICAL SYSTEM

Montenegrin social and political life was profoundly affected by these social groups, each of which had rather different functions which now need to be summarized. The members of a kuća owned their winter house and the pastures, fields, and forests around it and operated as a cooperative unit of subsistence involving as many as thirty or forty persons. The brastvo, which was sometimes localized but sometimes scattered, served as a military unit, as a feuding unit, and as a socially close community sharing the same moral reputation and military prestige. A brastvo could number anywhere from a few houses to several hundred, and even a medium-sized brastvo was a fearsome military machine. The pleme was both a moral community and a unit of territorial defense which, like the kuća or the brastvo, had its own chief. It also owned and regulated the summer pasture lands that were used by members of the tribe.

In all these units the leaders tended to be chosen from the same patriline as long as a competent male was available, but he was freely elected and could always be deposed. This provided Montenegrins with a political and social organization that had a hierarchical decision-making structure, a structure that enabled the tribesmen to cope with either internal or external problems in groups of an appropriate size and composition. As we shall see, this hierarchically composed segmentary political organization was useful not only in coping with external predators but also in coping with internal problems. As I mentioned at the beginning of this chapter, many kinds of smaller-scale or tribal societies exhibit feuding behavior, but for each of the more common ecological types, feuding seems to be optional: for example, some Eskimo hunting groups have vengeance killing, but some do not. The same is true of pastoral nomads, of shifting agriculturalists, of sedentary agriculturalists, and of various other types. However, among refuge-area warriors such as the Montenegrins, the Kurds, the Afghani tribes, the Riffians of Morocco, the Bedouin, and similar societies on other continents, the feud is much more constant. Later, after feuding in Montenegro has been analyzed, we shall inquire why this is so.

4

The Meaning of Osveta

The English term "feuding" suggests, among other things, a protracted state of homicidal aggression between two individuals or two groups that are consumed by bitterness and hatred.[1] To the extent that present-day Americans have a clear conception of feuding in its more serious manifestations, the above common-sense definition expresses this understanding quite fully. Our reference point, of course, is the Hatfields and the McCoys—people who lived in an isolated mountain area and settled their own scores, without governmental interference, by helping themselves.

In the next several chapters we shall draw much closer to this violent and complicated pattern of behavior in order to see how Montenegrin blood feuds actually worked. But to begin with, in comparing our own way of conceptualizing a feud with that of the tribesmen who did the feuding, we must look at the symbols that they used in speaking about vengeance.

DEFINING THE BLOOD FEUDS FOR MONTENEGRO

The Montenegrins with whom I lived had no one term that meant a "blood feud" taken as a discrete entity, even though they possessed a superbly rich vocabulary for speaking of different aspects of blood vengeance: *krvna osveta* meant "blood revenge"; *u krvi* meant "in blood," designating a state of hostility where the purpose was to take

51

blood revenge; a *krvnik* was "a blood revenge enemy"; *dužan krvi* meant "to owe blood"; *krvni umir* meant "pacification of blood revenge"; *platiti krvi* meant "to pay blood money"; and so forth. But unlike the Serbian words for warfare *(ratovanje)* and raiding *(četovanje)*, for feuding there existed no comparable noun which specifically designated the entire feuding process.

There was no ambiguity, however, among the three major domains of institutionalized violence that Montenegrins discerned, in that the concepts of raiding and warfare were clearly differentiated from the complex of events that attended the taking of blood vengeance (Boehm 1983). U krvi comes closest to designating a long-term feud as a discrete entity. But being "in blood" described a state of being, not a feud as a total event of a certain size, shape, and duration. Krvna osveta also came close, but "blood vengeance" referred to single vindictive acts or to the duty to take vengeance, rather than to the overall series of events that constituted a feud. These usages that I encountered in the field during the 1960s also hold for the traditional period a century earlier (see Karadžić 1935).

This semantic treatment on the part of the Montenegrins suggests that they did not perceive a feud as being a single entity in the same sense that a military engagement (*rat* [war], *bitka* [battle], or *četa* [raid; raiding party]) was a discrete event deserving a name of its own. Rather, krvna osveta assumed many different shapes, as do feuds elsewhere in the world. The distinction between our own concept and that of the Montenegrins of the traditional period is a subtle one. Our idea of a feud tends to focus on the bitterness and longevity of an interclan conflict. But for Montenegrins, krvna osveta or the state of being "in blood" could occur in a number of different contexts, some relatively brief but some protracted, some involving many retaliatory killings but others none; and to them the notion of taking vengeance as a solemn duty seemed to be the central focus.

Another term that the Montenegrins used frequently was *svadja* (quarrel). A svadja could involve merely a pair of men (or women or children) exchanging harsh words—for example, in an argument over property boundaries. Or a svadja could be a physical fight between two men, as in a drunken brawl. Svadja also applied to a conflict involving a larger number of people, as when two clans collected to back up some of their members who were engaged in a verbal or homicidal dispute. A svadja could even be a long-term homicidal fight between two clans which was based on obligations to take vengeance. So, the general term svadja could apply to either brief or protracted cases of krvna osveta, as well as to many other kinds of conflicts. But svadja never had the exclusive focus that "blood feud" or "vendetta" do in English, when they refer to a bloody Hatfield and McCoy or Mafia type of extended feud.

As we shall see, the Montenegrin terminology was not "incomplete." Indeed, when Montenegrins did wish to emphasize the long-lasting character of a particular feud, they simply said that two clans or tribes had been "in blood" (u krvi or *zakrvljeni*) for a very long time. The point is that the Montenegrin definition of the situation was different from our own because they were much more intimately involved with feuds than we are. For them, the focus was upon the duty and the need to take blood, not on some particular form that a blood-vengeance conflict took.

By contrast, for us the term "blood feud" provides a handy but limited idea by which to identify an exotic and rather baffling way of doing things, of locking into bloodthirsty conflicts with virtually no willingness to compromise. To understand the Montenegrin viewpoint it will be useful to set aside this narrow conception of a feud as a necessarily protracted or interminable bloody conflict between two clans and to think of feuding as a process. In this process, homicidal conflicts are acted out in a variety of ways, on the basis of cultural rules, well known by all parties concerned, that make perfectly good sense to the participants. In Montenegro, these rules not only created a charter for how to carry on homicidal conflicts but also provided a formal means for terminating or resolving such conflicts.

The next several chapters concern the more serious kinds of quarrels that Montenegrins used to engage in and the way in which those quarrels were resolved. Using the ethnohistorical materials, I shall reconstruct the basic sequence of Montenegrin homicidal quarrels, insofar as the events were predictable and followed a definite order. In making things as clear as possible for someone who has never been to Montenegro, I shall begin by describing these quarrels from the bird's-eye view of an outside observer trying to understand how Montenegrins defined and followed their own rules in enacting a feud. But later, in chapter 8, I shall draw closer to the indigenous perspective. There, I shall discuss this entire pattern of conflict and conflict resolution from the standpoint of the personal decisions that native Montenegrins had to make as they coped with their own feuding way of life. The focus will be on the alternatives among which the tribesmen had to choose in making these decisions, on the insights that they brought to situations of choice, and on the strategic criteria by which decisions were made in terms of both moral objectives and other kinds of goals. This will bring the reader a deeper understanding of the Montenegrin perspective.

THE PSYCHOLOGY OF KRVNA OSVETA: DEFINITIONS
BY PRESENT-DAY TRIBESMEN

In chapter 3 some of the psychological basis for feuding was established. The concept of honor was stressed and also the specific value that was placed on manly aggressiveness: no man would allow another man to trample him underfoot if he wished to retain the respect of his tribal moral community. In this chapter, before actual feuding behavior is displayed, it will be useful to explore in more detail how the compulsion to carry out krvna osveta was motivated in the Montenegrin mind. In the traditional period, no one ever thought to ask a Montenegrin: "What does krvna osveta mean to you?" But in the course of my own fieldwork I had a chance to do just that. Therefore, before turning to romanticized or negatively biased outsiders' descriptions of feuding in the traditional period, I shall let today's Montenegrins speak for themselves—and for their ancestors as well.

In 1966 I asked forty of my friends and neighbors in Upper Morača to assist me in the investigation of their values and beliefs, which I accomplished through a simple technique. I turned on a battery-operated Nagra tape recorder and read a standardized list of 256 cue words to my informants, telling them only that I would like to see how they personally explained the meaning of each word. With this minimal cue I hoped to avoid influencing their responses through my own biases.[2] One of these cue words was osveta, or "vengeance"—not "*blood* vengeance" (krvna osveta), but simply "vengeance." This term has the same general meaning in Serbian that it does in English, but about half of my Montenegrin informants chose to define the word in terms of homicide— that is, in terms of "blood." Such definitions often began with the idea that verbal insults or a blow were exchanged, but then escalated to include the exchanging of homicides as well.

For a people who have been prevented from taking blood for over a century, the idea of retaliatory homicide seemed to persist strongly in the same mold as earlier. This will be apparent from a few typical folk definitions, which one must realize were composed on the spot with brevity in mind and were simply intended to provide kernel ideas that identify a concept, not to serve as full explanations.

The late Savo Todorović,[3] who was well over seventy years old in 1966, explained the meaning of osveta thus: "Osveta, that means . . . a kind of spiritual fulfillment. You have killed my son, so I killed yours; I have taken revenge for that, so I now sit peacefully in my chair. There you are."

My neighbor Božidar summed up osveta very simply: "Osveta? Osveta. If I come to blows with someone . . . or he kills me, if he deals me a mortal blow, then it is known what must be. Then, he has to die as well. Right away, two people die. Not one but two, necessarily."

The late Milan Baošić, a good friend who died far too young, was a man of few words: "Osveta by my understanding means: if you have killed my brother or father, I look to take vengeance and so I kill one of 'yours.'"

My friend Jovan also gave a very brief definition: "Osveta means . . . when you have killed my brother, then I must kill you. That is the meaning of osveta."

Anica, the wife of an excellent singer of heroic epics, gave a long response which began: "Osveta means if you strike me a blow, I do the same for you and there you are: I have taken revenge. Just like those Turks and the Montenegrins in the old days."

A more vivid description came from my landlord, who was also a major political leader of Upper Morača tribe: "Osveta means people in some way have words with each other, or something, and seek vengeance. It comes under osveta when two men quarrel, one hits the other either with a stake or a rock or with his fist, or they shoot it out with pistols, one falls dead, and then osveta takes place if he is avenged. . . ."

A very dear friend and neighbor, a mild woman who dearly loved little animals, gave the following response, which I decided to follow up with some additional questions once I had secured her uninfluenced initial response:

"Eh, osveta! Perhaps someone kills my brother, and then I kill that one. . . ."

"Someone kills your brother?"

"And I take vengeance on him afterwards."

"Would you really do that?"

"I would."

"Would you?"

"Of course!"

"Really?"

"By God, if I were able!"

"But you are a woman. I haven't heard that women take vengeance like that."

"*I* certainly would, by God! And I've heard of one who did it over there in the White-Paul Tribe."

"Really?"

"Some man killed her husband, and she killed him!"

"Did she?"

"The wife killed; avenged her husband."

Kovilka Lukovac, the traditional Montenegrin woman who said that she
would want to avenge her brother personally, if he were killed. Kovilka is
spinning wool into yarn while she stands in her orchard and tends her herd
of sheep, which are out of sight. Kovilka and her husband, Milisav, were
my closest neighbors for more than two years.

"Is that so?"

"Yes, by God!"

"How did it happen?"

"I don't know; that was somewhere far away from here. I only
know she killed that one, and she was locked up for a short
time. . . ."

This information came at the end of my fieldwork, when I had
already asked many times if people knew of any contemporary cases of
blood revenge. This faraway example had never been mentioned by
anyone in Morača, even though I had heard about it in town. I believe it

was this spirited exchange between myself and a neighbor with whom I gossiped freely that brought out information she remembered only marginally. With respect to the very last thing she said, I have been told that modern Montenegrin courts are unusually hard on killings that are motivated by revenge except when it is a female who "takes blood." In such rare cases, women are so respected for performing this stressful male duty that in several instances they are said to have been let off with virtually no sentence at all.

These definitions, provided by modern Montenegrins who presumably have never taken vengeance, follow a common pattern. A verbal insult, a blow, or a killing is returned in kind; it may be returned either to the original aggressor or, in the case of a homicide, carried to his close male kinsmen by a close male kinsman of the original victim. Only one informant, old Savo, actually mentioned the depth of the need to take osveta and the satisfaction obtained from it; but the compulsive or obligatory nature of taking vengeance was implicit in many of these brief responses.

To avoid repetition, I have omitted a number of the folk definitions that simply followed this general pattern. But several of these typical definitions mentioned specifically that there is a considerable time delay between the original conflict and the time when blood vengeance is taken. There are also several remaining definitions that are not so typical and that reveal additional, important aspects of feuding. One young woman with a modern social perspective told me:

> Osveta is not a good thing. For example if you have done something bad to me, I take vengeance; that means with us: whatever it is that you do bad to me, I'll do it back to you, or maybe even worse if I am able to. Even worse than you did to me: if you have struck me, gotten me into some trouble, stolen from me, lied to me, placed some blame on me, I will be looking to do something even worse to you.

As we shall see presently, the tendency of quarrels to escalate on the principle that is outlined here is one of the most dangerous aspects of feuding.

Most of these definitions were spontaneous and contained little or no "tampering" on the part of the ethnographer, in that the mode of eliciting information was entirely open-ended. However, in some cases my curiosity got the better of me after I heard the original response, and I allowed myself to influence subsequent responses by asking specific questions, as in the case of the neighbor who told me about the woman's having taken vengeance over in the White-Paul tribe. In following up on a different informant's response to the same cue word, I asked one old woman whether a female could be killed in revenge:

> "That would not be proper. That would not be proper."
> "But why not?"
> "They wouldn't do that because, let's say, it is not within our customs to take revenge for a man upon a female!"

I then asked her how about killing the killer's brother, and she indicated that it was perfectly all right to kill the killer, his brother, or his father or, if he had no father, then his son or some other male kinsman, but never a woman. This agrees with indications from other informants that if necessary, one might simply kill any male in the clan of the man who owed the blood. But it was also clear that initially one started off by looking for the killer himself or a close male kinsman, preferably the brother.

Folk definitions by their nature are brief and therefore incomplete; so the agreement among my informants is quite striking. Since the cue word was simply "revenge," not "blood vengeance," and since half the informants mentioned homicide in their responses, it must be assumed that krvna osveta is still very much on the minds of Montenegrins who are living out in the tribal areas today. The idea is simple: if I am insulted or if someone strikes or harms me, I must retaliate in kind upon the person who hurt me. If I am killed, then someone close to me must kill my killer or some male genealogically close to him.

This one set of principles goes a long way toward explaining the logic of feuding in Montenegro, as far as taking action is concerned. But much of the emotional and moral side of the psychology of taking vengeance remains implicit in these responses. One thing may be inferred clearly: the feeling that an affront requires retaliation is present in a strong and certain form in the Montenegrin psyche even today. But to understand fully how the need to take vengeance was motivated, we must turn to accounts from earlier periods.

WHY TAKE REVENGE?

To fail to retaliate homicidally in many contexts used to result in severe damage to one's honor, in that the disapproval of the tribal moral community was so intense that it became almost intolerable. Mary Durham (1928) reports the story of a tribal leader who failed to take blood and thereafter lost his right to speak in a meeting of the tribe. For one in a position of leadership, this effectively invalidated his ability to lead, in addition to causing him supreme social discomfort.

However, the tribesmen did not take vengeance solely because as actors in the public spotlight, they feared the moralistic aggression of the tribal community. A nontribal Serbian named Medaković (1860), who had contact with the Montenegrins toward the end of the traditional period, eloquently describes the psychology of feuding in the following passage. Later, I shall point out some rather obvious ethnocentric biases in his analysis, but these may be discerned without my assistance.

> Osveta is something born into a man. It has to do with wounds to the soul and the heart. A Montenegrin says that he would rather die than live his life shamefully. And if someone does something to him, he is only too ready to pay it back. His consciousness is not highly enough developed so that he fully anticipates the consequences of osveta and bloody deeds, but rather he wishes to satisfy his own haughty pride, and on that basis counts himself as having done a heroic deed and a manly act. . . . Osveta is a terrible deed, worse than ordinary murder. Osveta is a deliberate and well-planned evil and sin. When he seeks vengeance, the *osvetnik* (vengeance taker) knows whom it is he will kill and why he will kill him. A still-worse form of revenge takes place when the feud continues and future generations must take part in it. Osveta of this kind may go on for twenty years. The osvetnik tracks the krvnik (the man who owes him blood), seeks him on all sides, falls upon him in some convenient spot or a defile; he cannot work, nor sleep in peace, until he has fulfilled his evil and bloody mission. The osvetnik may gather a party of kinsmen and go to an area where the krvnik is likely to pass, to await him there and kill him in ambush.
>
> First of all, the osvetnik will try to take vengeance on the krvnik himself; but if he cannot get at him, then he will kill his closest and most prominent brother or male kinsman. Osveta today is forbidden by law to Montenegrins, but in their social life they freely praise him who has taken vengeance. If a Montenegrin does not take vengeance . . . , he has no place and no honor among the rest of the Montenegrins. Then they say of him that he is no good and a worthless "nothing" if he has not avenged his own kinsman, and so the krvnik has taken away both his obraz and his status as a warrior. And women are equally eager for osveta; they too persuade their own men to take vengeance.
>
> When a Montenegrin takes vengeance, then he is happy; then it seems to him that he has been born again, and as a mother's son he takes pride as though he had won a hundred duels. Revenge has come down from an earlier time, and it does not allow itself easily to be extinguished. It happened frequently, that almost an entire tribe would be slaughtering one another, so that a Montenegrin would not be able to go from one settlement to another. There was not any governmental

power in existence to stop this evil which destroyed the people.
[Medaković 1860; see also Durham 1928:162–63]

In the above passage, written in 1860 by one who was part of the newly formed Montenegrin state, Medaković displays two biases as he portrays the psychology of taking vengeance. The first is the moral perspective of an educated man, who views the strong Montenegrin tribal sensitivity to honor as being a fault, even a sin, and who sees the tribesmen as lacking the development of consciousness that is necessary in order to realize the consequences of their own actions. This is the familiar bias of ''civilized'' people who think they recognize something of the impulsive child or animal in people whose level of culture is, in their view, beneath their own. A second bias comes out of his own close association with the same draconic central government, which was slowly managing to stamp out blood feuds as an obstacle to effective state centralization. This association prevailed at the time that Medaković was collecting his materials and writing his book, and it led him to view feuding as the antithesis of good government. Medaković did characterize rather accurately not only the desperate and persistent commitment of Montenegrins to the taking of vengeance but also the tribesman's vulnerability to the demands of honor and the deep sense of satisfaction that taking vengeance brought. But in giving vent to his biases, Medaković failed to appreciate either the complexity of the psychology of taking vengeance or the positive aspects of feuding.

As part of their accommodation to Christianity, the Montenegrins had the attitude that ''to take vengeance is to become sanctified,'' a saying heard in the Kući tribe, where people also said: ''Would that I not die before I kill my blood enemy'' (Miljanov 1901).[4] Mary Durham (1928) believes that revenge was taken in behalf of the soul of the man who was being avenged, rather than to punish the specific killer, and that as Montenegrins viewed it, vengeance also symbolically ''replaced'' to the victim's clan the blood that had been lost. Durham also believes that the taking of revenge reduced the sense of loss felt over the victim, and like Medaković, she stresses the fact that mothers coached their sons that when they grew up, they should take blood that was owed to their household. This kind of early training must be viewed as a special source of motivation which intensified the other motives mentioned above.

Milovan Djilas, writing in 1958 as a middle-aged man of letters and also as a native Montenegrin, tells of the effects of vengeance killing on his own family background:

> Though the life of my family is not completely typical of my homeland, Montenegro, it is typical in one respect: the men of several

generations have died at the hands of Montenegrins, men of the same faith and name. My father's grandfather, my own two grandfathers, my father, and my uncle were killed, as though a dread curse lay upon them. My father and his brother and my brothers were killed even though all of them yearned to die peacefully in their beds beside their wives. Generation after generation, and the bloody chain was not broken. The inherited fear and hatred of feuding clans was mightier than fear and hatred of the enemy, the Turks. It seems to me that I was born with blood on my eyes. My first sight was of blood. My first words were blood and bathed in blood.

Oblivion has fallen on the causes and the details of these deaths, but there remain the evening stories told around the fireplace, bloody and chilling scenes which memory cannot banish. Sparks scatter the ashes from the fire and the embers and flames flare up while words do not let the bloody deeds burn themselves out. [Djilas 1958:8]

It is obvious, from this rather poetic passage, that Montenegrins are not prone to forget a blood debt. The Djilas clan was atypical, in that it was small and in that its members "feuded" with the agents of Prince Nikola himself, who was the leader of the Montenegrin state after 1860. In so doing, they were nearly exterminated as a matter of deliberate genocidal policy which made sense in terms of the government's excellent understanding of the nature of feuding. The prince feared the strength of the Djilas clan's motivation to retaliate, and it was only by chance that a few members of this small clan did manage to survive an all-out attempt to kill every last male in one surprise attack.

After Nikola Djilas's father, Aleksa, was killed in the "feud," Nikola (Milovan's father) became an officer in the prince's army in Cetinje, then capital of Montenegro. Milovan describes Nikola's psychological state there:

His father's death constantly oppressed Nikola, both the pain and the unredeemed shame. The yearning for vengeance grew stronger and more unbearable in Cetinje, where he found himself near those he knew had dipped their fingers in his father's blood. Within him slowly ripened the thought, the intention, the purpose, to bring peace to himself through the satisfaction of revenge. [Djilas 1958:21]

Somehow Nikola Djilas's secret intentions were suspected, and he was placed in chains for a year and a day, during which time he was twice taken to the palace by night to speak with the prince, who "preferred to break men rather than kill them" (Djilas 1958:22). His son Milovan speculates on these meetings:

What did the Prince ask him? What did Father admit? Father told only this: The Prince took an oath that he knew nothing of Aleksa's murder—otherwise, the Prince swore, may I eat my roasted children on Christmas. Father believed in the Prince's innocence, or perhaps simply wished to believe it. The Prince's oath may have been a good way for my father to justify to himself and before others why he had foregone revenge forever—that most terrible and most sweet-tasting of passions, which still in those days stirred the breast of every Montenegrin. [Djilas 1958:21–22]

The psychology of revenge described above is still that of a free tribesman of the traditional tribal period. But the time was the late 1800s, and the unwritten tribal rules of feuding could no longer be freely applied, even though the accompanying emotions still ran so deeply.

If all these accounts are combined to explain what motivated traditional Montenegrins to take revenge, we must first of all discredit the strong ethnocentric biases exhibited by Medaković. For a Montenegrin tribesman, the taking of vengeance was a reasonable and eminently moral form of social action. Often the act of revenge would appear to be a way for an individual to compensate for a strongly felt personal loss. But in many cases this feeling was generalized to the clan level or, rarely, to the tribal level. Even at these levels, given the strength of social solidarity within the clan and the tribe, it is scarcely surprising that warrior "brothers" were prone to retaliate homicidally when any one of their group was killed. But in such cases the sense of loss became abstract and political, rather than immediate and personal.

Of course, the threat of retaliation extended the protection of the clan automatically to each of its members as a substantial benefit that was consciously appreciated. It also forced other clans to control the homicidal impulses of their members, since the entire clan was liable (see Moore 1972). Thus, in a tribal milieu in which the dynamics of power were well appreciated, these political concerns also helped to motivate or to regulate retaliatory killing.

From the standpoint of religion, osveta was rationalized in several ways. That the tribesmen may have believed that blood vengeance eased the soul of the original victim makes some sense. And particularly if one remembers that the local Orthodox clergy opposed the taking of vengeance homicidally on "innocent" people, this idea about easing the soul may well have been a belief through which the Montenegrins tried to defend their own customary practices against criticism by the church, by means of a favorable religious interpretation. Indeed, the Old Testament itself meets them halfway, since in various places it appears to promote the idea of taking vengeance.

For a self-assertive people who take obligations to kinsmen very seriously, an angry sense of loss did provide a strong motivation for vengeful actions. But I believe that the need for public approval by the tribal community usually played a more basic part in promoting blood revenge. Obviously, it is difficult to weigh these various motives and to balance them out; and it must be remembered that the motivational mix could vary from person to person and from case to case. But on the average, it is safe to say that in Montenegrins the motivation to take blood was very deep indeed and was developed primarily through informal means of socialization, including the kind of storytelling that Djilas alludes to. In some cases, however, teachings about revenge were quite deliberate, as when a mother repeatedly showed a container of her dead husband's blood to her young sons to remind them, as they grew up, that since there was no one else to do the job, they must avenge him (Jelić 1926).

In ending this discussion of the psychology of revenge killing, it is apparent that a number of different relationships were connected through the single symbol of blood, or krv. It was krv that was lost from the clan; it was krv that was owed; it was krv that was "pacified" by a blood court. As my own modern consultants demonstrated so clearly in their definitions, the concepts of revenge and blood were so closely connected that frequently it was not even necessary to ask them to define blood revenge: when they began to think about osveta, the idea of krv just naturally tended to come to mind as well.

There is one further aspect of the psychology of feuding which I have not discussed. The psychological stress created by feuding must be viewed as extreme according to our own standards. But surely in the Montenegrin view this was true as well, even though the tribesmen were far more habituated to taking mortal risks than most of us are. As I trace the course of a blood feud in chapter 6, I shall discuss psychological stress as a rather gruesome aspect of feuding that may have troubled traditional Montenegrin warriors deeply.

5

The Moral Legitimacy of Feuding

Vengeance killing predictably is outlawed in modern societies having formal legal systems with courts and laws. By contrast, in most segmentary tribal societies such as that of Montenegro the social-control functions of "law" are partly fulfilled by what legal anthropologists (e.g., Middleton and Tait 1958; Bohannan 1977) refer to as "self-help." In other words, the members of the tribal society consider it to be a legitimate moral prerogative of an individual or group to take homicidal revenge for the death of a close relative.

In chapter 11 I shall discuss feuding in societies other than Montenegro in some detail. But here I dwell on only two points: vengeance killing is viewed to be legitimate in such societies; and generally it tends to be an entire group that is eligible to take vengeance or against which vengeance may be taken. The functional explanation for the operation of the self-help principle is an obvious one: there exists no centralized political power to step in and control homicidal conflicts within the group. Indeed, members of feuding societies tend to be quite intolerant of having anyone order them around. Instead, they let the threat of private homicidal retaliation help to govern their social relations.

Writing for a sociological journal, Donald Black (1983) has demonstrated that self-help principles actually operate to a degree within the contemporary United States legal system. He analyzes cases in which citizens take the law into their own hands, to show that murder charges more frequently are dropped against people who moralistically kill

65

people who are known to themselves than in other cases of homicide. This tendency to grant moral justification to murder as a form of social control is not written into the law books, nor is it openly applauded by judges. But it is obvious that informally there exists a tendency to view certain instances of self-help as being legitimate.

In Montenegro, the situation was quite different. Even among the present-day men and women of Upper Morača tribe whom I quoted in the preceding chapter, it is obvious that the moral legitimacy of homicidal self-help is upheld by many, even though they know that the modern Yugoslav government is particularly severe in punishing vengeance killings and that many other people in the tribe sincerely condemn all forms of killing. For their forebears—the tribesmen who lived without any centralized governmental power up to 1840—blood feud was not merely acceptable and legitimate; for them it was a moral necessity that a man (or a clan) take vengeance, if a decent social status was to be maintained. There is on record no division of opinion about the legitimacy of vengeance killing among the traditional tribesmen: A man had to do it in order to keep the respect of his community.[1]

A main point that I wish to make in this chapter is that Montenegrins clearly differentiated between murder *(ubistvo)* and revenge killing (krvna osveta). Durham (1928) is very clear about this, as of about 1900; so is Simić (1967). This was true in traditional Montenegro and also in northern Albania (Karan 1973). If a man killed a member of his own tribe by night in order to steal the man's purse, this was viewed to be murder by the tribal community even though that community would not try to punish him. If a man killed the man who had killed his brother, this was considered blood revenge, and therefore was legitimate. In case of blood revenge, the original killing could be viewed as a murder or as justifiable (e.g., if an intolerable insult had been offered), or even as accidental. But in all three cases the act of retaliatory homicide was viewed as a legitimate form of self-help as long as the rules were followed. Later, I shall discuss a few forms of initial killing for which blood vengeance was not felt to be justified, such as a husband's killing a man taken in the act of committing adultery with his wife or an accidental homicide that was readily compensated for financially. But in traditional Montenegro the usual situation was that any homicide had to be avenged, or else honor was lost.

WORLD VIEW AND RELIGION

Traditional tribal communities vigorously upheld the moral legitimacy of krvna osveta. However, certain Eastern Orthodox bishops of

Montenegro tried to use the influence of their office either to discourage feuding or to settle feuds more quickly than usual, so as to better unify the tribal confederation that always was latent in Montenegro. By activating the confederation, they hoped to lead the tribesmen to a local Christian victory over the Islamic empire that for centuries had dominated all the Serbs except for the Montenegrins in their mountains.

The vladika was chosen by a meeting of all the warriors from several dozen tribes, and there was virtually no external control by the Eastern Orthodox Church. Montenegro's few small monasteries supported themselves, and the monks were the only literate people in Montenegro. Out in the tribes it was chiefly the pop who actually brought religion to the people. These nonliterate lay "priests" conducted simple religious services and served as upright moral examples in their behavior. They and their vladika went into battle like any other warrior.

After their conversion to Christianity in about the tenth century (Jovanović 1948), the Montenegrins oriented themselves to the one Christian God, whom they called Bog. However, they seem to have retained some of their earlier pagan beliefs, since they made St. Elijah into Bog's right-hand man as a deity who hurled lightning to earth to punish people for their sins. The ancient Slavs had a similar god (Wilkinson 1848).

The most salient aspect of Bog seems to have been that He was feared. I gained this impression from older people when I was in the field. Misconduct angered Him, and He punished in anger. His actions suggested furious retaliation rather than "constructive" punishment aimed at benevolent education and personal reform. He seemed to be particularly keen on receiving His due when it came to the special days set aside for Him, days when mortals were forbidden to work. Thus, God was not an impartial judge for a moral system in which merits and demerits were counted up toward a judgment day and afterlife. Rather, if persons offended Him, He might strike them angrily and any time. Such divine retaliation was by no means inevitable, but in the Montenegrin view it occurred frequently enough for a person to be careful.

Montenegrin religion may be seen as a system headed by one overarching patron and a number of lesser patrons. God and his saints were available for help with life's problems, so long as they were properly propitiated. Even the feast for the clan patron (which was called the *slava*) had its established rules, and if these rules were not followed, then retaliation was likely. Thus, the clan's own patron saint was potentially dangerous and had to be treated with care. This did not mean, however, that the Montenegrins stood in awe of the entire formal content of Eastern Orthodox Christian dogma, and particularly of all the moral prescriptions and proscriptions contained therein. To the contrary, they ignored many of these and in fact invented some rather unique uses for the church. For example, they conducted the ritual of blood brotherhood in church and swore solemn and terrible oaths in church in order to settle legal and political conflicts—all of which was against the rules of the church. These oaths will be described later as one important aid in resolving blood feuds. They also managed to all but ignore much of the church's formal program of social and economic control. This included its rights to collect tithes, as well as the entire system for advancement in the afterlife.

The vladika in Cetinje himself had to earn most of the respect he received as bishop. He found himself in a curious position: he was a political leader without any real coercive power who was also the chief representative of a religious ideology that the tribesmen resisted in many of its facets. In trying to resolve blood feuds, a vladika had to work against the indigenous Montenegrin code of honor, as he upheld the pacific values of the church. From an outside perspective this was useful, in that the feuding tribesmen themselves were virtually prisoners of their own warlike secular moral code, and therefore needed the moral leverage of a milder, competing set of values in trying to settle their feuds. Indeed, tribesmen who were not directly involved in the feud saw their vladika as someone who, through force of persuasion, might be able to help a tribal community out of these difficulties. But pacification was made very difficult by the fact that the participants themselves were at best extremely ambivalent about setting aside their feuds and frequently would ignore supernaturally based threats made by their vladika.

The vladika, like Bog above him, made use of force to the extent that this was possible. But unlike Bog, the vladika was limited to using devices such as threats of excommunication, which of course work much better when people believe strongly in the afterlife. More effective were his curses, which most often were aimed at a particularly tender spot. Above all else, Montenegrins were obsessed with the idea of producing male offspring within a given minimal lineage, that is, within a household or nuclear family. Every man geared his life to ensuring that he would have male issue; this was apparent not only in the ways that children were talked about, but by the behavior of the household when a child was born. If it was a son, there was joyous firing of rifles and exploding of other munitions. If it was a daughter, there was only a gloomy silence. This bias was well understood by the vladikas, who exploited it in trying to resolve feuds before they had run their course. When the vladika laid a particularly heavy curse upon a tribesman, its content was not merely "May you get leprosy in the face!" but also

"May the black flag hang from the ridge pole of your house!" Since this signified a future absence of male progeny and hence that the house's line would die out, the man would listen in fear. But even so, the person being cursed frequently would not obey but rather would continue the blood feud.

This poses a problem in interpreting the political role of the religious leader in Montenegro. The vladika is generally described as a theocratic leader (e.g., Denton 1877). However, this signifies a political leader who gets his power to rule from sources in the religious system; and in a way the opposite was true in Montenegro. As a religious political leader, the vladika was bound more closely to the moral code of the church than were the tribesmen and their leaders. This effectively limited the kind of political power the vladika could develop, since it was unseemly for him (as bishop of the Orthodox Church) to try to use methods that the Montenegrins did respect: namely, the direct threat of lethal sanctions.

Most Montenegrin vladikas traveled abroad, and carefully observed politically centralized state societies. Some were very eager to introduce to the tribesmen the joys of a formal legal system and, of course, the advantages of coercive sanctioning of behavior by themselves as political leaders. Their chief stumbling block was feuding, and for several centuries this remained a major bone of contention in Montenegrin political life (see Jovanović 1948).

THE MORAL CONTEXT OF FEUDING

To understand Montenegrin blood feud in general, and to understand the particular historically preserved cases of krvna osveta described in later chapters, it is necessary to appreciate the entire tribal view of morality. The highlights presented here will make the reader aware of the social and moral milieu in which traditional Montenegrins operated as they struggled both to stay alive and to maintain respect for themselves and for their clans in a sharply critical tribal moral community.

Like all other human beings, the contemporary Montenegrins whom I knew were perfectly capable of telling you eloquently and in a highly idealized way how a truly moral person should behave. Like any other people, they then went out to operate in real life on the basis of much more realistic values, coping in a practical manner with everyday situations. In traditional times these lofty "ideal values," as they are called, were partly contained in the written tradition of Christianity, notably in the Ten Commandments, and partly in the oral teachings of

Montenegrin culture. On the other hand, the "real values" by which Montenegrins actually operated were inferred from life itself, as individuals watched closely to see what other people actually could get away with while still keeping an acceptable moral standing. These moral values were like signposts for behavior, in that if a person too frequently went against the prescriptions, or did so in too extreme a manner, then social life could become painfully uncomfortable, or a troubled conscience might result. I shall discuss in detail the social and psychological mechanisms that kept people's behavior reasonably well lined up with the values of Montenegrin culture, but first it is necessary to examine the specific values that in traditional times set a standard for behavior. Because Montenegrins put so much stock in gender, I shall treat females and males separately.

A GOOD WOMAN: BASIS FOR ALL LIFE

In the Montenegrin view a good woman was one who provided her husband with sons and who nurtured his children and took care of the many other domestic tasks that were hers to perform. She had to be healthy and strong, preferably from a superior clan and house, hardworking above all, but also of good moral character as far as honesty and sexual behavior were concerned. The good woman was the very foundation of the household as the Montenegrins viewed it, the person who earnestly wished to bear sons and readily assumed full responsibility for child care, cooking, and cleaning and a goodly share of the heavier labor that went into obtaining a subsistence. Because Montenegrins feuded so much and because the men frequently went off on raids, women wound up doing much of the strenuous work, such as cutting down trees, splitting firewood, carrying water, raking hay, hoeing, and sometimes even ploughing. The only major subsistence work that was done exclusively by men, aside from raiding, was cutting hay and building houses. For a woman to be called *lijena* (lazy) was one of the worst moral statuses she could fall into, while being a *radna* (hardworking) person was highly laudable.

If a woman were to steal, the disgrace and also the economic penalties that came with detection would fall upon the *starješina* (head of the household) and upon the entire membership of her house. In this respect, the same values that were placed upon honesty applied to women as to men. These values required careful interpretation, because Montenegrins eulogized honesty as an ideal value but also respected cunning and deceit as real values. Early during my stay in Montenegro I learned that an individual must be careful in navigating the often ambiguous line between these forms of behavior.

Sexual behavior was one area of morality in which a very distinct double standard prevailed for the two sexes. Women were expected to be virgins at marriage. Public knowledge of nonvirginity drastically restricted a woman's opportunities for marriage, in that a "loose woman" was only fit to marry an old man who needed sons at the end of his life or a man who had some other defect, such as psychological liabilities or a pitiful lack of property. Sometimes a girl of tarnished reputation might manage to marry a man from a distant tribe, if his informal intelligence network did not pick up any very definite information concerning her reputation, which, after all, was often a matter of conjecture rather than a clearly established fact. Sometimes such a man might actually have learned of her reputation, but still might view her as something of a bargain in terms of health, strength, family, and so on. In his own tribe there would be some talk of her bad reputation "back where she came from," but people would judge him less harshly than if he were to marry a woman of dubious moral reputation from his own tribe, whose conduct would have been well discussed in the local gossip mills.

After marriage, women were expected to be faithful to their husbands, and there was far less tolerance for females' "straying off to the side" than for males. However, after marriage the double standard was not quite so extreme as before marriage, when males were looked on as healthy young animals who had natural needs and, in general, were winked at by most people for their exploits. If they succeeded with a willing young girl, they were prone to boast, which of course immediately ruined the girl's reputation. People then agreed that she deserved this for being a *kurva* (slut). The behavior of the young man was not subject to good-natured approval, however, if a truly virtuous girl was deceived and ruined, particularly if he showed no regard for the honor of the girl's house afterwards. It was ambiguity in this area that, as we shall see later, contributed to many of the misunderstandings that provoked the beginning of a feud.

Females generally were expected to be very circumspect concerning sexual matters, but once they were over the age of fifty-five or so, they gradually attained a freer status. Then they could smoke their tobacco instead of merely taking it as snuff, and they were able at last to indulge in the earthier kinds of jokes and metaphors that were socially acceptable for any male, including a pop, once adulthood had been reached. In addition, a Montenegrin widow could discreetly enter into nonmarital romantic alliances with far less stigma than a maiden or a married woman, and also with far less likelihood of creating a situation that might start a feud.

A GOOD MAN: THE HEROIC ETHIC

While it was crucial that a man be a *junak* (good warrior, hero) ready to go into battle or to go raiding, and that he be prepared to discharge his obligations in a blood feud, he was judged by other ethical criteria as well. A man was admired if his house was well kept and if its members lived well—that is, if they produced enough so that their daily subsistence was more than merely adequate. Montenegrins were seldom able to become rich by local standards, partly because of the scarcity of land and partly because their values in the economic sphere were geared toward "living well" rather than toward accumulating objects. If because of adequate land and a large, healthy, and productive family a man was able to head a household that lived very well, he was admired as long as he was also a good junak. But the latter consideration was primary: a poor hero received more respect than a rich man who was just an average warrior.

Hospitality was an important focus in estimating a man's moral character, for a good starješina both ran a good house and disposed generously of its products when he had guests. A good man also was honest; above all, he should never be caught stealing within his own tribe. The tribesmen had different words for raiding *(četovanje)* and stealing *(lupeštvo)*, and all observers agree that Montenegrins considered raiding to be morally desirable. Sometimes it was difficult to discern a clear boundary between these two forms of behavior when it was Orthodox Christian Serbs, rather than Moslems or Catholics, who were the targets of raids, particularly if they happened to be fellow Montenegrin tribesmen. This illustrates the fact that when morality becomes involved in everyday life processes, things frequently become not only complicated but ambiguous. When the ideal moral code of a culture is described simply as a catalog of values, as is sometimes done in an ethnographic monograph, such subtlety and complexity are frequently lost to view.

I have suggested that a man's sexual conduct before marriage was an area in which he was not very vulnerable morally. However, if he seduced a daughter of some house of good reputation, her starješina would be prone to retaliate homicidally or else to seek economic redress. But whether the starješina had the right to take vengeance depended upon the girl's reputation, and often this was quite ambiguous. After marriage, a man was merely winked at if he conducted nonserious adulterous affairs—that is, if the equilibrium of his own or someone else's marriage and the economy of his household were not likely to suffer as a result of his sexual escapades. Thus, while in the Montenegrin view, males were very free, in fact they operated sexually within known moral limits, just as females did. But their boundaries were far more liberal.

Of course, a primary moral concern was with a man's readiness to discharge his obligations to go to war or to conduct a campaign of vengeance should a member of his family or clan be killed. However, merely to discharge such obligations in a competent way was not to attain the greatest possible respect given a good man. Rather, a man had to know how to mix other moral values into the recipe for acquiring manly esteem, so that he might temper the demands of blood when other, competing values entered strongly into the situation. When properly done, such actions in no way threw the shadow of cowardice over the reputation of the man concerned.

This quality of being able to modify the demands of honor within the junak role through attention to alternative and more humane values is discussed in a book by the Montenegrin chieftain Marko Son of Miljan, (Miljanov 1901), a tribal leader who, as an old man, taught himself to write and proceeded to publish several works that have become classics in Yugoslavia. He focuses upon *čojstvo,* a term that is difficult to translate precisely, although it means something like "manly virtue." This concerns the highest level of moral behavior, in which the demands of heroism are tempered by a sense of humanity that is extended to one's enemy. In a later chapter, some of Marko's examples of čojstvo will be discussed in connection with feuding.

HOUSE AND CLAN AS MORAL UNITS

When a person behaved as a bad man or woman, this brought shame to him directly and also to his house or clan. The members of a brastvo were keenly aware of their clan's reputation as a form of communal "property," and they attempted to curtail behavior on the part of a member that was likely to tarnish the reputation of the entire clan. In addition, they would back one another up on any case in which moral ambiguity existed, and they tended to enter into quickly escalating disputes with those who made slighting remarks concerning the moral status of their clan.

Particular pride was taken in a clan member who distinguished himself heroically or in the fact that a clan traditionally carried the battle flag *(barjak)* for its tribe or supplied the tribe with other kinds of leaders, such as a pop, the vojvoda, or the "good men" (dobri ljudi), who arbitrated major disputes such as blood feuds. Indeed, it was blood feuds that placed an entire clan under the greatest moral pressure. When a feud began, the clan had to uphold its collective reputation in a very public way in a context that made it highly vulnerable to social evaluation and, if its members were soo slow in trying to take vengeance, to being condemned as cowardly.

HOW THE TRADITIONAL MORAL SYSTEM WORKED

The main values of Montenegrin morality have already been discussed. These values provided images of proper and improper conduct to which individuals could respond by deciding which of their impulses should be acted upon and which should be curbed. Had there been nothing to affect their behavior other than the knowledge of this moral code, it might be safely assumed that there would have been a great deal of disorder and disruption in Montenegrin society. For one thing, because of their love of taking booty, there would have been raiding between clans of the same tribe; so tribal political unity would have been destroyed. For another, the strict regulation of women, especially in their sexual behavior, would have been impossible had there been no "teeth" in the rules of conduct.

There were, in fact, many social and psychological mechanisms, direct and indirect, that conditioned and channeled individual behavior in conformity with the values discussed above. Such sanctioning mechanisms might be positively reinforcing, in the form of rewards, or else suppressive in that they involved negative conditioning. Some sanctions (such as public execution) were quite apparent, although they rarely come into play. However, as we shall see, many of the more usual negative sanctions and most of the positive ones were not terribly obvious to an outsider, even though Montenegrins felt their presence keenly.

INDIRECT SANCTIONS

The most basic sanction in Montenegro was a person's awareness of esteem or censure on the part of the tribe and the clan. At stake was one's own moral reputation or *glas* (voice). To have a *dobar glas,* or good voice, was to be respected among members of the tribe. To have a *loš glas,* or bad voice, was to be looked down upon by the tribal community.

Simply the desire to have a good name, plus the knowledge that the community was intensely interested in every individual member from a moral standpoint, were enough to make a person take care. He or she tried to see to it that all behavior that was subject to public scrutiny was such that a loš glas would not result. Thus, the esteem of the community provided a subtle but vital moral sanction in Montenegro, as it does wherever people live in small communities and spend much of their time gossiping about one another. Knowledge that a dobar glas would go to a person who was morally deserving had a positive conditioning effect upon individual behavior. On the other hand, everyone's acute awareness of the dangers of acquiring a loš glas had a very powerful deterrent effect, one that suppressed immoral behavior. In other words, a good reputation served as the "carrot" that led people on, while a bad reputation was one of the "sticks" that punished them.

DIRECT SANCTIONS

When a person is guilty of moral malfeasance, other people may take direct action to try to modify or get rid of the behavior. One effective mechanism is not to speak to the person. Ostracism produces social isolation and a feeling of profound discomfort. In Montenegro, ostracism sometimes took a peculiar form. When one member of a clan continually went against the moral code, his clan might formally disavow him insofar as retaliation in the name of clan honor was concerned (Bogišić 1874; Rovinskii 1901; Jelić 1926). By doing so, they publicly excluded him from the group, and they made it clear that if he were killed, his own clan would not seek to avenge his death. This extreme form of ostracism deprived a morally worthless troublemaker of the political backing of his own clan. It also saved the clan from the moral embarrassment of being associated with him and from an almost certain blood feud.

Another direct sanction was to criticize the person openly. This put pressure on him to change in a specific direction. In addition there were other heavier sanctions. A person might be exiled temporarily, or he might be permanently driven from the tribe. This did not deny the malefactor the right to live, since both in Montenegro and in the surrounding Turkish territory, people who were refugees from trouble of one sort or another continually were showing up and asking permission to settle. The moral code was such that whenever it was possible to award the desired sanctuary, this was done. But exile was still a very powerful form of direct sanctioning, because no one wanted to be uprooted.

In the most serious cases of moral transgression, execution was possible. This sanction could be applied formally, through tribal judicial processes that will be discussed presently. But it also might be a spontaneous act of the immediate community. In some cases, if very rarely, the method used was lapidation, or stoning to death. Usually, I was told, this was applied only to flagrantly dishonorable or evil women or to cowardly men who were seen as behaving like women or to people who had committed most serious crimes. The person judged to have transgessed was made to stand in one place, while rocks were cast by all members of the tribe. After a time, only a pile of stones was visible. The reason for having everyone participate in the execution was that this obviated the likelihood of a revenge killing to avenge the person who had been executed, which would have been feasible if a single person had acted as executioner.

Direct sanctioning also was involved with more formal kinds of judicial process. When the tribal elders formed a court (sud) and decided against someone in a dispute, he very well might have to pay damages in coin, livestock, or weapons. For example, if someone were found guilty of stealing from another member of the tribe, he would have to pay back several times the amount of the same goods that he had stolen. These economic sanctions resulted from a formal rather than a spontaneous judgment, but they applied only to a narrow range of behaviors, including treason and theft within the tribe. Sometimes an entire tribe would meet to consider formally the case of a tribesman who had been accused of treason (Jovanović 1948), and execution or exile was a possible outcome in such a case.

Of course, not all direct sanctions were dealt out by human beings. God, Saint Elijah, and a coterie of other saints might punish moral offenders who committed major antisocial acts, as well as people who did not give the deities their due, ritually speaking. It is difficult to reckon exactly how efficacious the religious sanctioning system that centered around confession and communion actually was during the traditional period. This system for the detection and correction of sinners did operate formally and was constantly available. However, as a sanctioning mechanism, it was definitely secondary to the social sanctions mentioned above.

THE MONTENEGRIN VERSION OF CONSCIENCE

In Serbian, *kajanje* means that you have committed some deed, and then afterwards you wish you had not done it (Boehm 1980). But by that time the evil deed cannot be undone, and feeling kajanje is of no practical help. The deed is likely to be highly immoral by Montenegrin standards: you steal within your tribe, lie to people close to you, or murder a fellow tribesman. This definition of kajanje comes, not from the traditional period, but from thirty-five contemporary informants in the tribe of Upper Morača, who defined the word for me during the spring of 1966. These definitions jibe nicely with the definition provided by Vuk Karadžić (1935) in his *Srpski Rječnik* (Serbian dictionary), which was compiled in tribal Montenegro in the early 1800s. Essentially, this word meant something very close to "regret" or "repentance" in English.

Every culture seems to have a word dealing with the fact that people sometimes think very intensely about their own past actions and the desirability or undesirability of such actions, as a sort of psychological feedback mechanism. In general, this device enables the native actor to analyze past mistakes and to pursue a more socially adaptive course in the future. This kind of self-awareness was particularly useful in a society such as Montenegro's, in which other people generally were quite unforgiving when it came to individual moral malfeasances. For major transgressions, there was really no second chance. Once it was publicly known that one had committed a major error, the social strain remained, and there was no likely means available for full atonement. If in theory the church offered such a means through confession, this was of little importance to Montenegrins. Rather, it was the public view of one's moral status that counted.

For this reason, it was important that people be self-aware and that they be able privately to take stock of their own moral transgressions while these still remained undiscovered or merely suspected. To fall into a pattern, let us say, of stealing within one's settlement or tribe, or of indulging in premarital intercourse if one were female, eventually was almost certain to lead to detection in such intimate communities, even though one was likely (with cunning and a bit of luck) to get away with it for a time. The Montenegrin version of conscience provided the individual with an intense and unpleasant psychological reaction, one that focused attention on the fact that an action could have resulted in danger to the person's moral status. This reduced the likelihood of repetition and eventual detection.

In addition, people might simply feel kajanje over the deed itself in a totally private way, because of having identified strongly with the moral values of their culture. Thus, kajanje was not only an early warning device but also a sort of internal courtroom in which one became dissatisfied with oneself, morally speaking, after the fact. If this happened, the anticipation of kajanje may well have acted as a double deterrent to repeating the same behavior, since it focused the attention of the moral actor not only on the danger of discovery, but also on the predictable internal discomfort that lay ahead if he or she were to transgress again and not be discovered.

Kajanje was not closely associated with religion in the sense that Roman Catholics must feel true remorse (as part of penitence) when absolution for sin is sought through confession. Nor was kajanje exactly like the entirely private guilt that torments many other kinds of Christians. For most Montenegrins, in the case of moral kajanje, the practical social consequences would seem to have been paramount, rather than a largely internal kind of moral agony. Because of the prominence of honor and shame in Montenegrin moral life, this particular blend of what Americans would call guilt and shame (see Piers and Singer 1971) is scarcely surprising.

HONOR AND SHAME

In general, Montenegrin moral faculties were sharp, and Montenegrins were quick to make judgments in cases of known or even suspected individual transgressions. As individual actors on the stage of morality, they were also very quick to anticipate, in their own self-interest, any adverse reactions that other people might have to their behavior. This focus on external sources of moral judgment is best represented in English by the word "honor."

Two words for honor were used very widely in Montenegro: *čast* and *obraz*. Čast meant much the same thing as the English word "honor"; it also designated the hospitality that was offered to a guest. Obraz, however, was a different kind of word, in that it was figurative. Literally, obraz meant "the cheek on your face." Figuratively, it was used in a special sense which was very important in Montenegro. Obraz stood for your moral reputation, your ability to hold your head up in the company of other tribesmen, to look them straight in the eye, to associate freely with people because you carried no major moral blemish that would make them view or treat you as a person who was socially unacceptable.

Bijeli obraz meant literally "white cheek," or better, "pure cheek." But *crni obraz* was the key term. Literally it meant "black cheek," which in the Montenegrin mind meant that a person's cheek had been besmirched through unseemly behavior. However, in Serbo-Croatian, *crni* (black) also refers to things that are red in certain contexts, as in the case of *crno vino,* or "red wine." Thus the metaphor would seem to have had another level, more nearly literal, in that "red cheek" signified that blood had rushed to a person's face to darken it. In Montenegro as elsewhere, this physiological phenomenon accompanies acute embarrassment. To face other people when they knew of one's moral transgression was painful socially, not only because their bad opinion was easily predicted and was sensed acutely but also because one's own social discomfort was physiologically obvious.

This bad opinion could merely fuel the local gossip mills without any direct expression of moralistic aggression. But there was also the possibility of ostracism. This spontaneous form of extreme avoidance was not required in order to make a Montenegrin feel terribly uneasy. Much milder forms of avoidance—ones that might not be noticed by a foreign observer—were enough to cause great social discomfort. These could take the form of a certain coolness in manner of greeting or a tendency of people to shorten the time spent in conversation with the alleged culprit. In extreme cases, however, the signal could be direct, openly critical, and psychologically devastating. For example, to reach behind one's back to hand someone a glass of brandy was an open insult that symbolically underscored his morally vulnerable status when he had failed to take vengeance for over a year (Rovinskii 1901).

Such sanctions had a very powerful effect in Montenegro. However, it must be remembered that the temptation to assert oneself in directions that were prohibited by the moral code could be very strong as well. For example, a love of plunder was part of the psychological make-up of any highly moral Montenegrin male, a value reinforced by heroic epics that extolled raiding exploits against Moslem enemies. It was very tempting to bend this ethic a bit, so as to "justify" the plundering either of Christian neighbors who submitted to the Ottomans or of tribal neighbors who happened to be blood-feud enemies. In addition, even though the Montenegrin sexual code was suppressive, particularly for females, culturally speaking, sexuality was an open and well-developed interest. The idea of love and loving was also prominent, even though it did not take the particular form that idealized romantic love takes in America today (Durham 1928; Djilas 1958). Given the prominent emphasis placed upon interpersonal sexual attractions in the culture, it is not surprising that both females and males did frequently try to enjoy life's greater pleasures, coping with the moral system through careful avoidance of discovery rather than through total conformity to its demands. Given these temptations and also a propensity to take risks, the avoidance of crni obraz was an ongoing and critical concern for most Montenegrins. In 1965 it was viewed as a difficult struggle that continued throughout life (Boehm 1972), and this view surely prevailed earlier.

This struggle entailed somewhat different behavioral strategies for males and for females. In the case of a male, the avoidance of detected theft and the pursuit of manly virtue in the violent fields of raiding, warfare, and vendetta were most important. Within the tribe, a man had to be reasonably truthful and should not behave submissively toward other men, since every tribesman was essentially equal as a man. Indeed, to be "trampled underfoot" was viewed as a signal dishonor. For a female, the avoidance of detection in theft or sexual misconduct was vitally important, as was the vigorous pursuit of the many household and subsistence tasks that a woman's life entailed.

For both males and females, honor and shame were closely connected. *Sramota* (shame) referred to the feeling or state in which a person could not face being in the presence of other people because they were aware of his or her moral misconduct. Public discovery was a salient aspect of the meaning of sramota, and in the Montenegrin view the social discomfort associated with sramota was very intense. One maintained a bijeli obraz largely by avoiding behaviors that would lead to sramota.

There was another term that meant almost the same thing as crni obraz, but it referred primarily to shame that resulted from committing a theft. This was *okideni nos,* or literally, "cut off nose" (Boehm 1972). Strictly speaking, this term was not entirely limited to being a metaphor. Mary Durham (1928) reports that in the early 1900s, when a wife was discovered being unfaithful to her husband, he literally might cut her nose off before divorcing her. The idea was that this would make her less likely to repeat this behavior with her next husband, if she could find one. Durham (1928) reports that her guide had seen such an unfortunate woman; but Durham never saw this herself during her extensive stays in Montenegro. However, cutting off a person's nose as a way of imposing moral indignity upon an enemy did crop up during the Balkan Wars and the First World War. By that time the Montenegrins had become responsive to the outside world's views on headhunting. But occasionally, an individual did cut off the nose and upper lip of an enemy to carry home. Mary Durham (1928), with her unerring eye for grisly detail, reports having seen in a hospital one man who had survived such an "operation."

What this verbal labeling suggests is that the taking of trophies—heads and noses alike—constituted both a symbolic and a literal disfigurement. This applied not only to a person in an enemy group, who was by definition the subject of ethnocentric hatred and hence of moral repugnance, but also to someone in one's own group who evoked great moral disdain.

At this point the reader has a good idea of the specific moral foci of the Montenegrins and of the ways in which these foci were taken into account by individuals. Following the orientation of the Montenegrins themselves, I have dwelt more upon the obvious negative side of morality than upon its positive features. However, it must be emphasized that positive sanctions, such as the according of respect to a person publicly, were extremely important in motivating individual Montenegrins to behave in accordance with the real values of their society. One good example is the funeral eulogy.

Although they did not believe very much in the afterlife, all Montenegrins anticipated the eulogy, which was certain to be part of their funeral service. In the eulogies that I heard, a series of men who represented their respective clans or settlements would boom out in their powerful Montenegrin voices a list of the good points of the deceased. All sins and misdemeanors were overlooked in eulogies; but even as the orator spoke, the entire tribe would think carefully upon the person's actual life and its moral qualities, both good and bad. In fact, just from the tone and content of a eulogy, I could usually tell whether the deceased was of good moral standing or not, without knowing the person's reputation. This funeral oration was the true Montenegrin "day of judgment," a worldly and democratic one rather than a supernatural one with judgment coming from on high. It was a final and utterly public summation of the tribal community's view of a person's obraz.

THE POWER OF GOSSIP

As I made my observations during the mid 1960s, I noticed that still another mode of judgment was on people's minds, a form of indirect social control that was likely to take place every day of one's life. This was the not-at-all public moral judgment that took place when various small groups of people got together socially and began to gossip. Because gossiping is universal and highly salient in small societies all over the world, I have no hesitation in assuming that the phenomena I observed in the recent past also prevailed in the traditional period before 1840. There is no ethnohistorical evidence concerning gossiping during that era, but such behavior seldom is recorded in the notebooks of travelers. In fact, gossiping is an intimate act, one that a foreigner is not likely to be privy to at all until after a long time has been spent in a small community.

In Montenegro, much gossip occurred in the context of "don't tell anyone I told you this, but . . . ." However, things really didn't work that way. The gossiper would then proceed to tell the listener a tidbit of information that someone else had passed on under exactly the same injunction of supposed secrecy. As in gossip systems all over the world, information that begins by being exchanged confidentially between people who are very close is passed along as a ''secret'' until eventually it falls into the hands of individuals who have little sense of obligation to keep it quiet; at that point it can quickly become community knowledge. This may well happen without any one person consciously taking responsibility for beginning to talk about the matter openly. The distinctive feature of an entire sysem of gossip in a small community is that intimate facts about individuals become widely known through a process that takes place in private. The people who originally dissemi-nate the gossip seldom realize the full extent to which the information will be disseminated; nor does the subject of the gossip often know how much broadcasting has taken place, unless a public accusation surfaces.

In Montenegro, as elsewhere (e.g., see Haviland 1977), gossiping constituted an entire system of gathering and processing information, by which a great deal of knowledge was organized in people's minds and memories. This information was concerned not only with the known or inferred actions of community members but also with their motivations and hidden desires. A goodly portion of this gossiping had a certain air of surveillance and detective work about it, and considerable energy went into trying to figure out unresolved crimes or into looking for moral malfeasance wherever such might be discovered or inferred. Because of this ever-present organ of ''crime detection,'' Montenegrins who wished to break their own cultural rules had to resort to elaborate schemes of deception. For example, in 1964 you might lean a rake against a certain portion of the barn as a signal to your lover that it was safe to visit during the next hour. Such ruses were discussed with me by young men in Upper Morača when I asked them how anyone could ever get away with anything in such an observant small community. Of course, activities connected with the herding of livestock frequently required people to spend time alone, and this did provide a certain amount of privacy. But for Montenegrins there remained the fact that one's neighbors could be counted upon to be curious, and many of them would talk, even if they were mostly guessing.

A gossip system involves a flow of information through social networks. While any given person may have only a few friends with whom the most intimate gossip is shared, in Montenegro these networks were sufficiently interconnected so that much of the ''news'' would travel quickly throughout the entire tribe or through large parts of it. In processing information concerning people whose moral standings were being evaluated, this network served as a kind of courtroom. Evidence was carefully sifted, and its evaluation from a moral standpoint took place in quite a subtle way. Fact and opinion were mixed in a fashion that would never be allowed in a modern court of law, and evidence of an extremely circumstantial nature could easily decide a case. This was particularly true where the community's opinion of the "defendant" was that the suspected misdeed was in fact likely, in terms of the person's clan background or personal moral character. Thus, one's personal moral track record, and also one's clan reputation and the moral standings of one's parents, played a major part in determining the conclusions reached by various individuals in the gossip system.

These decisions were made by a few individuals at a time, because the most intimate gossip took place in small groups. In fact, the conclusions that were reached would often vary from group to group. But the Montenegrin individual viewed the entire system as a unit, as a threatening mass of maliciously curious people who arrived at unanimous interpretations. A favorite expression was *"selo zna . . ."* (the village knows). If I would ask about the solution of one of the rare thefts that occurred locally in Upper Morača tribe, the reply might be that the authorities would never solve it because a lack of evidence prevented this, but "the village knows . . . ." The implication was that the culprit's moral reputation was blemished because the entire moral community had arrived at a decision independently of any formal legal process.

Members of the tribe tried not to provide this tribal gossip mill with anything too interesting about themselves. For example, a young girl of certain virtue would not allow even a young man who was sincerely interested in marrying her to draw her off innocently to a secluded place for as much as five minutes to speak with her privately. She would be afraid to provide the community with any information that it might tend to use as circumstantial evidence. In such a case, her fear would be well justified, since the young man might boast afterwards of things that in fact he had been unable to do, so as to enhance his reputation among the young men.

The very real fear of gossip, which significantly guided Montenegrin life, did not deter most people to the point that they would not take any chances at all; but it did make them extremely cautious. It also made them quite inventive in trying to realize a certain amount of satisfaction outside the confines of the moral rules, without losing their obraz. Many in fact succeeded. As a foreigner, I was sometimes entrusted with pieces of personal information that were known to only one or a few people in my settlement or tribe. These exceptional cases may not be revealed in print, even anonymously, because it is likely that people from Upper Morača will someday read this book. The local gossips would be quick to identify these people, no matter how well they were disguised; and the psychological consequences would be disastrous, because the individuals concerned would feel that they had been personally betrayed. In their view, the moral exposure would be utterly public, before a world-wide moral community, and therefore would be damaging to their obraz in a particularly monstrous way.

GOSSIP AND PERSONAL REPUTATION

In looking at the larger features of moral systems everywhere, gossiping is important as an indirect social control. But still more basically, gossip functions as a system through which the group's idea of what should be morally acceptable or unacceptable is continuously rehashed and refreshed through an endless series of case studies. Because in Montenegro the findings of this particular courtroom were seldom made public, gossiping, in most people's view, was a rather insidious instrument of morality. One had no right either to confront one's accusers or to argue one's case. In actuality, however, the same people who felt tyrannized by the moral curiosity of the community also participated in the system as gossipers.

It was, of course, personal participation in gossiping which made the individual so sensitive and so vulnerable to the working of the gossip system. No one who has been privy to a Montenegrin gossip session could remain oblivious afterwards to the fact that nobody escaped the scrutiny of the moral community there. As an indirect social control, gossip worked so well simply because almost every Montenegrin cared very deeply about how he or she was viewed by the community, independently of any direct sanctions or other manifest consequences.

At stake, of course, was one's obraz, because public opinion determined one's reputation, in general, and because one's moral reputation in turn determined the white or black state of one's "cheek." The fact that the community usually avoided and condemned moral confrontation in its more direct humiliating forms did not mean that an individual could not guess what was going on judgmentally when his or her transgressions were apt to be known or suspected.

In traditional Montenegro, gossiping as a sanction had different effects on different kinds of behaviors. In choices such as hospitality versus stinginess, honesty versus overuse of deceit in casual transactions between people, or sexual transgressions versus sexual propriety, gossip was the primary sanctioning mechanism. But in cases such as theft or murder, there were also other more-formal modes of investigation and punishment. For some more-serious crimes, a group of six, twelve, or twenty-four "good men" would meet to conduct a formal investigation and then deliver a sentence, while in cases of treason, the entire tribe might sit in witness and could decree death or exile. But even when sanctioning procedures became more formalized, gossip still played its part. The gossip system provided the network that helped to inform the people who sat in judgment, even though they also called in witnesses.

Thus, gossiping was a mechanism that was prominent in the Montenegrin mind because it determined the extent to which people's obrazes were black. But gossip also determined the degree to which obrazes were white. I must emphasize that there was an active interest in bestowing praise as well as blame when people sat down to talk about people in Montenegro. Individual moral actors were aware of this, too, and tried as best they could to behave accordingly. But it was the avoidance of social pain in the form of crni obraz that drove them the hardest.

THE MORAL SYSTEM AS BACKGROUND FOR EXPLAINING BLOOD FEUDS

In summary, this background discussion of the moral system and its operation in Montenegro presents a portrait of a people who were extremely sensitive in the matter of honor. This means that their lives and behavior were shaped very effectively by tribal public opinion simply because they were so vulnerable to that opinion. This concern of Montenegrins with their personal and clan reputations was the basis of feuding, in that the taking of blood vengeance was not merely morally justifiable but was morally necessary if one's reputation was to remain unblemished.

Gossip served as the major indirect mechanism of social control, even though gossiping was not done with any such intention. On the other hand, Montenegrins very deliberately implemented direct sanctions and knew how these worked, when they manipulated deviant individuals to make them conform. Thus, the moral system was consciously steered by the Montenegrin tribesmen as they applied whatever insights they possessed into the workings of their own social system to specific problems that arose. In this sense, morality can be viewed as a special guidance component, which steered the entire social system in directions that were valued by the members of the tribe.

THE MANAGEMENT OF CONFLICTS

In addition to sanctioning those who deviated, Montenegrins also manipulated groups of individuals when they could, in the interest of reducing tensions within the larger group, the tribe. Not infrequently, the Montenegrin capacity to identify immediate or potential dangers to the well-being or survival of the social group was focused on the disruptive conflicts that frequently erupted in a society of proud warriors. In many societies, conflicts simply are suppressed by force, where a political leader possesses the coercive power to do so. However, in Montenegro, no man was ever supposed to coerce another man within the tribe, even though the entire tribe could gather to try a major criminal. Therefore, it was necessary to use some other means to keep conflicts within manageable limits. In the absence of coercion, the means were limited to persuasion, even when a conflict became homicidal in the form of a feud and created extensive social disruption.

Management of conflicts frequently came through informal attempts to mediate disputes. But at other times it could be highly formal, with the kind of duly constituted body mentioned above, the Court of Good Men, seeking to find settlements that would be acceptable to both sides. In such cases, there was a clear and conscious diagnosis of a complicated social problem by the wiser men in a tribal community, which was followed by deliberate action in the form of a decision rendered. This decision was aimed at definitively resolving the problem at hand so that no further social disruption would take place. Both the methods and the objectives were clearly understood by all the native actors, since this took place in a shared cultural context.

I must stop here to explain that conflict management must be set aside from the more basic forms of moral conditioning discussed earlier. This is because the individuals who were involved in conflicts frequently were not seen as moral culprits. People who were morally innocent could and frequently did get into serious conflicts through honest misunderstandings or accidents. Such situations did not call for sanctioning people as individuals who were morally out of line, since Montenegrins did not define entering into a conflict per se as an immoral act. Rather, the aim was simply to keep the conflict manageable from the standpoint of the community's welfare.

The moral value that guided Montenegrins when they actively helped to resolve conflicts was one of the highest—a strong value placed upon social harmony *(sloga)* by shrewd tribal social theorists who understood quite well the dangers present in uncontrolled conflicts. Indeed, any individual who disrupted sloga without having a good reason could be severely sanctioned as an immoral person. But entering into a conflict because one's honor had become involved was viewed as a legitimate reason for disrupting sloga, so far as judging the behavior of the individuals was concerned. What remained was the conflict itself as a clear and present danger to social harmony and possibly as a real danger to the unity of the tribe itself.

Very often the management of conflict involved, not an attempt to resolve a conflict definitively, but rather a pressure brought to bear on the conflicting parties to limit their aggressive behavior so that this would not become dangerous to normal social life. An example that occurred only very rarely in Montenegro is the custom we know of as dueling. While dueling does not resolve a conflict before some violence takes place, the duel definitely is expected to terminate the conflict. This widespread practice, as a result of its well-followed rules, prevents homicidal disputes from erupting in locales where innocent bystanders might be hurt; at the same time it prevents a quarrel from spreading to include allies of the two disputants. This mode of managing a conflict situation does not involve a total suppression or immediate resolution of the conflict; rather, it involves a decisive limitation of its potential adverse social effects. Even if both parties survive, the conflict has been resolved as an affair of honor. As we shall see, the Montenegrin manner of handling blood-feud conflicts within the tribe bore important similarities to dueling as characterized above.

FEUDING AS CONFLICT MANAGEMENT

At this point I shall not discuss any further the management of conflicts as being a highly important extension of the operation of the moral system in its more conscious and deliberate aspects. But I do wish to emphasize that later in this book, the overall pattern of feuding will be interpreted as a major manifestation of the human capacity for deliberate social engineering. This emphasis comes because I am convinced that feuding everywhere is, in effect, an important and complicated form of conflict management. This may appear paradoxical at first, because in the chapters to come the reader will have to react to the exremely violent, compulsive, disruptive, persistent, and apparently uncontrollable nature of Montenegrin feuding behavior, at least as this strikes people who are cultural outsiders. But I shall argue that any Montenegrin feud that ran its full course necessarily contained two critical elements of conflict management discussed above: the deliberate limitation of conflict and a deliberate attempt to resolve the conflict. This understanding can come about only after one has become more familiar with how the Montenegrins themselves viewed and coped with the blood feuds in their midst.

FEUDING AND MORALITY

In many respects the morality of several thousand people who are living in a permanently settled tribal territory is unlike our own morality. There is less concern for legalistic maneuvering, and more for personal and clan reputation. There are no specialized police officers or judges, nor are there any prisons. But there are very powerful sanctions that shape behavior, and these operate both directly and indirectly, intentionally and automatically.

Feuding was essentially a positively valued institution insofar as the moral system was concerned, in that it involved the upholding of honor. In addition, I believe that feuding served as a kind of sanction, because it suppressed certain immoral behaviors that people knew were likely to start feuds. They also knew that feuds were dangerous, stressful, economically costly, and generally inconvenient from a practical standpoint. We must assume, therefore, that excessive quarreling and giving of insults, in addition to other provocative acts such as breach of contract, property disputes, and "fooling around" with the women of other clans, tended to be avoided because of the perceived threat of starting a feud.

VENGEANCE AS A MORAL ACT

Having read this chapter, the reader is in a better position to understand the Montenegrins and their ethics with respect to feuding. For a person who has never lived in such a culture, perhaps the most difficult aspect of feuding to comprehend is the way in which the tribesmen distinguished between homicide in which there was moral culpability and that in which culpability was absent. In this respect, their classifications differed significantly from our own. In Montenegro any deliberate or negligent killing of a defenseless fellow tribesman who had done the killer no harm created something like a criminal liability.

However, if two men quarreled and began to raise serious questions about one another's honor, an ensuing homicidal incident was not really viewed as criminal. The killing might not even occur in the heat of the moment; the insulted man might brood about things for a time and then simply shoot his enemy down in what we would call cold blood. While this has none of the chivalrous air that we attribute to dueling in the Western European tradition and while it would appear to be what we ourselves view legally as premeditated murder, the Montenegrins had their own way of looking at it. They felt that if the man was justified by their standards because his "blood was boiling," such a premeditated act, committed without warning, was perfectly ethical—and was laudable, as well.

This brings us to revenge killing. After a first killing had occurred, the retaliatory homicide that followed was considered not only to be reasonable and proper but also to be *morally necessary* by traditional Montenegrin standards. Anglo-Saxon standards of fair play simply did not apply, in the sense that we have a rather fixed view of a "fair fight" or a duel; indeed, the ethic that prevailed was more similar to our own for a commando raid made by American forces in the course of a wholly just war. Any amount of deceit was permissible, and killing could be wholly premeditated and aimed at any member of the enemy group without the need for any special moral justification. In this respect, dominant American ethical values are quite similar to traditional Montenegrin values, even though the particular contexts in which they are applied are very different.

There are two purposes for providing the reader with this rather complete perspective on traditional Montenegrin morality. One is to foster an accurate reading of revenge killing as an act that was morally justified—and even was morally required—by Montenegrin standards. The other is to provide a cultural context that facilitates the explanation of feuding as a political process in which individuals (and clans) had to make very complicated decisions involving practical and ethical trade-offs that involved their reputations. I turn now to feuding behavior proper, to trace the course of a typical Montenegrin feud from the first insult or killing to the pacification ceremony that, it was hoped, laid the feud to rest.

6

The Trajectory of a Feud

THE RELEVANCE OF HEADHUNTING

If one asks how a Montenegrin reached the point that he (or, rarely, she) enacted krvna osveta, the most general answer is that some kind of conflict usually started the process. One might ask whether headhunting provoked feuds, since cutting off an enemy's head constituted a dreadful insult and made burial very difficult emotionally for the victim's survivors. But in Montenegro, headhunting was mainly an adjunct of warfare and played a relatively minor role in raiding.[1] Particularly when raiding was targeted on people who lived close enough to feud with them, the raid was likely to be for sheep, not for heads. On the other hand, a large-scale raid in which many heads were taken would tend to be against Moslems who lived at a considerable distance, where the individuals would not know exactly who had killed whom in the engagement. As we shall see presently, these anonymous conditions precluded a blood feud's taking place, even though a series of such mass attacks and counterattacks might be based on generalized feelings of vengeance.[2] Thus, we may dismiss headhunting or raiding as a major cause of krvna osveta as this was practiced by the traditional tribesmen.

DEFENSE OF HONOR

Montenegrins were prone to get into seriously escalating disputes because so much of their behavior was acted out on a public stage and

91

because the warrior audience took such a dim view of submissiveness. Many disputes simply stabilized at a level that did not become homicidal: two men had words, as I did with Milanka, perhaps escalated things to the point of exchanging a few insults, and left it at that. Frequently, one party would suffer a moderate amount of humiliation rather than escalate the quarrel dangerously. But it was inevitable that in some verbal disputes the balance of insults would become seriously one-sided. When sensitivity concerning lost honor would become unbearable to one party, a truly intense hostility would focus upon the person who had done this serious damage to his reputation.[3]

Loss of honor is a difficult thing to repair in any society; to take someone to court for defamation of character, for example, may not entirely rehabilitate the honor of the person who has to rely on a court in fighting out his case. In traditional Montenegro, the mode of restoring honor that had been lost because of an insult was far more direct, and also more effective. You simply killed the man who impugned your honor. This is one important reason that Montenegrins, as a matter of personal self-interest, were careful about how far they went verbally in offering offense.

Among the tribesmen, to do excessive public damage to the honor of another Montenegrin was considered to be unethical, even if the person was a known moral culprit (Boehm 1972). This moral value, which restrained people from publicly damaging the honor of other individuals, was not upheld just because Montenegrins felt sympathy for a person whose honor was damaged; it was also upheld because they knew that such episodes were likely to lead to serious quarrels and also to homicides, which in turn led to further homicides and to serious disruption of the social life of the tribe.

VERBAL DISPUTES

In spite of this ethic, the tribesmen did rather frequently get into altercations at the verbal level, and these sometimes turned into disputes in which one party felt deeply that he had lost his honor or had been seriously "trampled underfoot," as the Montenegrins thought of it. This kind of situation was unpredictable, because Montenegrins did not necessarily escalate a dispute to the homicidal level at the time the verbal exchange took place, when both parties had an even chance to kill each other. Rather, the insulted party often restrained himself from trying to "top" the insult of his tormentor with a homicidal act while they were arguing face to face, but then he would brood about it for hours or days or even weeks, and finally would reach a state where he could no longer bear it. Then, if he either met his tormentor by chance or sought him out, he would simply kill him on the spot, without necessarily warning him in any way or giving him a chance to defend himself. The intention was to pay back the other person in kind and possibly a bit more, as was suggested in the definitions of my present-day tribal consultants. Because he had already accepted the verbal insult without retaliating adequately in the original dispute, to retaliate later with a mere insult would not have fully restored his honor. On the other hand, a man who was willing to kill another man over honor obviously had to be brave, since he knew that the victim's brothers, sons, or clan brothers would try to hunt him down and kill him wherever he might go.

In the following example from the autobiography of Milovan Djilas the "feud" took place after the traditional period and involved, not another clan, but a representative of the Montenegrin government, acting in an official capacity but also on the basis of a personal whim. Milovan's great-grandfather Marinko Djilas, the brother of Marko, was a mild and retiring man who had decided not to take on the captain who had killed Marko. As we shall see, Marinko's son Aleksa was neither retiring nor mild.

> It was spring and Aleksa was ploughing the field. His father, Marinko, was tending the flock on the mountain. Captain Akica Ćorović, accompanied by two soldiers, came riding by the field. He called out a greeting to the lad. Aleksa replied with a murky silence, the only fitting tribute to a murderer. Akica shot back, "Dog, why don't you return my greeting? For I could lay you out to dry as I did your uncle!" The lad left his plowing, hurried home to his mother, and tricked her into believing that his father had sent an urgent demand for his rifle to fight attacking wolves. His mother gave him a blunderbuss from the locked chest. Aleksa intercepted Akica, fired a shattering volley into his chest, and then, with a dagger, carved out pieces of his heart. [Djilas 1958:12]

In Aleksa's response to the insult of the man who deliberately had sought to "trample him underfoot" in public we have a good example of how a killing over honor might have occurred in the traditional period. The mortal verbal insult is avenged, afterwards, by a literally mortal physical blow that comes without warning. As my contemporary consultant said, you try to pay the person back in even better measure than he gave you. This is exactly what Aleksa Djilas did afterwards with his knife, with the inevitable result that his entire small clan had to flee Montenegro and settle for a time in Turkish territory.

In this case, it was words (riječi) that had inflamed a preexisting conflict to the point of homicide in spite of the fact that the consequences were quite predictably disastrous for this tiny clan. The unfortunate Djilases became better and better known for their valor as the blood continued to flow. From this point on, the "feud" that ensued was highly atypical of the traditional period, in that the government tried to wipe out every male in the small but obstinate Djilas clan. When this plan failed, Prince Nikola adopted a course of reconciliation, and the father of Milovan Djilas became rehabilitated as an officer in the prince's army. Earlier, I discussed the problem of his residual needs for vengeance.

This feudlike conflict had obviously begun and continued because of truly deep grievances. But during the traditional period, foreigners reporting on how Montenegrin feuds started tended to look at the overt causes of feuds as being highly trivial (e.g., Durham 1928), emphasizing that the initial killing might have come from a sheep's merely straying from the pasture of one tribe onto that of another, or some such minor incident. The implication was that Montenegrins were insanely sensitive in the matter of honor and were prone to having overly violent reactions. These foreigners missed the point that every year literally thousands of other straying sheep caused disputes that did not have any homicidal consequences. It was where there were already hard feelings or where someone had inadvertently or recklessly gone too far in offering an insult that a verbal quarrel would reach the stage where one party would feel that a mortal insult had been offered. In a later chapter I shall examine the difficult art of quarreling manfully and well in Montenegro without getting involved in a feud, from the special perspective of looking at the decisions that individuals had to make in this type of fast-moving and volatile situation. But here it is enough to say that while many recorded feuds did begin with angry words, in thousands of other cases (not recorded) similar angry words failed to bring on a homicidal act.

The following is a well-documented example of multiple vengeance killings in the traditional period,[4] which came about almost instantaneously because of "words." The dispute did not arise between two men but was a group affair between two clans, which was started by the disruptive behavior of children and women. A Venetian official took down a deposition from one of the participants, and Vrčević (1890) published it in his book on oral history and legal judgments. I rely here upon Mary Edith Durham's spirited translation:

> "Two years ago we celebrated the 'Karidad' (funeral feast) of the deceased Knezh Dumo. The whole village flocked to it and ate and drank all they could; and all at once two little boys started fighting like

A skup at which people have been happily dancing and singing is disturbed
briefly by a guzva. A group of men who are out of sight are restraining
someone who wants to fight, while members of a concerned community
approach the scene. The tribal community considers such a disturbance to be
unfortunate, and they will quickly return to their kolo as soon as the man is
quieted down.

two cocks and one of our 'odivas' (married woman) rushed to protect
her child, and the mother of the other one rushed up and hit her on the
head with a stone. Down ran the blood, and both women began to
shout awful accusations about each other's families. All our men
rushed with weapons in their hands to protect their sister. The men of
the other bratstvo[5] rushed to protect theirs, and there was a terrible
fight. We killed two of them and wounded two, and the woman who
had started all the trouble was wounded also. My father was killed and
I was badly wounded, and had the villagers not intervened there would
have been a blood-bath. We buried the dead and carried home the
wounded. Then the other bratstvo threatened me and my bratstvo
about the two killed; and they owed us for one dead head and two
wounded. In a few days the village gathered and wanted us to make
peace.'' [Durham 1928:89]

I interrupt the deposition at this point because we are discussing the ways
in which vengeance killings were initiated, not the entire course of a feud
through to its pacification. In focusing on the ways in which this
particular case of multiple homicide originated, two special circumstances must be noted. One is that this was a feast attended by members

The man who has become angry at someone is hidden behind the head of an observer. (His adversary has not become engaged in the conflict.) Members of the angry man's clan are moving in to control him.

of the same large local group or settlement. We may assume therefore that the intervention of the villagers was forceful and determined because they saw their own neighbors slaughtering one another and therefore felt that the social equilibrium of the entire group was at risk. Second, the fact that this dispute took place at a feast means that the adults were well into the process of drinking the grape brandy that Montenegrins produce. The danger of serious quarrels is particularly great at festive occasions because of the combined physiological and culural effects of alcohol.

During the 1960s I was present at several public altercations that were not called svadja but by a special term *gužva,* which means a sort of turmoil or mix-up. While rare, these occasionally took place at festive gatherings where an entire tribe or several tribes had collected to celebrate and drink. What happens with a gužva is that two men get into a dispute, and when it appears that they are close to coming to blows, the bystanders come in to restrain forcibly the more aggressive party, or both parties if necessary. I have seen occasions when eight or ten strapping young Montenegrin men were just barely able to restrain a single enraged comrade, the entire cluster plunging and swaying crazily as he desperately tried to get at his opponent. On one occasion I took a photograph of a gužva, and the reaction of the tribesmen was unexpectedly hostile. They wanted to know if I planned to emphasize to the outside world the

In this picture the aggrieved party is struggling to free himself from those who are restraining him. The two men with mustaches, who are both members of his clan, have firm grips on him. But in his efforts to shake free, he carries along from place to place the entire group of men who are trying to hold him. In a few minutes, the episode will be over.

way in which they quarreled when, in fact, the entire tribe had gathered for a national holiday to drink, dance the *kolo,* and be sociable.

My purpose in taking the picture was to see whether it was chiefly the members of the disputant's clan who restrained him or whether it was random members of the tribe. My hypothesis was that in the old days a clan would carefully restrain its own obstreperous member in order to keep him from getting them into a feud unnecessarily. Obviously, this threat no longer existed under the modern government. But I suspected that the pattern of behavior might be a kind of cultural holdover, of a behavior through which the clan protected both an inebriated brother and itself as a wider liability group that either could have to take vengeance or could be targeted for vengeance. When the picture was developed, my guess proved to be correct, in that it was almost exclusively members of the man's own clan who clung to him so desperately.

Out of deference to the wishes of certain people of Upper Morača tribe, I am tempted not to include that fascinating and dramatic picture with those that illustrate this book simply because those people are extremely sensitive about the honor of their tribe. However, I was later told by a spokesman for the clan concerned that the picture was not injurious to the clan's reputation, and in my own opinion this picture shows Montenegrin character at its very best. The man who is being restrained has been drinking, and he has a grievance against another

Here the would-be quarreler, who is hidden behind the dozen men who are actively trying to stop his movement, is finally under control. The chief administrator of Upper Morača tribe (wearing a modern hat with hat band) is showing his concern. Almost all of the men who are restraining the quarreler are members of his clan and therefore are expected to watch out for his welfare. In traditional times, if he had injured or killed someone, his own clan brothers might have been liable for retaliatory homicide.

member of the tribe—something that can happen anywhere in the world. Almost all of the men who are restraining him are clan brothers who do not wish to see him damage his own welfare or the good name of their clan by attacking someone inappropriately when he is inebriated.

In publishing this picture and writing about quarrels, I do wish to reassure my Montenegrin friends and my neighbors back in Morača that anyone who reads this book will view them, not as people who are given to quarreling—indeed, all people quarrel at times—but as people of the very highest moral character who actively try to control quarrels when these inevitably arise. Indeed, if one takes into consideration how important honor continues to be to individual Montenegrins, it is amazing how few quarrels there are there today.

Another example of a possible fight that was contained by the men around it took place when people from a number of tribes gathered together to sing, dance, socialize, drink brandy, and generally to have a good time up on the mountaintop in the summertime. The photographs show these events, along with the throwing of large rocks, by which men

This skup is on a mountaintop. While several hundred men and women join arms to sing and to dance very slowly in a giant kolo, individuals within the circle dance in pairs or cut in on those who are dancing together. People at this skup come from three or four tribes, but many have stayed behind because they are working in the fields down in the valleys, near the winter villages.

exhibited their strength and asserted their dominance amicably. At the end of this meeting of perhaps a thousand people, when the men were mounting their horses to ride home, it appeared that one man had a grievance against another. These men were not from Upper Morača tribe, and I did not know them or the cause of the trouble. But the photographs speak for themselves. The theme, as in Upper Morača, is one of carefully controlling the potential for violence.

In the historical case quoted from Vrčević, one reason that there was no quicker success in stopping the series of killings was that there were no earlier warning signs in the usual sense. It was not men who had begun to quarrel, but little boys. Again, one could not begin to count the number of little boys who have come to blows at festive occasions in Montenegro without starting a major altercation. So just as in the case of a stray sheep, there was no good basis to predict a potential homicidal outcome unless, perhaps, one knew the history of relations between the groups involved. Indeed, in this case, apparently the words of the two women were critical in escalating the quarrel. Their insults and the subsequent blow transformed it into an affair of honor in which two clans become homicidally involved, because two clans happened to have their men on the spot and because everyone was drinking. In this case the confrontation was utterly public, and clan honor was keenly involved in that the entire local community was present as an audience.

In traditional Montenegro, any conflict situation involving land, women, or money could have led to angry words, insults, then homicide.

This traditional dance emulates the eagle, or oro. Lengthening shadows indicate that the day's festivities are nearly over, and soon people will be walking or riding horseback to their katuns, where they keep their sheep during the summer.

But in some cases the conflict situation itself was so insulting to honor that retaliatory homicide became likely in the absence of any verbal exchange. Probably the one most regular cause of trouble came from the ambiguous Montenegrin definition of sexual morality discussed earlier, which all but encouraged the free-ranging young male "eagles" to prey upon the morally restricted young female "rabbits."

The pattern worked like this. A young man and a maiden would be attracted to one another and would manage to meet clandestinely. The young man would lead the girl on with promises of marriage, and sometimes she would decide to trust him. Even in the 1960s there was no way to obtain reliable research data on this most private aspect of Montenegrin life, but it would appear that some young men did marry girls whom they otherwise might have "ruined," while others simply strung the girl along and then dropped her. If the youth was discreet at that point and did not boast of his conquest, the maiden's loss of virtue still might remain undetected. She could then try to convince her fiancé, once a marriage had been arranged, that she really was a virgin, or at least she might try to get him to accept her damaged status without telling anyone about it. But since Montenegrin young men were prone to boast,

Hurling a rock for distance. This competitive sport occupies some of the
stronger and more competitive young men, while others sing and dance, sit
in sociable drinking groups, or promenade.

it was also very likely that the girl's reputation would be ruined, in which
case she would become all but unmarriageable. The honor of the house
would be damaged accordingly.

Earlier, when the culprit was unambiguously identifiable and the
ruination of the maiden was public and definitive, homicides did result
from this kind of damage to honor (Jelić 1926). But if the girl had
engaged in premarital intercourse with previous partners, then the young
man who was discovered to have slept with her could not be blamed very
seriously for damaging her honor and that of the house. Of course, these
facts were difficult to determine because, for females, premarital sex was
utterly clandestine and never admitted and because so much empty
boasting was done by males. All of these factors in combination led to a
great deal of ambiguity, to differences in interpretation of the facts, and
therefore to the likelihood of serious misunderstandings, verbal disputes,
insults, and killings.

In case the girl became pregnant, the honor of the house was very
much on the line, and a young man of good intentions would immediately
marry her (Jelić 1926). In a rich case history, which will be presented in
its original form in the next chapter, there are statements from the father

The promenade, or corso, is where unmarried young men and women get a chance to look one another over as they walk back and forth on the cool mountaintop. Sometimes their glances result in intertribal proposals of marriage. Lengthening shadows indicate that it is now about time to go home.

of a girl who became pregnant and from the father of the boy who made her that way, each arguing that the other was at fault for the dishonor to her house and for the fact that her father had killed the boy to avenge the dishonor (see Vrčević 1890). In another case that I heard about, which illustrates how ambiguity could lead to the starting of a feud, a boy was hired out by his household to a household in a different tribe. The barn in which he and two sons of that household slept burned down, but only the hired boy was burned to death. The circumstances of his death were ambiguous in the minds of his own clan, since only he had died; but because they were not certain that there had been foul play, instead of taking vengeance they made it known that they might accept money for his dead head. In effect, the clan that had hired him was thus obligated to ''go to court'' in order to prove that there had been no malice or negligence. Its argument was convincing, and a killing was averted because the death was defined as noninsulting to honor. In this case there was no hostility to begin with, and no verbal dispute had taken place. But without the intervention of the Court of Good Men to resolve the ambiguity, there would have been a revenge killing instead of merely a payment of blood money to cover an accidental death.

THE FIRST HOMICIDE AS A MAJOR OPENING MOVE

Insofar as a blood feud was a competitive contest strictly controlled by rules, feuding may be likened to a game played by two sides. In the following sections I shall lay out the course that a typical feud followed, dividing the process into stages that make sense to me as an ethnographer. In introducing this treatment, I must issue a warning, insofar as this outline is somewhat idealized. For one thing, it is clear from Hasluck's (1954) book on the unwritten laws of the northern Albanians that sometimes there were substantial variations in feuding practices from one tribe to another. Where the law is unwritten and no central governmental control exists, this is predictable. For another, I have sometimes built upon fragmentary evidence in order to put a piece of this sequential puzzle in place. I shall not interrupt the text to indicate every point at which my interpretation is somewhat tentative; rather, certain interpretations will be discussed further in notes for the benefit of readers who are interested in the finer points of ethnohistorical method.

Arbitrarily, it may be said that feuding usually came into play with a single or multiple homicide that, according to the rules of feuding, could honorably be avenged in blood. Few homicides were exempt, although to kill a rapist, adulterer, or thief who had been caught in the act obviated the need for further vengeance (Jelić 1926). And as we have just seen, when a death carried a strong possibility of being unintentional, it was not proper to take revenge immediately but rather to let a Court of Good Men decide if it had been accidental (Jelić 1926). If it was, then there would be solely a financial liability, and honor did not require vengeance in blood so long as blood money was paid.

I have already suggested that the causes for blood revenge lay in a complicated mixture of religious and fraternal feelings and also in the highly developed retaliatory responses that could be expected in a warrior society, all combined with a keen and compelling sense of honor. This last produced both a low personal tolerance for insults and a strong tendency to insult other people in the name of manly fearlessness. Most feuding began through such an insult to honor, which resulted in homicidal retaliation. This could be initiated by a verbal insult, by a direct nonverbal communication that was insulting, or through some action that intentionally or inadvertently besmirched the honor of a household or of a clan. Prominently mentioned in the historical sources are abduction of a maiden to marry her, seduction of maidens, adultery, runaway wives, and breach of betrothal agreements, as well as disputes over pastures (Vialla de Sommières 1820; Wilkinson 1848; Jelić 1926; Durham 1928; Dragičević 1935).

The man in the leather hat is having a problem with the tall man next to the horse at left, who is standing his ground but obviously does not want to promote the quarrel. With considerable physical force, the man in the white shirt is restraining his companion and trying to persuade him to go home peacefully.

Angry words continue after a brief—but violent—scuffle between the man in the hat and his companion in the white shirt. The latter appears to be perfectly sober and has managed to restrain his friend without any assistance.

In this dramatic photograph, the man in the hat wants to go after his
adversary, who finally has decided to leave the scene. The man in the hat is
now being restrained by four companions. This successfully concluded the
episode without a fight actually having taken place.

In every case the parties to the dispute had to be from different clans
for a feud to take place. If a conflict resulting in homicide took place
within a clan, there was no possibility of further retaliation, because
according to Montenegrin cultural logic, homicidal retaliation within the
clan simply did not make sense (Jelić 1926). The tribesmen were jealous
of the fighting strength of their clans, and they realized that an
internecine feud would weaken their own clan relative to other competing
clans. But the cultural rationalization by which they operated was simpler
than this practical logic: by the rules of feuding, a clan, by definition,
could not owe itself blood, because to take another life would further
reduce the clan's own blood.

In discussing how feuds began, I must say something concerning the
ethical status of acts that brought on a blood-vengeance homicide. If you
insulted a man cruelly in a verbal duel, he was liable to kill you either
then or later. Yet the offering of insults was a normal part of such dueling
and was considered to be ethical, even though it was risky. On the other
hand, if you promised a man's daughter to marry her, took her virginity,
and got her pregnant, but subsequently decided that you did not wish to
get married after all, then, as viewed by the tribal moral community, you
would have behaved very unethically and in a way that you knew would

dishonor her father's house. This means that while feuds very often began out of neutral situations in which there was no moral culpability for either party, in some cases one or both parties were at fault morally. This ethical consideration did not make any difference in the conduct of the feud itself. But when it came time for pacification, then a party that was judged to have been unambiguously disobeying moral rules would have to face an economic penalty, depending upon the judgment of the Court of Good Men.

We stop here with the first mortal insult or the first homicide, which I take to be the classic opening move of the feuding game if the homicide was one that by the unwritten law was legitimately subject to retaliation. The killer, of course, had to make certain that his new blood enemies knew that he was the killer (Jelić 1926). As these kinsmen of the victim declared that the killer and his kin owed them blood, the feud approached what I shall call the middle game.

EARLY MOVES IN THE MIDDLE GAME

Once the initial homicide or other serious affront had taken place, the closest kinsmen of the man who had been killed had an obligation to take blood (Karadžić 1922). Exactly how they went about this would depend upon a number of factors, the most important being whether the enemy clan was within the same tribe or outside of it and whether their own clan was much smaller, about the same size, or much larger than the clan of their blood enemy. The homicidal initiative rested solely with the clan that had suffered the first homicide or affront. When blood was owed within the tribe, then by the rules of feuding, it appears that the clan that needed to take blood could immediately mount an attack on the house of the killer and could seek to destroy that house quickly (Jelić 1926).[6]

If the killer and any clan brothers who were aiding him could succeed in defending the house for several days, the feud would then de-escalate to the stage where single individuals would be ambushed. If the killer and his clan brothers felt that they could not resist the attack, then they were obliged to flee the tribe. Usually, however, other members of the tribe would try to persuade the aggrieved party to desist and to wait for pacification without engaging in further killings. A well-documented pacification at this early stage will be discussed in detail in the next chapter.

If this early pacification attempt was successful and the right to take blood vengeance was renounced in favor of a payment of blood money by the killer's clan, then feuding would reach only minimal proportions. In

This house in Kuči tribe on the Albanian border is old enough to have the loopholes through which muskets could be fired; several of these are visible at the end of the house. Loopholes were built into all four walls, so that gunfire could be aimed in all directions in case of a siege (see Thurner 1956). Some houses near this region had stone outhouses extruding from the second story, with pipes through which excrement fell to the barnyard below. These pipes were deliberately bent in such a way that an assassin could not fire through the pipe at anyone who was using the outhouse.

such a case the conflict would end at the very beginning of the middle game. I should mention that when early pacification did take place, Montenegrins always considered it to be a painful loss and a dishonor to have stopped before blood retaliation had taken place. They submitted to early pacification only if their feeling of respect for the strong wishes of the remainder of the tribe was more powerful than their desire to restore their honor by taking revenge, or else if they faced some overwhelming disadvantage in numbers (Jelić 1926).

If an immediate truce was not obtainable and if the aggrieved clan wanted to attack the killer's house and drive him out of the tribe, it had to possess enough strength to attack a house defended by the killer's clansmen (Jelić 1926). If the enemy clan was very large, a smaller clan that was seeking revenge was more likely to bide its time and seek to kill its blood enemies singly or even to agree rather quickly to pacification and a blood payment.

The killer's household could simply flee before the attack if his clan was small and the enemy was very large. After escaping, it might sue for pacification later, after its property had been destroyed, and might be able to rejoin the tribe if the enemy clan eventually would accept blood money. Otherwise it could receive refuge from the Ottomans, who would provide the members with land and then ask them to bring back a Montenegrin head from a raid to prove that they were worthy of being Turkish subjects (Karadžić 1922). For a small clan that was hopelessly outnumbered, seeking refuge with the Turks was not even looked down upon; in truth, their only viable alternative was to emigrate to a distant place.

If the killer's household and clan decided to defend the house, crops, and livestock from devastation, then it appears that according to the unwritten law of blood feuding, they needed to do so for only three days.[7] If a successful defense lasted that long, it guaranteed them freedom from any further all-out attack in which large-scale clan warfare might take place. After that, they were subject only to the usual assassination through ambush on an individual basis or, at worst, on a small-group basis. This means that once they had successfully defended themselves in an all-out clan war of limited duration, the tribe was obliged to suffer a feud in its midst.

If more than a single homicide had taken place, the feud was very difficult to terminate, unless the blood score between the clans, which was kept very carefully, became exactly even (Jelić 1926). Otherwise, the clan that was behind would pointedly avoid the agony and sense of dishonor that came with foregoing vengeance. It usually took considerable time for tribal social pressure to result in a willingness to pacify on the part of a clan that had the lower blood score.

There were also feuds that began between clans from two different tribes. As I have emphasized already, a feud simply could not occur between two members of the same clan. And within the same tribe, while feuds did often prevail, a feud between two clans was subject to strong social pressure for pacification, especially if they were located close to each other. But in the case of a feud between a pair of clans from two different tribes, the pressure was significantly reduced. This was partly because a feud at longer range was less socially and economically disruptive and partly because the need for political cooperation was usually less critical between tribes than between clans within a tribe.

When the initial homicide involved clans of different tribes, there appears to have been no phase in which the killer's house was attacked. Rather, the victim's clan immediately began to hunt down a clansman of the killer, preferably a close kinsman. These intertribal feuds sometimes spread. If the killer's close kinsmen were inaccessible, then more-distant relatives of the killer were ambushed, drawing the entire clans intensively into the feud. And under certain circumstances, it appears that the clan that was seeking blood might even try to kill any member of the enemy clan's tribe, whether or not he was a member of that clan.[8] Such events occasionally brought two entire tribes into a state of feud. Although this seldom escalated to a state of warfare, it did give any male of either tribe a license to hunt for males of the other tribe.

Just as with feuds within the tribe, these intertribal feuds were extremely disruptive both socially and politically. The Turks could exploit a state of feuding so as to dominate a tribe temporarily because one of its usual allies was now its enemy; and sometimes the Turks could enlist the active military support of a Montenegrin tribe against its blood enemy (Jovanović 1948). The Montenegrins did have a fairly effective system for making temporary truces so that they could join and fight together for a specific purpose. But unfortunately, the ability to make truces frequently was hampered by very hostile feelings that accompanied feuding and that led to a deep desire to see injury done to one's blood enemies.[9] The bishops were always seeking to pacify feuds permanently or to legislate against them, and Stephen the Small, during his brief reign in the late 1700s, suppressed all feuds in order to build Montenegro's strongest confederation. But the normal state of affairs was that the tribesmen feuded intertribally and relied on truce making when it became expedient.

In spite of many reports that Montenegrin tribes were beset with long-lasting internecine feuds, I believe that the writers who made such statements failed to realize that within the tribe the great majority of vengeance killings were pacified quite rapidly. While ethnohistorical records cannot really decide this question, I suspect that it was mainly the long-distance feuds between different tribes that went beyond the opening moves of the middle game and that caught the attention of these writers.

THE LONG MIDDLE GAME: KILLING BACK AND FORTH

When a revenge homicide did take place, it became true that "two must die, not one." My definition-making neighbor was absolutely correct in this respect. But this state of parity did not necessarily end the conflict. More often, the second death was only the beginning of the feud's middle game. Whenever the score remained unequal, the side that had the lower score always attempted to ambush its opponents. Although I have no direct evidence of this, it seems logical (according to

Montenegrin logic) that after the second killing, it was up to the clan of the more-recent victim to retaliate.

The conditions of existence for people who were obliged to feud were truly terrifying. If the feud was with neighboring Albanian tribesmen, their favorite mode of assassination was to creep up on the house and climb onto the roof (Wyon and Prance 1903). They would remove a shingle and then would kill their victim where he slept, at short range. Montenegrins tended to fire their rifles from ambush, outdoors. But any mode of killing was considered fair.[10] Once a man had succeeded in taking vengeance, it was vital that he himself survive; otherwise, obviously, the blood score was not advanced in favor of his own clan. For this reason, northern Albanians carried charms to make them "light of foot" during the escape (Hasluck 1954). But in addition to a careful accounting in blood, there were many other rules that governed this violent middle-game activity.

RULES FOR KILLING OR NOT KILLING

Margaret Hasluck's book on Albanian unwritten law provides the most complete information on the rules that governed Balkan feuding, even though Jelić (1926) has synthesized much of the information presently available for Montenegro. These sets of rules were both comprehensive and specific. I have already said that keeping an exact score was very important in a blood feud. In fact, this activity defined the phenomenon of blood feuding, since careful scorekeeping regulated the roles of the two sides so that one took up the offense and the other the defense. Scorekeeping also was a sign that ultimately a payment of blood money could be reckoned for pacification. Scorekeeping was taken so seriously that should there be doubt as to who had killed a blood-feud victim, the killer would announce it from a distant hillside to the victim's clan (Jelić 1926).

This careful, fair scorekeeping even involved animals called house dogs. Albanians and Montenegrins kept dogs that were deliberately trained to be vicious, house dogs that were unchained only by night so that they could circulate around the house and kill an intruder. They could be handled and chained solely by the one person who fed them. If you were to approach my house at night, at a time when you obviously had no proper business with me, and my house dog then killed you, your clan would have no right to exact revenge. This killing would be justified, just as killing a thief or rapist caught in the act was justified. However, if you were to kill my house dog close to my house, where he was properly on watch, then my clan would seek to take blood for a man, since such a dog counted as a man if it was killed while on guard duty. But if my house dog were to attack you on a public path, where the dog had no right to be, then if you were killed, your own clan could kill a man from my clan in return, since in this context the dog would count as a warrior of my clan and the initial killing would not be justified.[11]

In Cetinje in 1964, one of my close Montenegrin friends who lived in a big house had a large enclosed yard with two fierce dogs in it. I noticed that he always carried (secretly, he thought) an enormous revolver whenever he came to visit with us in the evening. I also noticed that he was quite cautious about leaving our garden for the street if he visited after dark. He never explained this to me, but I subsequently learned from a neighbor that several decades previously my friend had killed a fellow Montenegrin while working in America. He now feared the man's brother, who lived twenty-five miles from Cetinje and needed to take vengeance. The neighbor said that the dogs were to keep down the probability of an ambush. So the Montenegrin house dog is not yet entirely gone, even though the old rules about dogs no longer apply. Apparently, however, the idea that "two must die" is still very much on some people's minds, sometimes even when they live in town, not out in the tribes.[12]

In the old days, women were free to come and go as they chose under feuding conditions, since taking their blood did nothing to help the blood score and also counted as a dishonor, morally speaking. Thus, their normal daily activities could continue. But men were sorely pressed when it came to doing any work other than herding, which allowed them to stay under cover with a rifle ready at all times. In 1965 it was for this reason that women still did so much of the heavier work in the fields, or so I was told by slightly apologetic Montenegrin "male chauvinists," who viewed this as a once-necessary custom formed in an earlier era. During the traditional period it also made sense, from the standpoint of economics, for Montenegrin men to go raiding a great deal. By engaging in this activity they were contributing to the household economy, and in a raiding party, whatever its risks, they at least were safe from attacks motivated by blood revenge. But whatever might happen to the men during a feud, the women were always free to keep the household economy going because the rules of feuding were taken so seriously by the opposing party.

With respect to the sanctity of women, it was even possible for them to enter directly into combat during the first stage of a feud, when the killer's clan shut itself in and the victim's clan attacked the fortified stone farmhouse, which had loopholes everywhere. With no fear of being harmed, women could carry straw and firebrands up to the house to try to burn it. Also, women of a besieged house could go outside at night carrying torches, to light up the enemy so that their own men could shoot at them (Jelić 1926). This exemplifies the strength of these particular rules: to shoot a woman was a source of shame (sramota) for the entire clan.

THE ESCALATION OF FEUDS

Once instant pacification had been rejected and the attack, if any, had passed its third day, the feud was on. Conceived of idealistically and very mechanically, a series of single killings back and forth would follow, with neither side ever getting more than one head ahead in its score and with pacification coming at some point when the scores were even. But as we have seen, sometimes the initial killing would be multiple or would involve uneven losses on the two sides. Actually, this would not prevent the neat pattern mentioned above from taking place, once parity had been established; but the nature of Montenegrin heroic values made absolute parity unlikely. This was because instead of simply paying back an insult or a homicide in kind, Montenegrins tended to pay back in better measure than they were given. Aleksa Djilas did this by cutting out the captain's heart, thus adding insult to injury. A lesser insult could also upset the sense of parity even when the actual number of killings was equal.

Since taking blood was not just a matter of duty but was also an affair of honor, it should come as no surprise that Montenegrins tried to insult the krvnik as well as to take his blood. An ultimate (but rarely used) insult was to carry away the head of one's victim so that he could not be properly buried. When the agents of Prince Nicholas eventually took their revenge upon Aleksa Djilas, they cut off his head, took it home, and threw it out on a field to rot or to be gnawed on by animals. They dishonored his body in order to pay him back for the unusual damage he had done to Captain Ćorović. Only a young girl of the Djilas household, Aleksa's daughter Stanojka, could safely go to bring back his head. She was sent on this mission, did her job, and remained emotionally impaired for the rest of her life from the gruesome experience. According to Djilas (1958:15–16), to retrieve and preserve the head of a slain clansman ''was like the retrieving of one's honor and pride, almost as though a man had not been slain.'' In this case, all that the unfortunate Djilas clan could retrieve of its honor was the head, since further vengeance was all but impossible in this highly unequal and atypical "feud." But normally it was an insult such as taking a victim's firearms or killing a person of high status that helped to keep a feud going even when the score had become equal.

For the traditional period, the middle game of feuding is the phase that we know the least about. In the pacification documents, which are our best detailed sources, by far the most attention is given to the blood payment at the end and to fixing culpability, if any, for the starting of the feud. However, the overall pattern of the middle game is fairly clear. The clan that had the higher score stayed on the defensive while being hunted by the clan that felt its honor was besmirched because of its lower score. The more blood that was owed and the greater the sense of insult to honor, the greater the zeal of the "losing" clan. Obviously, a very uneven score increased the likelihood that the "losers" would take blood from more-distant kinsmen of the man who had started the feud, killing whoever was accessible. Or as mentioned previously, in an intertribal feud the "losers" might take blood from a man who was not even a member of the enemy clan but was merely a member of the same tribe, thus escalating the feud to the intertribal level.

In theory, when the scores became even, the two clans or tribes were then ready to pacify. But I have discussed two reasons that feuding did not necessarily work in this way. One was that each clan tended to overperceive insults that it had received and to underperceive the insults that had been suffered by its blood enemy. The other was the tendency to pay back in greater measure than was received. If the opportunity arose, this could be done by killing two men instead of one, when killing just one man would have evened the score. To take more blood than was required to even the score, and thus to continue the feud strongly, was considered to be truly heroic. But more usually a clan that was behind by one "head" would kill just one of its enemies, to even the score, but would simultaneously perpetrate some symbolic insult so that if the other side accepted pacification at that point, it would feel humiliated, even though technically the blood score was even. The tendency to overperceive one's own loss of honor of course exacerbated such assessments, and the possibility of spontaneous settlement, which was already slim, became impossible without outside intervention.

SOME HELP FROM THE *NEW YORK TIMES*

To assess what the effects of the middle game of feuding were upon the daily life of traditional Montenegrins and upon their psychological well-being in particular, I shall turn to a rather unexpected source. The following passage is from the *New York Times* of 1 December 1972. It relates to a province in Yugoslavia where a million Albanian tribesmen live outside of their own country, having been placed in Yugoslavian Kosovo by the peace settlement after World War I. Until recently, Kosovo has continued to be an underdeveloped and relatively autonomous area within Yugoslavia, but is now being developed through increased educational opportunity and industrial investment.

> PRISTINA, Yugoslavia, Nov. 23—An ancient blood-feud tradition among Albanians, requiring a death for a death to uphold honor, is stubbornly resisting official sanctions in the autonomous Yugoslav province of Kosovo.
>
> The feuds are proving a hindrance to ambitious economic and social efforts in the province, three-fourths of whose 1.3 million inhabitants are ethnic Albanians.
>
> Fears of falling victim to an avenger's bullet are confining about 8,000 Kosovo inhabitants to walled-in, fortresslike households. Fields and vineyards go untended. Workers in new factories dare not go to their jobs and teen-age boys hesitate to go to school. Families suffer from long confinement, malnutrition and lack of medical attention as well as nervous strain. . . .
>
> Although education and economic development have made sizable strides since World War II, blood-feud killings have increased. In 1955 the total was 36, with 41 attempts. By 1969 the figure had risen to 100, with 147 attempts.

In many ways, this situation is similar to that in Montenegro under the later rule of Bishop Rade Petrović, who was trying very hard to form a centralized state after 1840. In Kosovo, police powers are such that some killers are apprehended, even though this does not really terminate the feud. But the government in Kosovo is also providing the same kind of service that the Montenegrin bishops had tried to provide—namely, an external agency that will come in and try to get the principals to the feud to set aside their feelings and to pacify immediately.[13]

If these two situations are directly comparable, and I believe they are, then obviously for the traditional period the accounts that imply that almost all Montenegrins were feuding almost all of the time clearly are exaggerated. In Kosovo, only perhaps 1 percent of the total population is actively involved in feuding. Before 1840 we might assume that the average figures for Montenegro were several times as great and that they might have been as high as 5 or possibly 10 percent when a bishop was ineffective as a peacemaker. But this is still a relatively small proportion of the total population. For anyone who has read the accounts of visiting foreigners, these figures will seem very low indeed.

A contemporary Albanian feud that was described in the same *New York Times* article follows the classic Montenegrin lines developed in this chapter. A member of the Taci clan slaps a Mazreku shepherd lad for refusing to get his sheep out of a Taci wheat field, and the incident progresses from insults to beatings to fights. Finally the Taci kill a member of the Mazreku clan, who are also Albanians. All 190 members of the Taci clan then take refuge in their twelve houses, which are surrounded by a brick wall. At the end of three years a Taci man, with cunning that is also typical of the Montenegrins, decides that on New Year's Eve the enemy clan will forget about the blood debt and go home to celebrate. He sneaks out to tend his vineyards, but the Mazreku clansmen hear about this, and six of them come to exact vengeance. Now the feud apparently escalates, since over the next two years a series of killings results in eight dead on each side. At that point, a pacification is agreed upon, and the feud ends.

The *New York Times* article succeeds rather well in portraying feuds as being morally necessary from the indigenous standpoint, but it may tend to overemphasize the economic deprivation involved. The women are still able to work, and these Albanians live in large extended households in which there is highly efficient labor specialization. Also, the article deplores the killing of young boys (age eleven is the youngest), but in the indigenous view this is merely something to be avoided if possible since it does not bring much honor; it is morally acceptable by the rules of feuding (Hasluck 1954). The same was true in neighboring Montenegro, where the avengers, if seriously thwarted in trying to kill adult males, might turn to subadults.

The Taci and Mazreku clans spent five years in this enactment of a moral and heroic drama between hundreds of persons who were organized into two homicidal vengeance groups. They paid an economic penalty, because their men could not work and their boys could not go to school. But aside from the loss of life, probably the greatest penalty that they paid was in the form of psychological stress; for one side always knew that its adult and subadult males were targeted for killing from ambush at any moment.

A FEUD IN KUČI AT THE TURN OF THE CENTURY

Fortunately, we have a more graphic account of how an individual responds to this stressful situation, written by two Englishmen who traveled extensively in Montenegro just after 1900, Reginald Wyon and Gerald Prance. They tell (Wyon and Prance 1903:234–39) how Kečo, a

Montenegrin who lives adjacent to the Albanian frontier, has his cow stolen by a Moslem Albanian named Achmet. In a public marketplace the Turk not only tells Kečo that the cow's milk is of good quality but also that the cow is too good for a Christian dog like Kečo. Kečo does not give in to the boiling blood that urges him to kill: "To this hour I wonder that I did not strike him dead. My rage rendered me powerless to move or see. It was as if a black cloud descended over my eyes. When I recovered, Achmet was gone." Kečo, who is too wise, in spite of his passion, to kill a Turk in a Turkish market, where use of firearms is prohibited, is taunted again when Achmet tells him publicly that the cow has borne a fine calf. Kečo seeks legal redress from the Turkish authorities, but with no result. So he gets two friends to go with him to get his cow back.

> I did not go at night, like a thief, but when the sun was highest and when all could see me. I left my comrades outside Achmet's house and went in alone. There I found my cow and her calf, but only the women were present. So I drove the cow and the calf out of the door towards my comrades. Then, lest any should think that I was afraid, I fired my rifle into the air. Very soon the men came running from the fields, and amongst them Achmet and his son. When they saw me and my cow, they came towards me firing, but being unsteady from running, the bullets flew wide. Then I took careful aim and shot Achmet dead, and then his son. We then ran quickly, and though men pursued us, they were afraid to come too near lest I should shoot them likewise, and so we came back to Fundina in safety. Since then the men of Dinosh wait for me, and they will kill me soon, for the insult is very great that I have put upon them, and the fame of my deed has travelled into all lands.

Wyon and Prance ask him why he remains in a place so close to his enemies, and Kečo, with a characteristically Montenegrin lack of modesty, answers that men know him to be a hero; so what would they say if he ran away and sought safety elsewhere? In his opinion, he would be a double coward if he fled, for he would be leaving his brothers to inherit his fate. Kečo is determined to wait for his avengers until they come, and he affirms that they will not find him sleeping or unprepared: "See every night I make my bed in a different place, sometimes in one room of the house, sometimes in the bushes outside. They never know where I shall sleep for these dogs love to kill their enemy in the night."

When the authors and a friend who was a Montenegrin doctor first met Kečo, this self-praising Montenegrin warrior struck them as a "small and insignificant man . . . with haggard looks and grey hair."

As he took the tobacco tin which was proffered him, his hands trembled so excessively that the rolling of a cigarette was a work of art. "His nerves are gone," explained the doctor. "He lives in hourly danger of his life."

Kečo tells about his present state of being:

"Though my hands tremble and my hair is growing white," he began, "Yet I do not fear death. We must all die, and I know that my fate must speedily overtake me. This house I have built for my wife, and stocked with what money I had, to provide for her. They shall not kill me easily. Twice they have tried. The first time I was in the fields when men fired at me from long distance. I took my rifle and made a detour, and, as my enemies recrossed the border, I was there waiting for them. But I did not hit one. Another time seven men hid themselves only thirty yards away from my house, in the evening, but they dared not shoot then, for my wife was by my side."

The reasoning behind the last statement was perfectly logical from the Montenegrin standpoint. It was such a shame to kill a woman that no one would risk the shot. The Albanian code of blood-feud rules was, of course, identical to the Montenegrin code in this respect.

Kečo's story must remain unfinished. But the aggressive provocation that he offered and the fact that he owed two bloods made it unlikely that the feud would be pacified at that point. It may seem curious that his deliberate insults ensured that his blood enemies would scarcely be able to submit to pacification before they themselves drew blood, since apparently it was they who had wantonly insulted him in the first place. But this provides a good example of how the two sides could overperceive the insults that they themselves had received.

These more-recent accounts of the middle game are assumed to be relevant for the traditional period. While there are few early descriptions that even approach being this graphic, we do know that feuds not infrequently involved more than twenty deaths on either side at the point when they were settled and that they sometimes went on for twenty years (e.g., Stanojević 1955). Some of these large scores, however, may have been the result of duels in which opposing clans met with the intention of letting just a few of their members fight it out.

DUELS IN MONTENEGRO

Earlier, I likened feuding to dueling in the Western European tradition, as a well-controlled means of channeling an unavoidable conflict so that its ill effects would at least be contained. Traditional Montenegrins actually had a name for a duel *(dvoboj)*, and while the practice bore some resemblance to Western dueling, it was quite different both in form and in efficiency. Marko Miljanov (1901) recorded from oral tradition a dvoboj in which twelve men from each side showed up with their maces, each challenger sending an apple to the man he wanted as a partner. Kovaljevski, a Russian observer in the early 1800s, states that such duels were over women, theft, or injury to honor and that they took place with or without witnesses (Kovaljevski 1935). Two men would drink a brandy together, load their guns, and duel. In one case they seem to have fought to the death, to Kovaljevski's horror. Such duels tended to prevent large-scale warfare, and in theory they were conducted in private. But the populaces involved tended to hide in the woods to watch, so escalation to a general conflict always was possible. In one case, two tribes lined up and fought over a runaway wife. In one document (Vuković 1971) sent to the tribesmen involved, Bishop Petar Petrović urges the two tribes not to duel because he fears that each party will bring his "army" and a slaughter will result.[14] Thus, Montenegrin duels appear to have escalated rather easily.

Somewhat later, just after a state had been formed, duels were actually used as a cover for feuding (Miljanov 1901), since krvna osveta was punishable by death. But in the traditional period, duels must be considered as a rarely used means of conflict management, one that apparently worked less efficiently than the long-established feuding system. It is unfortunate that more information is not available on the dvoboj, since its relation to feuding remains unclear. But it may have provided an alternative means of settling scores at either the early or the middle stage of the feuding game.

TRUCES

If the middle game continued long enough, then feuding came to involve people who had nothing to do directly with the original homicide that had started the feud. Particularly when a feud became intertribal, many of the participants in feuds did not even know one another personally. But a feud never was carried on dispassionately. Even when a solemn temporary truce was concluded in order to discuss the beginning of pacification, there was always the possibility that one side—almost always the side with the lower score—would be consumed by the desire to take revenge and would simply start shooting. Montenegrins recognized "boiling blood" as a very special and all-consuming psychological condition; and as a moral justification, boiling blood went far in exonerating a person if he broke a truce.

In one instance related by Jovanović (1948), Bishop Petar Petrović came to Ljesanska Nahia to try to pacify a feud early, but the two clans opened fire. The battle raged for two hours. In another case in Cetinje a similar battle erupted, while the furious bishop stood in the middle of the mêlée, alternately cursing the evildoers and pleading with them to stop. When they did, there were around twenty dead or wounded (Jovanović 1948). These instances, like the duels that got out of hand, demonstrate the extreme volatility of tensions between feuding clans or tribes in Montenegro. It was because of such volatility that rules for feuding were so important in maintaining the tribal social fabric, and in view of the ease with which Montenegrins went for their guns, it is a tribute to the system of truce making that it worked as well as it did.

In spite of such reverses, then, truces usually worked rather well at strategic points as a way of reducing the political, social, and economic damage caused by feuds. Often truces were made for reasons of expediency—for example, to form military alliances in desperate cases of endangerment from outside enemies (see Jovanović 1948). Truces were also concluded in order to harvest hay (Jelić 1926), since using a scythe was men's work; the same was usually true of ploughing.

A more common kind of truce was the automatic one that came when a guest was present in the house of a man at feud. Marko Miljanov's (1901) story about the Albanian who killed his own brother because the latter had killed a houseguest exemplifies a rule that also held strongly in Montenegro. Another major reason for agreeing to truces was to open up the option of pacifying the feud, but this will be left for the next chapter. Otherwise, the most important truces were those that were agreed upon in order to maintain military solidarity within a tribe, if the feud was within the tribe, or to make possible a temporary military alliance between two tribes if the feud was intertribal.

The possibility of making such truces has already been shown to have been only partly effective. When Montenegrins were locked into the stressful middle game of a feud, they were not always successful in putting aside their differences when external danger arose. Indeed, it was often by means of exploiting tensions that existed between tribes because of feuding that the Turks were able to isolate and dominate many of the tribes, even if they were unable to conquer them totally. This the Turks managed, even though the mechanism of truces was available to the tribesmen.

THE END OF THE MIDDLE GAME

The middle game was the part of krvna osveta that corresponds best to the image of a stubborn and vicious conflict that is called up by the English phrase "blood feud." However, as I emphasized previously, the minute that someone was killed and blood vengeance became appropriate, then insofar as the Montenegrin view was concerned, krvna osveta was at issue. The game had entered its first stage. Whether the next step was immediate pacification, an attack on the killer's house, flight by the killer's household or clan, or a successful revenge killing followed by more killing back and forth, the process involved krvna osveta because the duty to take blood had been activated. Any of these outcomes constituted a feuding situation by Montenegrin definition. If the feud did reach the middle-game stage, it was possible that it might go on for many years; in fact, there is one case, recorded by Wilkinson (1848), of a pacification in which the middle game had raged for so long that even the oldest man in one of the opposing settlements could barely remember the exact circumstances under which he had been told that the original killing had taken place. This feud was probably so protracted because the two parties lived in Montenegro and on Venetian territory, respectively, and therefore had no reason of social or economic cooperation or of political alliance to resolve the conflict. But in Montenegro proper, I was told that one feud between Ceklin tribe and Njeguši tribe had gone on sporadically for over half a century, threatening at times to divide the old Montenegrin tribal confederation (see Boehm 1983). Thus the middle game potentially was of very long duration. This meant that potentially it also was very costly in terms of political, economic, and psychological resources, as well as of male lives.

7

The End Game:
Management of Conflict

In discussing the moral system of Montenegro, I have pinpointed the management of conflict as being one particular area in which all humans actively apply their intelligence in a practical way in order to help their own social systems to function. When people tolerate as much violence as the Montenegrins do, one is prone to wonder whether there could be a prominent role for such efforts. But Montenegrins themselves considered blood feuds to be highly disruptive from a social, economic, and political standpoint, and they tried to intervene actively whenever they could in an effort to control these morally legitimate quarrels in their midst.

Here, we examine in some detail the pacification of blood through the payment of blood money. First, we shall try to understand how it was that a feud within a tribe sometimes could be headed off early while the participants still had their blood "boiling" strongly. Then there is the problem of explaining how, after many years, two weary but stubborn clans were able finally to cut their losses and settle their differences. In Serbian the expression is *miriti krvi,* "to pacify the blood."

THE COURT OF GOOD MEN

Before a Court of Good Men could be convened to settle a feud, it was necessary for the two feuding parties to declare that they were open to pacification. When a homicide took place within the same settlement or when the blood score quickly became even, then if the parties could be persuaded to agree to a truce, the court could meet quickly and try to effect an early settlement. However, once a feud had entered the middle game and had intensified, it was very difficult to make the transition from the state of feuding to the state of truce, which was needed for pacification. This was because usually the blood enemies and the people with the lower score, in particular, were too aroused to meet face to face. For this reason the Montenegrins did not try to bring the parties together for formal pacification procedures until two renewable truces had been agreed upon and kept. This sequence gave the feuding clans at least several months to let their feelings quiet down.

The clan with the higher blood score had to initiate the truce formally (Jelić 1926), since it could afford this sign of weakness due to the fact that its honor was in better shape. But often people who were not involved in the feud had to persuade even this "winning" clan to sue for a truce, since it felt it was giving in to the attacks of the side that had the lower score. It was best not to attempt this move while the feud was really raging or while one side had a big advantage in score; it was strategically better to wait until the blood score approached a state of equality between the two clans. However, once the feud had gone on for a very long time, eventually outside social pressure might combine with weariness on the part of both clans, and a truce might be arranged. Whatever the conditions of truce leading to a pacification attempt, everyone knew that this was an extremely delicate situation. Once the first truce had been agreed to, the second and third were likely, but not certain, to follow. It was only after the third period of *vjera* (truce) had begun that the court was convened (see Durham 1928; Jelić 1926).

I have emphasized already that the judges *(kmets)* had to be of high moral status in their tribes and had to maintain a reputation for being nonpartisan in their work as kmets (Durham 1928). This ensured that the thinking of the judges would be in accordance with the mainstream of Montenegrin moral tradition, which may be inferred readily from historical documents. Fortunately, there is a wealth of documentary evidence on Montenegrin blood pacifications (e.g., Jelić 1926; Vuković 1971), and many of these seem to reflect an ancient mode of judgment. This unwritten tradition flourished before pressure was effectively brought to bear by Bishop Rade Petrović after 1840 to punish blood-vengeance killers as they would be punished in a centralized state—by a death penalty. These written depositions were recorded, usually by monks from Cetinje, and provide not only an excellent source for figuring out the content of the oral legal code but also a way of seeing how the legal code was applied in real-life situations.

The legal hearings were public (Vrčević 1890) and followed a prescribed order. There was a fact-finding phase, and there could also be a special method of testing for truth, when the testimony of one witness or party was at odds with another or when the interpretation of facts was in a state of doubt that made resolution very difficult. In one test for veracity, a group of men on the side of the person whose word was in question went into a church along with the group of men on the other side of the dispute. A spokesman for the latter group uttered extreme curses, invoking affliction with disease and absence of male progeny upon anyone who told a lie, while the group on the side of the man who was testifying swore to his veracity under the threat of these dire curses (Karadžić 1922). Such a test sometimes had the result that a man who had testified falsely would refuse to enter the door of the church, so the test did have some effect in terms of fear of supernatural sanctions. But asking a group of the man's honorable allies to put their own health and descendants on the line also was a way of getting them to assess privately whether he was telling the truth or not. If they refused to take the oath with him, then his testimony was discredited, whether he was telling the truth or not.

A CASE HISTORY FROM NEIGHBORING GRBALJ

The brief outline of Montenegrin judicial process gives the reader some idea as to how it differed from or was similar to the modern systems with which we are more familiar. But it does not convey the distinctive flavor that such procedures carried with them in Montenegro. Since I believe that exposure to one such legal case in its entirety can tell the reader more than an entire technical ethnographic chapter on judicial process, I reproduce here a legal case written up by Vrčević (1890). This case occurred in a semitribal area named Grbalj, which lay just below the highest mountain in Old Montenegro on a plain down on the coast. The people there were culturally Montenegrin, but they were under the nominal jurisdiction of the Venetians and later of the Austrians, both of whom allowed them to resolve disputes through their own indigenous legal institutions. We may assume that the spirit and application of the unwritten law in this case applied to tribal Montenegro as well. The event took place in the heart of the traditional period, and Vrčević entitled it "Court of Good Men between Two Feuding Families in Grbalj, around 1820." Vrčević obviously followed oral tradition closely, but he also relied upon written depositions as he arranged the case history in a format that is consistent with oral-tradition style in Montenegro.

1. Introduction

Let it be known that today we have gathered at the meeting place in front of the Church of the Holy Lord, and we the undersigned elders [*kmets*] are present in the full number of twenty-four men, selected and summoned by the two powerful households of Rajković on the one hand and Vučetić on the other, which are "in blood." The Rajkovićes have killed one Vučetić because he blackened the cheek of one of their girls. We have sworn that we will unanimously (by justice and our souls and not through any partiality, as best we see fit) make a judgment on the basis of testimony from both sides. Above all else we acknowledge the name of God, in whose hands are the source of justice, truth, and reason, under whose name we today must uphold and administer the law. We decree that Nikola-son-of-Stanko (father of the late Miloš) and Djuro-son-of-Savo (father of the girl who has been dishonored) come before us and that in the name of their clan brothers they speak and all others listen and that no one utter a word except these two. We call up Nikola-son-of-Stanko and order that he speak first with his complaint, and Djuro is to listen and not say anything until Nikola has finished.

2. Trying the Parties before the Court

First Kmet: Tell us, Nikola, why you have something against Djuro; only, speak clearly that we may all hear and understand.

Nikola: I ask Djuro, who was once the sharer of my bread and salt but who now is my blood enemy, why it is that he killed my only son who was old enough to bear arms, and therefore harmed my house and snuffed out my hereditary line so that I have no descendants.

Djuro: But how can you ask me this, when you yourself know everything just as I do? Have you not done me more than a little shame, which your son visited upon me? And have you not blackened my cheek so that my house is mentioned as one which is blemished, from this time forward, forever, in the entire world? I am left without any lips to open before such honorable judges, nor eyes, that I may look at them, for your deceased son blackened my cheek and did mischief wantonly, even though he did not harbor any kind of personal malice. But what he looked for, that he found! But then, you should testify first; your side was the first to put the grain in the mill and grind it.

Second Kmet: Do not speak in that manner, Djuro, but rather answer the question. A curer cannot heal wounds before he sees them, nor can a barber know which tooth to pull out before he knows which one it is that hurts.

Djuro: If that is how it must be, then it is my duty to tell about my own blackened cheek. Miloš-son-of-Nikola for a year has been hovering around my daughter Savica like a "devil" fluttering around the barren limestone rocks: after her in field and forest, after her in the market and at the spring and all around the settlement. The entire village knew of this, but I and her mother were the last to know. We both advised her to stay away from this boy from another clan, and by God we also threatened that we would beat her bones to pieces within her skin. She always answered us like this: "What can I *do* about him? Whenever I try to get away from him, he just moves in closer. There you are, and there he is; just by telling him to do so I cannot make him go away. And anyone with eyes can see that he simply does not know what shame becoming to an upright man really is." I asked the young man three times to allow my girl to pass by him without courting his and my own evil undoing, but all for nothing. He would not curb himself. It was, judges, five months ago when my wife (if you will excuse the expression) told me that Savica had become pregnant because of Miloš-son-of-Nikola and that the entire village already knew it. That lightning from heaven should strike me or that an enemy's hand cut off my head—this would be just the same as such miserable news. So I at once ran to the village priest and to the knez, the leader of our village, and swore to them that they must find some kind of "medicine" for my cheek, before the blood began to flow between our two families. The late Miloš was called by them, and as though they were his own brothers, they urged him to marry Savica while it was still possible to be "on time" and with the least possible trouble. But he from the first fell into lies and oaths that he had not done it. "And even if I had"—he said to the pop and the knez—"she should have looked out for herself. It is fit for falcons to go hunting," he says, "and for the prey to try to take care of itself." They answer, "But that is not how it is: a pregnant girl can no longer wait in her own father's house. Rather, when you have committed a sin, then you must also make amends. Marry her as your own, and let your child be born in your own house." Instead of listening to the advice of the pop and the knez, like an honorable young man, and submitting to them, just listen (pardon my repeating the language) to what he answered to them: "Whenever the cow gets loose, the house will have a calf." When I fully comprehended what he had said, my mind turned upside down, and my blood boiled beneath my Montenegrin hat; so with my brother and my one son, I went out one day, then went out again the next, to lie in wait for him and kill him. I ask you, Kmets, did I do this out of wantonness, or out of a monstrous and heavy necessity becoming a true warrior? When a man has lost his obraz, he has lost his mind, and he does not take into consideration either his own life or his property.

Nikola: Have you heard that, Kmets? My blood enemy knows how to dream his own dreams at length, but the water runs back over his own mill, and the wheel itself creaks. What blood do I owe him, when he is the one who owes me? He tries to find his own honor, and my son is

left dead in the end. He wants to equate my own evil misfortune with
the fact that his cheek has been blackened. A man would say that he
does not know what I and all honorable and upright men know—
namely, what the duties of a husband and father are. Every man, even
he who does not even own his own meadow, keeps cows or sheep on a
tether, so that a wolf or a mountain brigand may not carry them off
when they stray. Does not every person build some hedges and walls
around his own vineyards and crops and meadows, so that nothing on
four legs may break in? Which father and husband is it who does not
take care of his own wife and daughter, watching where they go and
with whom they keep company and how they behave themselves, and
then does not deal with them as one must with a good Arabian mare,
holding the reins firmly in his hands? When someone does not take
care of his own obraz and his own mother, let no one but himself be
held at fault. When things are allowed to develop without restraint and
care, he eventually will be unable to escape from evil events, for a dog
will always come to lap up milk that is left out. Djuro knew, as the
entire village knew, that his daughter was right out in front of the
house winking at people, so why not advise her to keep her eyes
straight ahead, like every modest and honorable girl when a young
man from another clan passes by, and not to take in every single one
with an appraising glance? We know that where a black devil is to be
found, its mother is not going to be white. Djuro has fallen prey to
dishonor and shame, but my own house has had to bury a male head.
In this misfortune, who is at fault? Both of us, if, Kmets, you judge
only on the basis of how it all started and whether a girl must guard
herself from a young man or he from her. But Djuro is really at fault:
when he heard of the evil that had taken place, why did he not come to
me on time, so that we might have talked it over in a brotherly way and
come to an understanding in such a way that this misfortune might
have been averted. He wouldn't, may God judge him, but right away
he killed my only son, a true grey falcon, and so exterminated the
candle that I burn for my clan ancestors at my patron saint's feast. For
that reason, again in your fair judgment, I ask of this blood enemy that
he pay me for the head of my son Miloš! Oooo-h, my Son! My heart is
torn out! Oooo-h, Son! My house is buried! (Nikola cries out like a
dog that has been wounded, then falls silent as though stricken. The
kmets release the two parties to the dispute and tell them to sit down
peacefully beside one another.)

3. Reaching an Agreement among the Judges

First Kmet: Indeed, Brothers, this is a very difficult affair. And our
duty is to finish it whether it is easy or difficult.

Second Kmet: It is not merely difficult but most difficult of all! It is in
fact with reason that Nikola-son-of-Stanko seeks a head from Djuro-
son-of-Savo. But how can all the blame be placed upon Djuro's

daughter Savica? It seems to me that this is not so. Every woman's head is long-haired and small-brained,[1] and every girl is both impetuous and deceitful. If they look at young men, that is the profession they are born to; they hunt young men just as a hawk hunts birds in the field. There has not been born today a girl who by force made a young man commit a sin or forced him to contribute to her own shameful downfall. Since Nikola seeks redress for his son's head from Djuro and since from Nikola, Djuro seeks redress for the honor of his daughter, there exists a hard pine knot, upon which the sharpest of all axes will break; the threads of this case are extremely long and tangled. . . . The main thing, Brothers, is that we think of a young man and a maiden as being the same as gunpowder and sparks from a fire, that they should not get together, that they should always be in their own separate places. Evil has taken place, we know exactly how, and we see that both of them are at fault and have broken their own necks. But to us it remains, above all, to make a choice: Which of the two was the first to make sparks come off the flint—Savica or the late Miloš?

Third Kmet: Nothing easier: The metal striker was in Miloš's hands, and Savica's eyes acted as the flint. For me both are at fault. But I find Miloš much more at fault than Savica. The stronger party may easily lead the weaker one astray, and the wiser one may deceive the more foolish one. If Savica trusted that Miloš would marry her, then why did he shame the cheek of a girl of another clan, when he knew that he had no intention of marrying her?

Fourth Kmet: That is the living truth!

First Kmet: It is easy, Brothers, to set the compensation for a dead head, since its price is well known (124 sequins). But then we may fall into another kind of evil, when what we want is to do justice. But here we are with this miserable work before us. Savica is saddled with a burden, and when the child is born, what do we do with them? If we put her in the house with her father, as is appropriate, she will have a place to comb and braid her grey hair. But then, we cannot place on him the burden of someone else's bastard child. In that problem a wolf lies in wait for us!

The Oldest Kmet Present: I think, and I do not deceive myself, that for every one of us who is here today this is not the first time that we have sat in the circle of blood judgment. Rather, each of us knows how to judge the most weighty and difficult cases. Never is judging going to be, for one side or the other, exactly what they want; but rather it must be according to what people know and are able to do and to discover. It would be an evil thing if one party to a legal case were to go home singing and the other lamenting. There is no one in the world who has not given someone else a meal out of his own bag. We may neither bring back Nikola's son from the grave nor return Djuro's honor to him. For us, the task is to see clearly with our minds and to make the decision that we see as being most appropriate, to ensure that two embroiled brastvos come to peace with one another and that other honorable men will not look askance at what we have done.

(Now the jurors come to their final deliberations and finally agree upon the following written decision.)

4. The Judgment of the Elders

We have heard and understand how evil things took place between two families, notably the houses of Nikola-son-of-Stanko of the Vučetić clan, and Djuro-son-of-Savo of the Rajković clan. We are convinced that Nikola's son, the late Miloš, blackened the honor of Savica, Djuro's daughter, and then did not wish to marry her, even under the advisement of the pop and the knez. For that reason the Rajkovići killed him. The girl was "left sitting" to be an old maid, pregnant and shamed before the world. We acknowledge that neither Nikola nor Djuro was guilty of any other malicious acts, but simply that their misfortunes were born in evil, in which Miloš paid with his head and Savica with her obraz, and for which each party respectively owes to the other, by our judgment. And we judge as follows:

First: If Nikola-son-of-Stanko of his own free will wishes to take the child as his own when it is born, then Djuro-son-of-Savo has to pay a woman to nurse it, however much two honorable men decide is appropriate. But if Nikola does not wish to receive the child, then Djuro-son-of-Stanko will not be obligated either to pay for having it nursed nor be due any payment to Nikola for the head of Miloš.

Second: If Nikola-son-of-Stanko does not want either a male or a female child, when it is born, to take as his own, we judge that half will fall to Djuro and the equal share will fall to Nikola, to pay for Savica-daughter-of-Djuro and her child for food and clothing. This is to be however much two well-esteemed villagers in their own souls may determine to be appropriate, as long as she lives or until she marries, and the child until it reaches the age of sixteen.

Third: If Savica by chance in the meanwhile should marry or if the child should die, then Nikola and Djuro need give no more. And may God promote good speed, that between the two families both the angels of peace and brotherly love may reign, just as among us today there is harmony as we give this judgment. Amen

Having read chapter 5 on the moral context of feuding, the reader should be able to understand much of the above document in terms of what he or she presently knows of Montenegrin culture. However, the final terms of the settlement require some further interpretation. First, one must realize that in the opinion of the Court of Good Men, Djuro's homicide was justified morally because Miloš had led Savica astray and then had refused to take any responsibility for his action, thus wrecking Djuro's good name. According to the Montenegrin view, Djuro's blood had been set to boiling over the damage to his honor, and so he was subject to no moral censure, only to payment of blood money. This financial obligation was based simply on the score between the two parties, in which he happened to be higher by one head if only human lives were counted.

The ruination of Djuro's daughter was also taken into account as a form of damage. The court made a decision that left certain options open to Nikola, obviously in the hopes of making a viable social position for the child. This was done because illegitimate children were at a disadvantage socially and economically in Montenegro. Nikola was given a large economic incentive to take the child on, since in that way he would receive blood money for his son's head. This put the child in the position of being adopted formally as a fully privileged member of a good house; whereas if it were to remain with its mother, it would always be viewed as a *kopiljan,* or bastard-child. If Nikola refused to take the child, then the girl and the child together were to be taken care of financially by both houses, and Nikola would have to forfeit the large amount of 100 sequins that he would otherwise have received for Miloš's head (the remaining 24 sequins would go to the kmets for their lost day's work).

What the kmets did was, first, to distribute the liability to both parties but in no very precise manner. Then, in the final details they used economic sanctions to give Nikola a good rationalization for setting aside both his anger and his predictable inclination not to be associated with an illegitimate child. If he were able to do this, he would have a chance of acquiring another male descendant directly into his own bloodline, depending, of course, upon the sex of the child. This is an issue that the kmets were aware of when they specified that he could make this decision after the child had been born.

Unfortunately, the sex of the child and Nikola's decision are lost to history. But the criteria used in arguing and judging the case remain, as ethnohistorical gems that shed a special light on the ways in which Montenegrins reasoned morally. This kind of insight takes us far beyond the mere spelling out of the structure of the moral code and the specifying of various sanctions that reinforce that code. In following this legal case, one has the opportunity to use the knowledge provided earlier in this book, to see how past actions of moral ambiguity were rationalized in moral self-defense as Djuro and Nikola carefully manipulated facts and interpretations, each in his own self-interest.

The particular form of moral ambiguity was that which predictably attended the case of any virtuous young girl who disgraced herself by becoming pregnant. In such cases, it was necessary to interpret the entire context of her having become pregnant, and this example from Grbalj highlights a classic Montenegrin dilemma. The nature of the dilemma can be implied from Nikola's insinuation to the effect that Savica was sleeping around "with the entire village." If in fact she had been doing this, there would have been no certitude that the child was fathered by Miloš. But the kmets obviously decided that she was a virtuous girl who had been led astray by the typical ruse used by young men in that society: a promise of marriage, which was taken more seriously by the girl than by the young man. The kmets' knowledge undoubtedly came in part from assumptions that they made concerning the moral character of her clan and her parents, but more through weighing information in the local gossip system. Had Savica in fact been a *kurva* (slut), this would have been "known" or at least very widely suspected. Since a Montenegrin girl could never be placed on a witness stand and be expected truthfully to tell the shameful facts if this were so, the judges were obligated to rely upon inference. Their decision to treat Savica as a virtuous girl who had gone astray with only one man tended to repair Djuro's honor somewhat, as well as to provide Nikola with a possible male heir. But this interpretation never would have worked had Savica been under heavy suspicion of sleeping around with more than one man. Nikola's honor would not have allowed it.

From the tone of these proceedings, one may also get a sense of the deep respect that Montenegrins had for the judicial process itself. Particularly evident was the feeling of the judges that the basic purpose of their arbitration was to bring about a compromise. This contributed to the social harmony of the entire community, as well as helping the households and clans that were directly involved. In this particular legal case, the danger of a major blood feud was not yet great. We may assume not only that Nikola realized that his son had offered some serious provocation but also that because the families had been close, he desisted from opening up the middle game with an immediate attempt at retaliatory killing. His statement to the court shows that there was a case to be made for his son. Indeed, the arguments given on both sides clearly illustrate the complexity of ambivalent Montenegrin attitudes toward premarital sexual affairs, in the terms of the respective roles of males and of females. But while young falcons were winked at for preying upon young birds who truly were promiscuous, such predatory behavior was moral only if the girl was essentially bad and ready to be led astray. If the falcon gained the favors of the bird through deceitful promises and if the bird was otherwise honorable and acted out of gullibility, then things became highly ambiguous. They also became dangerous, because predatory sexual actions of young falcons that damaged a maiden's virtue were certain to harm the honor of the girl and her house, if discovered.

To avoid wilfully damaging the obraz of another person was an important ethical value in Montenegro, and one that the late Miloš had failed to respect. Except in cases of rape, a maiden's fallen virtue was always ambiguous in Montenegro; therefore Miloš, once he had had the bad luck to be discovered, attempted to hide behind this ambiguity. He thereby tried to ignore the damage that he had done, once Savica was known to be pregnant. It was due to this kind of moral ambiguity that there was such ample opportunity for feuds to begin in matters concerned with courtship and engagement. What the ambiguity did was to feed a sense of self-justification on both sides, as each party to the dispute tended to overperceive his own moral rightness. In court, this tendency was exacerbated as each party consciously tried to manipulate the moral context in his favor. The difficult job of the court was to intervene in order to unravel the facts, to apply traditional moral interpretations, and then to resolve the entire affair from a practical standpoint as well. This was done in the best interests of all parties concerned, including the local community.

In the proceedings before the Court of Good Men, a great deal of the information concerning moral precedent was either taken for granted or was made apparent through indirect means. Much of the basic psychological foundation for measuring human actions and motivations was expressed in a special idiom that was ever-present in Montenegro, notably in the form of folk aphorisms, or sayings. So many of these exist that a foreigner who is trying to master the Serbian language spoken in villages may come to feel rather hopelessly that the number of such sayings is infinite. Indeed, in the field, I finally came to realize that new ones were continually being coined, even through there was also a very large stock of standard sayings that metaphorically expressed certain psychological truths about human nature as the Montenegrins viewed it. This flexible system of metaphorical interpretation was referred to continually as the witnesses and judges attempted to build up a context through which a decision might be reached.

Montenegrins took inspiration particularly from their own subsistence activities in generating these metaphors concerning human behavior: mill wheels turn, dogs lap up milk, straying cows become heavy with calf, sparks from the flint strike the gunpowder, and so on. The reader may also have noticed a general tendency of Montenegrins to hyperbolize—to exaggerate things when expressing feelings and to use the superlative mode freely. This was simply the usual Montenegrin way of expressing things that were felt strongly; it was not any special "manipulative" language that was employed solely in the courtroom.

COMPROMISE AS THE SPIRIT OF THE LAW

Of particular interest for understanding Montenegrin morality and its relation to feuding is the final portion of the text, where several of the judges—particularly the senior man among them—made explicit some of their own legal philosophy. Direct mention is made of the clans, as well as the immediate families of the disputants. This shows that the kmets were consciously concerned with the possibility that a blood feud might start and then escalate to the level of involving entire clans. It must be understood that Nikola, in spite of his willingness to submit to arbitration, would have been honor-bound to take vengeance if successful arbitration had not headed this off.

In view of the substantial moral ambiguity with which they were forced to deal, the judges took care, in formulating their judgment, to find neither party to be the guilty one. As the senior judge said, they had to see that neither party went home either singing or lamenting. This expressed perfectly the spirit of Montenegrin mediation of disputes. Compromise, rather than a guilty versus not-guilty decision, was viewed to be more useful from the standpoint of the entire community. In Grbalj, this moral community was the size of a tribe living up in the mountains. Had this conflict been settled in Montenegro itself, the moral community in question would have been the particular tribe in which the dispute had taken place. But in either case, the spirit of compromise existed as a practical solution to a well-perceived problem: long-term disruption of the larger social unit was being imminently threatened. In the tribes, such disruption was known by the tribesmen to be a dangerous source of weakness in the face of outside enemies such as the Turks. It also made the tribe as a whole vulnerable to territorial incursions, by which summer pasture land could be lost to predatory Montenegrin tribes with whom frontiers were shared.

In looking at this legal case, it is also interesting to see how religion played a role in reducing disruptive aggressive behavior. Insofar as ideology was concerned, Eastern Orthodox Christianity lent itself strongly to the curbing of aggressiveness and to individual submission to processes of conciliation.[2] The Montenegrins sometimes made use of these particular Christian values in trying to curb or channel the predatory or violent responses that, for a male, were also a moral necessity of life. For example, early in the conflict, the village pop was immediately turned to as one of the mediators. Also, considerable formalistic obeisance was paid to God in setting the general context for the administration of justice in what must be viewed as a basically secular context.

There was no physically coercive force behind the decisions of the Court of Good Men when it dealt with powerful latent forces that could easily have erupted into a long-term feud. It was for this reason that the court had to bolster its already considerable moral influence with every ingredient that the moral system had to offer, including the sanctity of religion.

SOME OTHER PACIFICATIONS OF BLOOD

I have exploited this detailed account of a settlement of a blood debt in order to illustrate for the reader the principles and processes by which a tribal court came to its decisions. In this particular case the conflict had barely started, and many of the findings concerned the welfare of the girl and the child, rather than the actual blood settlement in terms of a final score converted into a monetary blood debt. But this was true of many such pacification decisions, in that feuds usually involved contingencies that went beyond the simple mechanical reckoning of dead heads and wounds.

We may continue now with the other deposition, which Mary Durham translated from Vrčević, adding some clarifications of her own. This pacification is of the quarrel in which the little boys began to fight, the mothers jumped in and one assaulted the other, the men of the two clans started killing one another, and then the rest of the tribesmen jumped in to stop this violence in their midst. At this point the brastvo with the lower score threatened the one that was ahead, while the one that was ahead angrily reckoned that the other one owed it "for one dead head and two wounded." We continue here with the deposition related by a member of the "winning" brastvo, which had killed two men.

> "In a few days the village gathered and wanted us to make peace. We sent men to them and asked for the first truce till St. Dmitri's Day (October 26th); and so soon as it came we asked for a second till Christmas, which they granted after much begging. At Christmas we asked, as is the custom, for both truce and arbitration ('kmetstvo')." (If a third truce were granted this meant that arbitration would be accepted. If a third truce were refused the feud raged as badly as ever.) "We fixed it for St. Sava's Day (January 14th). They gave us the names of twenty-four men, and off went I over wood and rock to beg them to come, and luckily none refused. St. Sava's Day came. I killed two oxen and six sheep, took four hams and bought two barrels of wine. I gathered together my bratstvo, my Kums, and my pobratims (sworn brothers), and, God forgive me, they helped me with money

and bread, and so I had all that was needed. And the men sat down and gave judgment thus. They held the head of Nikola Perovo as equivalent to that of my dead father. The head of Gjuro Trpkov they valued at 120 zecchins. One of their wounded was held equivalent to my wounds and the other was valued at seven bloods'' (one "blood" was 10 zecchins, i.e., about £5; the judges valued the wounds by this standard), "and that woman's wound was reckoned as three bloods. And they decreed that I should bring six infants" (in order that a man of the other bratstvo shall stand godfather to them and thus cement peace by a spiritual relationship), "and that I should hang the gun which fired the fatal shot around my neck and go on all fours for forty or fifty paces to the brother of the deceased Nikola Perova. I hung the gun to my neck and began to crawl towards him, crying: 'Take it, O Kum, in the name of God and St. John.' I had not gone ten paces when all the people jumped up and took off their caps and cried out as I did. And by God, though I had killed his brother, my humiliation horrified him, and his face flamed when so many people held their caps in their hands. He ran up and took the gun from my neck. He took me by my pigtail ('perchin') and raised me to my feet, and as he kissed me the tears ran down his face, and he said: 'Happy be our Kumstvo (Godfatherhood).' And when we had kissed I, too, wept and said: 'May our friends rejoice and our foes envy us.' And all the people thanked him. Then our married women carried up the six infants, and he kissed each of the six who were to be christened.

"Then all came to us and sat down to a full table." (They are waited on by the head of the house and his men, who do not sit down with the elders and the plaintiff. At the head of the table sits the most respected of the elders. After the meal he proposes the health of the new Kum and of the master of the house, and they drink to the newly established peace. The payment of the fine is then called for.) " 'By God, my brother,' said my uncle, 'we have but little money. But we are a fine bunch of brethren, each with shining weapons. Here they are and here are you. Another time we shall do to you as you do to us. Here are the weapons. Take what your honour permits you.' Kum Nikola was indeed a man. He took the gun which had shot his brother and kissed it on the muzzle. The other weapons he gave back, saying: 'Take them, O Kum. I give them you as gift in return for the six Godfatherhoods; and I give you my brother for the gun.' " [Durham 1928:89–90]

The reason that it was safe to wait a few days to establish the original truce is that the quarrel was within the same village, and it was generally understood that honor must bend in the interest of social harmony. Those first few days surely had been spent in burying the dead. The blood settlement itself involved enormous amounts of money, probably more

This illustration of the pacificaton of a blood feud appeared in a book
published in 1820 by Vialla de Sommières, a French colonel in Napoleon's
army, who was allowed to visit Montenegro extensively a decade earlier.
Given the large number of inaccuracies in his published work, this
illustration cannot be trusted entirely. But the krvnik's crawling toward his
victim with the killer rifle slung around his neck jibes with later accounts, as
do the separate groupings of the two clans. The conciliatory role of the
Orthodox priest is also appropriate.

than three hundred United States dollars per "head," at a time when a
dollar was something like a week's wages. In spite of the enormous blood
debts that were run up by both sides and the substantial residual amount
owed by the "winning" clan, it turned out at the end that the blood-
money payment was largely symbolic, since only the rifle, as the actual
instrument of death, actually changed hands. Otherwise, the rifles,
pistols, and broad swords in the pile were returned to their owners.
According to Jelić (1926), this was not atypical in Montenegro.

The enactment of the pacification drama involved constant humiliation for the winning clan, beginning with its having to beg for a truce and
for pacification and ending with the groveling request for the losing clan
to accept the large sum of blood money that the winner had to pay. These
actions were truly hard upon honor. That they were built into the
standard pacification procedure is a testimonial to how strongly the
"losing" clans always felt about not taking vengeance in actual blood.
Obviously, one reason that pacification was difficult to achieve in the

absence of overwhelming public pressure was that both clans, not just the "losing" one, were necessarily humiliated by the process.

A SECOND PACIFICATION IN GRBALJ

In the year 1890 Pavle Rovinskii, a highly competent Russian ethnographer, visited Grbalj and witnessed a blood pacification there. It was a curious feud in that the killer, a brash quarreler, escaped after killing a well-respected villager and was himself killed later on by parties who were not involved in the feud. The sons of the killer's victim were thinking about the killer's sons as targets when the community asked that the traditional procedure be used to pacify the blood debt. This request came in spite of the fact that Grbalj by then was subject to regular police control.

According to Rovinskii (1901), the Bojković clan owed for a head, so the Zec clan got to appoint the kmets to the Court of Good Men. The court found that the sons of the Bojković killer and his clan had to do the following: (1) pay 163 sequins, 2 grosh, and half a para (all coins) for the head; (2) hold a dinner for the Zec clan to the tune of honoring three hundred guests; (3) conclude twelve godfatherhoods with the Zec clan; (4) conclude twelve great and twelve little blood-brotherhoods between the two clans; and (5) transfer the rifle used in the killing to the Zec clan, with all due self-humiliation.

At the ceremony, the two clans stayed away from each other "like two hostile regiments." Rovinskii describes the ceremony in detail:

> A short moment of silence falls, and then a group of people steps out from the other side. The son of the murderer, in a single undergarment, barefoot and without a cap, creeps on all fours. And on his neck hangs a long gun on a strap (it is always a long gun, for a greater effect, even if the murder was just by pistol); two *kmets,* also without caps, support it from the ends. Seeing this, Zec hastily runs ahead in order to shorten this severe, humiliating scene. He runs to Bojković in order to raise him up more quickly, but at that very moment Bojković kisses him on the feet, the chest and the shoulder. Taking the gun off Bojković's neck, Zec addresses him with the following words: "First a brother, then a blood enemy, then a brother forever. Is this the rifle which took the life of my father?" And not waiting for a reply, he hands the gun back to Bojković, expressing by this the full forgiveness of the past, and they both kiss each other, embracing each other like brothers. [Rovinskii 1901:386]

This did not conclude the ceremony. After the feast the godfather-hoods and blood-brotherhoods had to be concluded, and we discover that great blood-brotherhoods are relationships in which the same men become simultaneously blood brothers and godfathers to one another. The point of creating these ritual kinship ties, between men who were not really kinsmen by blood, was perfectly obvious to Montenegrins. It was to cement positive bonds between members of the two clans, since there were sure to be residual feelings of anger and vindictiveness. Once these bonds were formalized, what remained was to pay the blood money.

Since money was scarce and since Montenegrins at this time still kept much of their wealth in fine weapons, the Bojkovićes had to amass a pile of pistols, rifles, and short swords in front of Zec. He kept making them add more until he was satisfied with forty-two guns and fifteen swords. Next, the organizers of the dinner feast were given two guns. After a dramatic pause, Zec returned all of the other weapons to the member of the Bojkovićes who was to become godfather with him. This was expected, although he did have the right to retain all or some of the valuable weapons. Then the godfatherhoods were finalized, and the day's work was ended with the reading of the sentence *(sentencija),* or settlement, which is summarized above. The following day, two copies of the sentence were prepared, each with half of a Turkish coin, a para, attached. This accounts for the single para mentioned as part of the payment for the dead head. With this, the pacification was completed.

OTHER PACIFICATIONS OF FEUDS

In 1965 I was told about a similar pacification that took place in Rovca, a Brda tribe whose territory borders on that of Upper Morača tribe. There was a killing involving a prominent clan, and a similar traditional ceremony was used to cement the social order back together at the clan level. I have not heard of a more-recent blood pacification in Montenegro. This one took place in Velje Duboko, in a remote portion of Rovca territory that remained as isolated as Upper Morača and in 1936 was far from the surveillance of the Royal Yugoslav government that existed at that time.

No account exists of the pacification of a long-term, very active feud that approaches these excellent contemporary descriptions of feuds that were resolved very quickly. But there have been recorded many formal sentences from the traditional period, all of which follow a similar pattern (see, for example, Milović 1956; Vuković 1971; Jelić 1926). Sometimes only a few heads and "bloods" (wounds) were owed; or there might have been as many as ten or even twenty on each side. Where the score was large, the feud was likely to have lasted a long time; and these stubborn feuds often required the intervention of the bishop or, if two tribes were involved, sometimes a special court made up of leading men from a number of different tribes. The normal pattern of settlement was first to cancel out the number of heads and wounds shared by both sides on a one-for-one basis, then to reckon up, at the going rates, the additional heads and wounds owed by the winning clan (Jelić 1926). Next, any special factors were taken into consideration. For example, if the feud had begun because a member of one clan had abducted the wife or daughter of a member of the other clan, the Court of Good Men might find that this was culpable, and they therefore might levy an additional fine. Usually, any arms taken from men who had been killed during the feud were to be returned, and if the clans had damaged each other's property, restitution might be necessary if there was no justification for the damage (Jelić 1926). All of these expenses were tallied up on a single bill, which was owed by the clan with the higher final score.

When the feud mentioned earlier between Ceklin and Njeguši tribes in Old Montenegro was finally pacified in 1797, it had raged for at least thirty-two years (see Dragičević 1935) and had several times resisted what was supposed to have been definitive pacification (Boehm 1983). In 1797 Bishop Petar Petrović personally presided over this important pacification, and the court consisted of chieftains from all over Montenegro who begged and implored the two parties to come to terms. These two tribes were a day's walking distance from each other, so it was not terribly disruptive to their everyday life for the feud to prevail, even though it meant that the members of the two tribes were constricted with respect to traveling in certain directions. And because they were not contiguous, their need for defensive alliance was not so critical. But Bishop Petar at this time was building what was to be Montenegro's most extensive permanent tribal confederation. The settlement of this particular feud was crucial for its success, since it involved two of the most powerful tribes of Old Montenegro.

By 1797, Ceklin tribe owed eight heads to Njeguši tribe, while the Njeguši owed Ceklin six. But because a member of Njeguši clan had killed an important Ceklin man while a truce was in effect, the two heads owed to Njeguši by Ceklin were reduced by half a head. Then came the wounds. After canceling out five wounds on each side, the court added up the remainder: one serious Njeguši wound, valued at half a head but canceled out because a member of the Njeguši had improperly taken away the wife of one of his blood enemies. A few more heads were assigned to particular clans on either side. And finally, all loot and plunder were to be returned, although every last detail was not spelled out. This sentence ended with an admonishment that the tribes should live in brotherly love and that all of Montenegro would be against them should they return to feuding. And finally, each tribe was to pay a quarter of a head's worth of golden sequins to the kmets, to recompense them for the job they had done. All this was duly recorded by a pop from Ceklin.[3]

There are many other "sentences of pacification,"[4] but the reader now has an excellent idea of how the scores were tabulated and of the feelings, values, and beliefs that guided the kmets in doing their difficult work. These settlements were very similar, whether they took place within the tribe or between tribes. But one must not get the idea that the conclusive results that were written down as part of a settlement guaranteed that the feud would end forever. The failures for the most part are lost to history, but we do know something indirectly about them, as in the case of the prior settlement between Njeguši and Ceklin tribes. We may also assume that when a bishop served as a court of appeal for very stubborn feuds, this sometimes was because normal pacification procedures had broken down or had failed to work permanently.

THE BISHOP AS SUPREME COURT JUSTICE

For legal cases within a tribe in which the tribal kmets were unable to reach a decision that was acceptable to the disputing parties, or when an already pacified feud had flared up again, the problem might have to be taken to the bishop in Cetinje. Bishops Petar and Rade Petrović were both arbitrators who had earned the manly respect of their fellow tribesmen on the battlefield. They administrated justice in the open air under a special tree beneath which this judicial tradition had persisted before written history (Wilkinson 1848). It must be emphasized that while bishops had little or no coercive force to command any politically autonomous Montenegrin to abide by their decisions, they did have on their side the fact that the people so greatly respected judicial process itself. People also respected their Eastern Orthodox religion very deeply, as long as its officers did not attempt to interfere in their political autonomy. Thus, in submitting to arbitration before the bishop, there was already a strong commitment to try to accept his decision simply because this was an assumed part of any mediation process. But the actual decision was binding only in a general moral sense.

The Montenegrins took what they wanted from the ideology and values offered by the formal written tradition of Eastern Orthodox Christianity. When they were free from outside interference, they had no great sense of conflict between their own values and those of the church, even though these differed sharply in some basic respects, especially concerning the moral status of homicide in general and of revenge killing in particular. The tribesmen realized that the available ideology of the church, along with the active pressure exerted by some of its officers in favor of pacific behavior, was a necessary ingredient for the settlement of the feuds to which they were prone. In fact, they appreciated these pressures and utilized them enthusiastically as long as they themselves were not directly involved in a feud, because as members of the tribal community they sensed that feuds threatened their own immediate and long-term interests. It must be assumed also that even the parties who were directly involved in a feud ambivalently appreciated the help that they could get through mediation, if they had reached a potential stopping point.

Once they had decided to seek the mediation of their bishop, the tribesmen truly appreciated his potential intervention. This need was particularly likely to arise when a feud had started between two different tribes, because there were really two different moral communities involved. Unless two tribes had a particularly strong tradition of political alliance, the concern for social order was much weaker than when a dispute involved two clans within the same tribe. In fact, intertribal conflicts actually tended to galvanize each separate tribe into greater than usual internal social cohesion. But at the same time, the ability of the wider tribal confederation to defend itself against powerful external predators was impaired.

In such cases, the felt need to rely upon the bishop's moral authority could become great, but only when the two tribes had become sufficiently weary or threatened that they wished to set aside considerations of honor and feelings of emnity. Because the longer-range benefits of intertribal confederation were often rather unpredictable or otherwise difficult to see clearly, this time was often long in coming. The more-active bishops went out into the field and worked tirelessly to convince quarreling clans and tribes that for the common good, they should submit early to pacification.

THE THREAT OF VENDETTA AS A
PERCEIVED SOCIAL PROBLEM

The speed with which intratribal feuds could ignite and escalate necessitated highly decisive intervention. As the main organ for the formal management of conflict, the Court of Good Men had to try to nip such possibilities in the bud. However, as has been emphasized previously, such legal tribunals had no absolute or even coercive power to impose a decision upon two parties who were "in blood." It did, of course, have this kind of power if an individual had committed some heinous crime and the tribe had decided to try him or her formally; then it could impose sanctions such as exile or execution. But usually, neither of the parties to a feuding dispute had committed any such crime. Thus, the decision of the judges was in no way binding, even though the parties agreed in advance to accept the decision. In spite of the moral pressure to accept such decisions, members of either party, in practice, could change their mind and go back to feuding. The point is that the tribe as a whole was powerless to force the parties to a feud to desist.

In the account of Djuro and Nikola's case, it was quite evident that the judges were worried that they might not find a compromise that would work, and they strongly implied that ultimately, peace between two powerful clans was at stake. It also was obvious that they were fairly confident that they would be able to manage that particular conflict effectively.

Less-formal mechanisms for conflict resolution also were important for averting feuds at earlier stages in their development. Had Miloš listened to the pop and the knez in the first place, he would not have been killed. His father, Nikola, at least was willing to compromise his honor and his own very strong feelings about his only son's death, which cried out for vengeance, by submitting to arbitration before killing in revenge. There can be no doubt that the entire local community informally put pressure on him to do so, at the same time trying to convince him that this was not the end of his honor. This made "submission" easier for him. It is also possible, living as they did under an Austrian protectorate, that the parties to the dispute in Grbalj had it in the backs of their minds that the Austrians ultimately might intervene with military force if a feud were really to get out of hand.

During the traditional period, this last factor, of course, was absent up in tribal Montenegro proper. There, the threat of prolonged feuding was always present whenever sparks of any kind flew in human affairs. As we have seen, the likelihood that a single killing would escalate into a prolonged vendetta depended upon a number of different factors. But whatever the other contingencies might have been, in traditional tribal Montenegro the availability of a formal means of mediation may be viewed as having been absolutely essential for the continuing effective existence of the segmentary social system. This was true at both the tribal and the intertribal levels. As I shall emphasize further in chapter 8, this well-developed tradition of conflict management required leadership by men who had a highly sophisticated understanding of the requirements of their social system.

In this chapter we have seen how the basic moral functions that suppressed antisocial behaviors in individuals were supplemented by an elaborate tradition for resolving conflicts. Processes of mediation and judicial settlement constituted a highly specialized aspect of this basic system of social control, in that they went far beyond merely conditioning individuals to curb their favorite impulses. There was a deliberate and purposive effort made by the community, whether it was a clan or a tribe, to contain and resolve internal conflicts, regardless of whether moral culpability was present.

The management of conflict, unlike many other aspects of the basic system of moral conditioning, did not operate independently of the conscious desires and objectives of native actors. Rather, it represented a self-conscious kind of social engineering, in which the older and more mature members of the community tried to manipulate a homicidal conflict in such a way that it first could be contained and then could, it was hoped, be resolved on a permanent basis. Given the potential for conflict in Montenegro, we must give the indigenous Courts of Good Men a great deal of credit for helping their own social system to work effectively.

8

The Importance of Decisions

As we have seen, feuding in Montenegro involved very deep feelings. Perhaps the most basic were self-assertive emotions that favored violent retaliation for a serious affront to one's own person, but the same feelings were quickly applied to the killing of a close agnatic kinsman. Because this was taken not only as a loss but as an insult, the emotional need for revenge was closely involved with the social need to maintain honor (and to avoid shame) by not accepting a serious insult passively. To satisfy both of these needs,[1] a man could not merely ensure that vengeance was taken. He also had to be certain that the actions he took were in conformity with the unwritten Montenegrin "Geneva Convention"—the rules for homicidal conduct contained in the oral legal code.

While revenge was extraordinarily sweet for a Montenegrin in that the need was felt intensely and its fulfillment was a great source of relief or satisfaction, this culturally patterned psychological compulsion very seldom made the participants blind to the rules of the game. For example, one would not give in to the impulse to kill a woman from the clan with which one was "in blood."[2] To do so might bring satisfaction emotionally, but it would harm honor, because it was an act viewed as being morally reprehensible (see Wyon and Prance 1903). Furthermore, one knew by the rules of feuding that her blood would not even count from the standpoint of scorekeeping. What it would do, however, was to involve one's own clan in a bitter second feud with her father's clan (Jelić

1926). Thus, there were sanctions other than tribal public opinion that protected females and encouraged people to play by the rules.

More generally, to keep a feud honorable, the native actor constantly had to make rational calculations as to how his actions, which were always very public, would come off on the tribal stage. The audience, as we have seen in chapter 4, was a highly critical moral community. However, calculations in feuding did not end with the steering of a proper moral course. There were also nonmoral, practical considerations having to do with economic and political goals that impinged at every stage of a feud. Various combinations of moral and practical alternatives presented problems that necessitated the making of highly complicated decisions as to how to behave, and every decision was somewhat different from the last one, even though the great majority followed a common pattern.

Describing the structure of a decision-making process is more difficult than, say, describing the structure of a clan or a tribe as a social group based on genealogical connections. But in Montenegrin feuds, I have discerned five predictable points at which the individuals or groups who were involved were obliged to make critical decisions. Before treating such decision crises in detail, I shall briefly outline the overall sequence.

The first decision point came whenever someone felt inclined to offer a provocation to another person who belonged to a different clan. If a provocation seriously impugned the honor of his potential adversary, he had to deal with the possibility of a retaliatory killing. The second decision point involved the person receiving the affront. If he decided not to take the life of the man who challenged him, then the feud was averted, possibly at the cost of his own obraz. If he killed him, the feud was now on, and the third decision point arrived. At this point, the decision-making process widened to the households of the two protagonists and possibly to their clans. These groups had to decide upon specific strategies of passivity, flight, or offense. At this third decision point they also considered the alternative of having the dispute mediated, so as to end it right there, at decision point three. However, if the two clans did settle down into a pattern of killing back and forth, decision point three could be repeated a number of times. The fourth decision point began when at least one side decided that it wished to end the dispute, and the other side then had the alternatives of agreeing to a series of truces or else continuing the feud. Finally, after both sides had agreed to attempt a pacification, a formal court would meet to decide upon a fair settlement at the fifth and final decision point, which, it was hoped, would terminate the feud. We shall turn now to these five phases of decision making, to examine the options and the risks that confronted Montenegrin decision makers at each of these important junctures.

DECISION POINT NUMBER ONE: THE ART OF INSULTING ANOTHER WARRIOR

A Montenegrin male, and to a far lesser extent a Montenegrin female, had to take into consideration the possibility of starting a feud whenever he asserted himself in such a way as to impugn seriously the honor of another person. While offering insults was an expected mode of maintaining honor, he also knew that his stronger provocations might get him killed. In the eyes of the tribe, this was exactly what made aggressive behavior commendable in many contexts. Thus, in any verbal dispute, a miscalculation in any direction could harm a person's honor if he were to give the appearance of being "trampled underfoot"; but a serious miscalculation in an aggressive direction could get him killed.

Decisions as to how to behave in disputes were both complicated and critical. An adult warrior would have to calculate on the spur of the moment just how sharply to deride another man in public, in a situation in which both men were likely to become incensed and carry things too far. In deciding what to say, a man had to determine exactly how important personal and clan honor were to the particular opponent he was confronting. The immediate aim was to be certain that other people did not view him as a *kukavica* (coward); so if he offered insults that came close to requiring homicidal retaliation, then no one would doubt his courage. But because no Montenegrin was foolish enough to invite his own death unnecessarily, he would try to avoid giving the ultimate insults that few Montenegrins could bear, unless he was certain that his adversary would take such humiliation and would still refrain from killing him on the spot or at some later time.

The ethnohistorical materials back up this assessment. Very few feuds began through the ultimate types of insult, such as touching the mustache of one's adversary or hitting him with one's long pipe *(čibuk)*. If anyone did this to an honorable man, the latter would simply have to kill his provoker or totally lose face. Rather, it can be assumed that the immediate provocation usually was verbal, less extreme, and therefore ambiguous. It would not drive the victim to instant homicidal retaliation;

rather, he would brood about it for a time and then perhaps would give in to the need to kill his tormentor after a period of desperate ambivalence. For each recorded case of this kind of delayed reaction, we must assume that there were many others in which a man would come close to killing the person who had insulted him but then refrained from doing so because he did not wish to involve himself, his close kinsmen, and possibly his entire clan in a feud.

The exchanging of insults, then, was a very delicate art that involved ultimate risk taking. Decisions as to what to say next were potentially matters of life and death, since simply to maintain one's honor, one had to take at least some small risks of being killed. But if Montenegrins were not foolish enough to deliberately commit suicide by offering ultimate insults to other Montenegrins, we must ask why there were so many feuds resulting from verbal disputes. One reason was that decision makers were fallible and therefore could miscalculate something as complicated as another person's reaction to an extreme insult. Another was that the decision maker himself could be emotionally carried away because his blood was beginning to boil, so that his capacity to make lightning calculations was impaired. If he were to overdo his manly performance, the risk of getting himself killed would obviously increase.

Thus, keeping insults within bounds at the same time that in public a person was courageously pushing his adversary almost to the brink of homicidal retaliation was a game that required an astute decision-making capacity under fire, and also a good control over the emotions. I myself have participated in minor verbal duels in Montenegro, in the form of semihostile joking with other males in which both sides calculated very carefully what they could get away with without provoking real enmity. Indeed, as I explained earlier, I was willing to take such risks only at the end of several years, when I felt secure enough in my command of the language to be certain I would not overinsult someone unintentionally. Had I been there in the old days, I doubt that I would have become involved at all in such joking contests, but in 1965 these were no longer viewed as potentially homicidal conflicts. In fact, they did sometimes get out of hand, resulting in fistfights or lawsuits. The latter, of course, are the modern equivalent of a retaliatory homicide. But in the old days a man would not have sued for defamation of character; he would simply have drawn his pistol and blown his antagonist away, either on the spot or later when they met.

Thus far, I have spoken of disputes as though they occurred simply because two men happened to rub one another the wrong way. Many feuds do appear to have begun because trivial grievances had led to verbal exchanges that then got out of hand. But very often, some more-substantial prior conflict underlay the argument. It might have had to do with territory, in that pasture disputes were a prominent cause of feuds. But most often, as we have seen, women were involved. In addition, a past history of having been "in blood" with another clan automatically would intensify any such dispute, even though "complete" pacification supposedly had taken place.

This means that the first decision point in a potential feud was not limited solely to the manner in which direct insults were exchanged, verbally or nonverbally. It also was possible to insult a man mortally in a less direct fashion: for example, by ruining his daughter, by making a cuckold of him, or by seriously mistreating his daughter, if she happened to be one's wife. The decision to enter into such behavior brought the same risk of homicide as a verbal insult whenever honor was directly involved. Since certain Montenegrins continually tried to encroach on one another's property and to ruin other men's daughters, it must be assumed either that many of them were very lucky or else that they knew which situations had lethal possibilities and therefore calculated the risks rather carefully.[3]

Individual differences played an important part here. Obviously, those who took the largest risks were most liable to get caught up in homicidal consequences. But there were other differences, as well. Some Montenegrins deliberately chose to behave rashly because such men were esteemed, up to a point. This was a matter of honor. Others simply may not have been so good at foreseeing the consequences of their actions and therefore miscalculated their chances. Others, carried away by emotions of greed, lust, or anger, stumbled into situations in which an outraged father or husband or father-in-law felt obliged to kill him.

DECISION POINT NUMBER TWO: TO KILL OR NOT TO KILL

After the original instigator decided what kinds of risks he wished to take in offering an insult, the recipient had to decide what he was going to do about his own threatened social reputation. This brings us to the second decision point, which differed from the first in several respects. For one thing, the decision might involve a homicidal act. For another, if the actor decided on homicide, he faced the near certainty of further homicidal retaliation, not only against himself personally but against other males in his clan. At this second decision point the affronted man's decision became more complicated if the clans of the two adversaries were of markedly different size. Particularly if his clan was relatively very small, his action could result in the clan's being seriously decimated or of its having to emigrate and resettle elsewhere under a new name unless early pacification efforts succeeded. If his clan was relatively much larger, then it was possible that the smaller clan might not dare to retaliate.

No matter what the relative size of the clans, the second point of decision making had potentially far-reaching practical consequences for large groups of people. If the clans were evenly matched, then a prolonged feud would eat away their supply of energy that was available for subsistence purposes and would reduce the fighting strength of each clan as warriors were killed. At the very least, it placed some or all clan members, but in particular the males who were prime targets, under a truly unwelcome degree of psychological stress. These disadvantages were increased or decreased, depending upon which clan was the stronger or the weaker in size and in aggressiveness. In any event, the consequences of starting a feud were dire, from either the Montenegrins' or our own perspective. For these reasons, affronted individuals often struggled with extremely powerful feelings of need for retaliation for days or for months, and often for years. Frequently, but not always, members of smaller clans would swallow their pride, even though they would often rationalize things so that they could feel that they were merely putting off homicidal retaliation for a better opportunity in the future.

This brings up a major difference between the first decision point and the second. The first decision was made in a variety of contexts, often in the heat of a verbal conflict, on the basis of assessing the probability that one might be shot in retaliation. Because of individual personalities and moods, there was sufficient uncertainty in predicting outcomes in this area so that people regularly took calculated risks without actually being reckless. However, at the second decision point, the dilemma of whether to kill or not to kill brought with it far less uncertainty. If one killed and if the clans were both fairly large, then the feud would go into full swing. Thus, it became much easier for the affronted person to predict the further consequences of lethal retaliation than it had been for his adversary, at the first decision point, to predict what reaction an insult might bring.

Once the affronted person had given in to his emotions and had retaliated homicidally, he knew that eventually there would be an additional killing of either himself or a male kinsman unless pacification were to take place. What became uncertain, at this second decision point, was exactly who would be killed next. This became a matter of opportunity, since the entire household or clan was now on guard. While the man who had taken revenge himself would be the prime target, he was by no means the only acceptable target.

At the second decision point, where the alternatives were to kill or not to kill, decisions necessarily became difficult. One had to face directly the strong likelihood that all of one's male relatives would become involved in a stressful and bloody affair of honor, a conflict that could also disrupt the life of the entire tribe. For this reason, I assume that many potential feuds simply never took place because wise decisions were made in favor of these other considerations, rather than in favor of honor, at the second point of decision making.

DECISION POINT NUMBER THREE: A TIME FOR LIMITED WARFARE

The third decision-making juncture arrived immediately after the initial retaliatory homicide had taken place. At this point, the original individual protagonist no longer made the decisions. It was now time for the households of the two adversaries and, usually, other close kinsmen in the male line to become involved in the decision-making process. If the two clans were located in different tribes, the chances were that they would simply decide to feud, unless they perceived some very special reason to try for an immediate reconciliation. If the two clans were from the same tribe, they would have to decide upon their respective strategies: assuming that the killer had sought refuge with kinsmen, the victimized clan had to decide whether to mount an attack or not; and the killer's clan had to decide whether to resist an attack, if this seemed likely, or to emigrate.

Simultaneously, the entire tribe now recognized the certainty of either losing some of its fighting strength, if one clan would be obliged to emigrate, or else of suffering the politically divisive effects of having a feud right in its midst. At the beginning of a feud within a tribe, the remainder of the tribe knew that it could intervene only when the time was ripe. In this delicate situation, once the attack had begun, the principals were not likely to be persuaded to set aside their differences until the period of siege had passed and the feud had settled down into a series of killings back and forth.

Often, as in the case of the killing in Grbalj in 1820 between neighboring clans that had always been friendly, it seems likely that it was decided early on that the attack phase should be left in abeyance. This might be followed by a drawn-out series of interventions by outside parties, resulting in truces. Such a delicate process required that a number of mini decisions be made by both the principals to the dispute and by other tribal personages who had intervened. If the attempt succeeded, the feud was terminated by the same kind of formal pacification decisions that will be discussed at decision point five. But if these negotiations were to break down, then the usual series of killings back and forth would result, although for feuds within a tribe there would be a constant pressure, coming from other members of the tribe, for the two clans to pacify.

DECISION POINT NUMBER FOUR: THE READINESS TO QUIT

Let us assume that a conflict has settled down to an active middle-game pattern of killing back and forth. With this state of affairs the arrival of the fourth major decision point—whether to end the feud—could not be predicted very easily. However, because of social pressure, native actors would feel far more constrained to set aside a feud within the tribe than one between clans of different tribes. This fourth point involved a simple and clear dilemma: whether to submit to pacification procedures or to continue the killing. The dilemma was particularly difficult for a clan that had a serious deficit of heads and wounds on its scorecard. To take money at all in place of blood compromised honor to a degree that was painful. To take a great deal of money for many heads that were owed was all but unbearable.

With respect to the above-mentioned social pressure, I must emphasize that the tribal moral community at large was genuinely ambivalent about a feud in its midst. On the one hand, parties who were external to the feud badly wanted the social order to be restored. On the other hand, they deeply respected a clan that stubbornly kept trying to even up the blood score so that it would not have to compromise its honor.

At this fourth decision point it was possible that the feud might have spread beyond the immediate households of the original adversaries, to include both clans in their entireties. This, too, involved an important decision, because the killing of a more distant agnate would predictably increase the number of people involved and might result in their targeting one's entire clan. We must assume, in the absence of data, that Montenegrins were judicious about escalating feuds beyond the immediate households involved.

Even when the adversaries had made the choice to submit to arbitration, this decision was only tentative, since it was symbolized by entering into a short-term truce. This was only the beginning. Actually, there were a series of three separate decisions, each resulting in a new short-term truce. And it was only when the third truce had been agreed upon (see Durham 1928; Vrčević 1890) that the two parties committed themselves to arbitration. At that juncture, the fifth and final decision point had finally arrived.

DECISION POINT NUMBER FIVE: THE GOOD MEN RENDER THEIR JUDGMENT

The fifth decision point brought up a decision that was the responsibility, not primarily of the disputants themselves, but of the Court of Good Men, whose decision the two parties had agreed to abide by in concluding the third truce. The Good Men's decision was a highly formal one and was not limited to the simple mechanics of counting up heads and wounds. This decision-making body of twenty-four honorable men also had to decide whether the feud involved any moral culpability, either at its inception or along the way. As I have said already, the initial exchange of verbal insults followed by a killing was viewed as being morally neutral; neither side was in the wrong, and the final blood payment simply accounted for the excess heads and wounds owed by the clan that had the higher score. But other kinds of conflict situations involving proprietary rights over women, or rights to territory or other property, produced great moral ambiguity. These required a fine ability to make decisions that might be acceptable to both sides, as did cases in which the very rules of feuding had been violated.

Of course, we must not ignore the fact that once the court had handed down its decision, both groups then had to decide whether or not to accept the settlement. In theory this decision was made in advance; and

if the groups did accept the settlement, the feud was terminated. Though
their willingness to submit to arbitration was a sign that they were
prepared to set aside their differences, in the Montenegrin mind the
decision by the "loser" to accept money rather than to even the score in
blood always was a difficult one to make, in spite of the fact that the
"winning" clan could be counted upon to humiliate itself ceremonially.
And even if the Court of Good Men had done its job well, there always
was a real danger that the losing side might be emotionally unable to
accept the settlement and that the feud would therefore begin again. Thus
the necessary compromise at this fifth point was both delicate and
potentially quite complex. As the oldest kmet in the Grbalj case said,
neither party should go home singing or lamenting.

For Montenegrins, the successful resolution of a long and bloody
feud was seldom definitive. Whenever a new dispute erupted, if the
disputants were from clans that previously had been at feud, the
likelihood of instant homicide was increased. Thus, an apparently well
resolved decision at point five was still fairly likely to lead to a
recurrence of the entire decision-making chain, as a new feud arose out
of the ashes of the old.

THE RULES AS CONSTRAINTS UPON
DECISION MAKING

The decision points that I have identified all involved moral values
and practical alternatives that were quite clear to Montenegrins. The
decisions themselves ranged from individual ones, in which demands of
honor were weighed against personal and collective considerations of
energy, stress, and bodily risk, to collective decisions based on similar
considerations. The latter were guided by an awareness that feuds
between entire clans or tribes impaired the quality of social life and could
seriously weaken the ability of these groups to form a defensive alliance
in the event of an external threat, in spite of the possibility of expedient
truces.

This analysis of decision-making stages provides an eloquent
testimonial to the fact that Montenegrin blood feuds were highly
patterned. Thus, they were not random and willful manifestations of the
passionate capacity that these self-assertive warriors had for defending
their honor through homicide. The rules of the game, embedded in a
tradition composed of past precedents that Montenegrins felt morally

obliged to follow, were what made it possible for this explosive violence to be expressed without doing serious harm to the overall adaptation of the tribesmen. These rules included the announcement of each killing so that both sides knew the exact score, the targeting of males only, the killing of adults except under very unusual circumstances, the exemption of guests from feuds, the honoring of truces, and so forth. These were the main rules, although there were also more-specific ones, such as those applying to house dogs.

Without such rules the tendency for conflicts to escalate would have created constant and widespread clan and tribal warfare, which would have resulted in the destruction of the segmentary political structure. This segmentary tribal structure, of course, was what enabled the predatory Montenegrins to live in stable territorial units and to remain free of the powerful Ottoman Empire, an external predator that was always ready to take advantage of tribal weakness.

DECISIONS AND ALTERNATIVE VALUES

I must emphasize that the rules for moral behavior that were inherent in past precedents for feuding were by no means simply a fixed cultural tradition, followed mechanically by individuals who were strongly governed by conformity. Rather, this tradition provided a context within which both individuals and groups were constantly making choices among the alternatives that they perceived. At some decision points the potential choices were many, while at others the alternatives were relatively few. But it must be stressed that these decisions almost always were active and reflective, even when they gave the appearance of being highly routine or of being determined by chance events. Sometimes, they were highly inventive, and in fact, it was possible for a man to forego revenge and still to enhance his honor under certain circumstances, if he played his cards correctly.

Marko Miljanov, the famous chieftain *(vojvoda)* of Kuči tribe, learned to write very late in life, after the leaders of the new Montenegrin state had removed him from power. He then published several books on tribal custom. Vojvoda Marko tells about a major clash between two clans of the Kuči tribe, in which a Montenegrin warrior deliberately decided not to take blood when he had a good opportunity:

> Tomo Popović son of Petar from Medun, when the Kuči tribe fought among themselves at Roga, encountered Grujo son of Luka, who had

killed his brother. Tomo raised his rifle so as to kill Grujo and avenge his brother Rako, who lay nearby, dead. But Tomo saw two of Grujo's brothers where they lay dead, then he thought it over: "Was it better to kill Grujo, the third brother, or to leave Grujo alive and his own brother unavenged?" His companions berated him as he did this, crying, "Fire, Tomo, he killed your brother." Tomo said: "His two brothers have been killed, Pero and Radulje, so I am not going to shoot this third one and leave Luka son of Mijat without a single son!" And so he paid no attention to his kinsmen's remonstrations and left Grujo alive and his own brother unavenged! [Miljanov 1901:44]

Tomo emerged from his decision as a respected man, rather than as a coward, because he made his reasoning public and because he knew the moral code well enough to make a very fine interpretation. The reason that this pacific action was socially acceptable to traditional Montenegrins was that in spite of the sharp demands of junastvo (the quality of being a true warrior), there also existed higher values, represented by the word čojstvo, which signified "humanity" or "manly virtue." I doubt that his humane act would have taken place if old Luka had had only one son. But to make a man lose all three of his sons in a single day was stretching the demands of blood too far, in Tomo's mind, even though it seems to have been specifically Grujo who had killed Tomo's brother and it apparently had not been men of Tomo's clan who had already killed Grujo's two brothers. No one would have censured Tomo for killing the third brother; in fact, this deed would have won respect. But since he made the basis for his decision clear, his unpredictable action brought him the respect of the tribal community. And this in turn may have established a precedent for future decision making under the same or similar circumstances in which similar cultural values came into conflict.

SOME OTHER EXAMPLES FROM VOJVODA MARKO

For decision makers in the feud, there were two kinds of decisions that were patently wrong. One was a decision that was certain to be viewed as cowardly. The other was one that would escalate a feud and its practical consequences to a degree that not only was socially or politically impractical but also was not called for by reasonable demands of honor.

One of Vojvoda Marko Miljanov's examples concerns the leader of the mighty Vasojevići tribe in the Brda, Vojvoda Miljan, who sent his wife home to her family—a clear cause for homicidal retaliation. When

This carved stone piece helps to frame a doorway of a house in Kuči, the tribe to which Marko Miljanov belonged. I was told by a member of this household that it commemorated an incident in which an ancestor had caught a thief in the act and both men had shot and wounded each other. Rather than killing the thief, the head of the household had nursed the other man back to good health and had let him go free. This was considered to be an example of čojstvo.

people asked her brother why he had not taken revenge, he answered: " 'I can't leave the Vasojevići without a single Miljan. If there were another to take his place, then this one would not remain alive on this earth!' " (Miljanov 1901:57). The ostensible (and magnanimous) reason for foregoing revenge was that the tribe could not find another such leader. But since vojvodas generally came from very powerful clans, one must wonder if other expediencies were more important in governing the decision.

In another case, a tribesman from Morača is targeted, an important man in the tribe. The avenger literally has him in his sights, but then kills a lesser man, justifying his action by saying that he has at least killed at the same status level and that in this way the important man's tribe will still have a useful leader to help it rise against the Turks (Miljanov 1901). A similar rationalization is used by the Vasojevići to justify sparing the son of a vojvoda: the avenger tells the son to hurry home before the avenger's clansmen arrive to kill him.

In these stories and others, individual Montenegrins negotiate their moral statuses with words as well as with actions or the absence thereof. The theme is an obvious one: although one may legitimately kill a man of much higher prestige than the victim, and thus enhance one's honor, there is such a thing as carrying a good thing too far. In backing off, one speaks to the issue altruistically so as to enhance one's own obraz or to defend it. But there is also the awesome practical problem of very seriously escalating the feud—a threat that goes unmentioned.

In addition to this prominent theme, there are many other examples that may be used to highlight the fact that decision making in feuding was both active and, at times, quite inventive. In one case, the victim abandoned all caution and exposed himself to assassination so flamboyantly that the avengers asked him why. When he answered that it was to escape from his marital problems, they refused to kill him (Miljanov 1901). My interpretation is that they felt that such an easy prize would not have satisfied honor: indeed, killing a person who was mentally defective, while technically counting as a "head," could only soil the honor of the avenger (Jelić 1926).

In another case, a Montenegrin entered an enemy's house at night but simply couldn't kill his enemy while he was asleep. Instead, he left his sword under the pillow to show that he could have killed him (Miljanov 1901). In still another case, a Montenegrin woman lost her son by homicide, and later the killer was captured in combat and brought before her to atone for her son's blood. She quickly gave the killer a piece of bread, thereby transforming him into a guest, who could not be killed. She then insisted that his life be spared.

These and other examples recounted by Miljanov are exceptions to the rules: in these cases the participants were indigenous actors who managed to make and to rationalize "aberrant" decisions that nevertheless worked for their honor. Other values that competed with the very strong value place on homicidal retaliation were either ones supporting tribal unity or simply ones of Christian mercy. Given these kinds of options, it becomes still more apparent that in enacting krvna osveta, native actors were playing by ear a very complicated game that had many moral rules, and that a number of these rules were in direct contradiction with one another.

COMPLEXITY OF DECISIONS IN REGARD TO FEUDING

When the possibility of making a choice exists, mistakes will always be made. We must assume that in some cases, individuals who were in the grip of "boiling blood" simply acted upon a revenge impulse in the heat of the moment and later wished that they had taken a more sensible course. But most feuds were begun primarily under the aegis of moral necessity, the judgment having been quite rational and calculating even if it was accompanied by intense emotions.

Honor, of course, was very much on the mind of the decision maker. But for Montenegrins a proper decision about feuding also involved calculating the possible disruptions in the person's basic subsistence mission—that of maintaining a piece of property, livestock, and a family. Obviously, a person would exercise particular self-restraint in a conflict that, if it should escalate to homicide, might result in his having to emigrate. However, the preservation of honor also came very close to being a basic necessity of life. In the history of the small Djilas clan we have seen the kinds of material, psychological, and biological sacrifices that some Montenegrins were prepared to make in the name of honor. There we also saw the sharp differences that particular personalities could make in the destiny of an entire clan.

The often-complicated decisions that were made along the way, through the five stages of decision making that I have identified, depended upon a shrewd capacity for evaluating social, psychological, and logistical contexts. To work, the blood-feud system required that this kind of analytic and decision-making competency exist on the parts of ordinary individuals, whose intuitive and sometimes very rapidly made decisions deeply affected the welfare of entire clans and tribes. There was also a need for experts to serve as decision leaders, and entire kin groups functioned as collective decision-making units. Some of these decisions were enormously complicated. But given the well-developed general ability of Montenegrins to undertake life-and-death decisions as warriors and raiders, it is not surprising that such a sophisticated decision-making competency was to be found in ordinary individuals.

Some decision dilemmas required that considerations much broader than the immediate self-interest of a person, clan, or tribe be taken into account. For example, the disadvantages and dangers of severe political divisiveness within a tribe, or between two tribes that normally were allies, were obvious to all adult tribesmen. As I have already shown, the greater the reason for two feuding groups to cooperate, the greater was the pressure from people who were not involved in the conflict to persuade the adversaries to pacify. And the greater this pressure, the greater was the likelihood that they would decide to do so. But when the potential for cooperation was low, a feud could go on almost indefinitely.

These behavioral patterns resulted from the practical application of rather sophisticated assumptions about the nature of political life in contexts that were quite complicated. The assumptions were shared by every Montenegrin adult, male or female. They were applied intuitively in decision making by ordinary Montenegrins, while the legal experts who sat in court sometimes were able to make them not only explicit, but eloquently so, as did the oldest kmet in Grbalj as his words came down through seventy years of oral tradition.

PREDICTABILITY AND UNPREDICTABILITY OF DECISIONS ABOUT FEUDING

Imagine yourself to be an ordinary Montenegrin tribesman. When you find yourself in an antagonistic confrontation with a member of some other clan, you must intuitively add up the entire score in just an instant, before you try to stand your ground and perform like a good warrior in the exchanging of insults. In spite of the strong emotions that you feel, you must try to calculate the relative strengths of your enemy's clan and your own, and you must reckon the likelihood that he might be more sensitive than most people to an insult. Many things are riding upon your ability to make these reckonings. First of all, your very life or possibly your ability to remain in the tribe where you have grown up is directly at stake, as well as the lives of your dearest relatives in the male line in case you should decide to flee. But beyond that, the possibility of your entire clan's remaining in the tribe could be at issue, if it is by far the weaker one. Furthermore, if pacification should come quickly, that pacification might be very expensive for your clan. On the other hand, if the opponent is from another tribe, then there is the possibility that the two clans will take pot shots at each other, raid mutually for livestock, and even possibly hunt heads from each other over a long period of years. You may even start a full intertribal vendetta if you kill a person whose death is likely to escalate the feud.

Of course, if your clan is powerful, you may be more inclined to throw your weight around in an argument, since men from other clans may shrink from retaliating in blood for an insult. And if your clan is powerful and someone deals you an insult that really wounds, you may be quicker to retaliate homicidally if the opposing clan is weak, since the chances are that they will procrastinate about taking blood. (I know of two such cases, in which blood was taken by a markedly weaker clan more than a hundred years later.) But such a possibility would scarcely deter you in your immediate decision to retaliate against members of a weaker clan as long as your own clan was very strong.

These are some of the more prominent constraints within which I believe decisions were made on the basis of known risks. The moral community that overlooked these public disputes was also aware of these considerations, and it judged less harshly a man who swallowed his pride if his clan was very small. But knowing these constraints by no means provided a person with definitive predictors of what might happen in a given situation; they only established some probabilities that were used intuitively in the reckoning of both disputants as to where they would go next in a conflict. The killing of Captain Ćorović by Aleksa Djilas has already shown us that conflict situations could contain a considerable element of unpredictability, depending upon the individual involved. Aleksa's father had swallowed his pride concerning the avenging of his brother's death. So had young Aleksa, Captain Ćorović obviously thought, until he pushed Aleksa too far by wantonly trampling on his honor.

As a self-assertive Montenegrin warrior, then, a man's mission was to maximize his own reputation and honor at the same time that he minimized the risk of getting himself killed from ambush or of getting his kinsman or tribe into deep trouble. Many Montenegrins took only moderate risks and had to be content to maintain only a moderately honorable reputation. Some knew how to push their opponents to the verge of homicide without getting themselves killed, and as long as they did this under provocation, they were respected and admired. Others were known as quarrelers *(svadjalica),* and while there was a certain admiration for their aggressiveness, there was also substantial disapproval for their provocations because of the danger that these posed to their clans and to the social order.[4] But every good Montenegrin knew that in situations involving confrontations, it was better to be a brash svadjalica than a fearful kukavica. With a warrior people who played this game very hard, it would not be surprising if there were quite a large number of feuds; indeed, what is remarkable is that there were relatively few.

THE IMPORTANT WORK OF EXPERTS
IN DECISION MAKING

When it came to making delicate decisions that required a sophisticated ability to read possibilities for pacifying a stubborn blood feud, it was the experts who stepped in. These specialists were leading men in their clans or tribes. They were selected for their general ability in what might be called sociopolitical analysis, for their ability to negotiate solutions to difficult conflict situations, and also for their moral uprightness and bravery. As astute applied social scientists, they were responsible for sensing when a propitious time had arrived for triggering the resolution of a feud: this could be at either the third or the fifth decision point. But even once they had intervened as go-betweens and the idea of arbitration had been accepted, they knew that the feud was far from settled.

At the final decision point, the Court of Good Men had a very delicate task before it. This is why the largest possible court of twenty-four kmets was gathered for the formal pacification, or *umir,* with the court being made up entirely of tribesmen who had been personally successful in navigating the many perils of trying to stay morally respectable in Montenegro. This purely personal decision-making capacity gave them a special credential for serving on a committee that had such important and difficult work, in which success hinged on the need to satisfy the honor of both parties in a conflict that amounted to a less-than-zero-sum-game.[5]

From the perspective of how major decisions in regard to feuding were made, we have seen that these were made sometimes by the individuals at feud, sometimes by feuding households or clans, and sometimes by entire tribes at feud, while special external decision-making groups were set up at certain predictable points when the disputants had expressed some willingness to negotiate. These decisions all depended upon a common conception of honor and of the morally appropriate enactment of retaliatory homicide. But within this shared cultural context, Montenegrins had many alternatives to choose from as they negotiated the often perilous course presented by their own tradition of feuding.

While every tribesman had a reasonably good grasp of the social and political factors that entered into making decisions about feuding, we must assume that it was the leading men who perceived these constraints most clearly and who continued to shape the rules so that the overall system could work. It was no accident that the rules of feuding limited interclan homicide to a degree such that protracted full-scale warfare between the larger clans was avoided. Tribal leaders knew very well that such behavior would result in the extinction of clans and the serious weakening of the tribe. They also knew that the Turks were always poised to finish off the job, once serious divisiveness had appeared in a tribe, and that when territorial competition was severe, a similar threat existed from unfriendly Montenegrin tribes. What I am stressing here is that the more astute tribesmen were shrewd enough to anticipate these potentially disastrous outcomes and that such insight was important to the operation of the system of feuding. As a result of this perceptiveness, over a long time the kmets gradually built and refined a set of rules for feuding that made these adaptive disasters unlikely. But they did this without ever trying to reject entirely the valued forms of homicidal self-assertiveness that seemed natural to them as honorable tribal warriors.

WHY EMPHASIZE DECISIONS?

As a way of bringing home an important point to the reader, I have summarized the entire pattern of feuding in terms of decision making.[6] One might cling to the impression that Montenegrin society was anarchic or that the tribesmen were impulsively and recklessly or even immorally prone to violence. But even though such impressions were voiced by almost every outsider who observed the Montenegrins during the traditional period, none of these characterizations is accurate. Rather, being devoted to the principle that no man may rule or coerce any other man, the Montenegrins quite carefully controlled the same sword by which they lived. In the absence of a centralized government possessing the coercive force needed to settle disputes arbitrarily and to execute, punish, or incarcerate those who seriously disrupted the social order, Montenegrin individuals were guided by their own communal sense of morality. This generated a moral pressure that was sufficient to maintain the well-known yet unwritten rules of conduct that regulated feuding.

Believing deeply in the moral necessity of blood revenge, the Montenegrins were well educated in a cultural tradition that made it natural to see a feud not only as a logical and necessary series of dire events but also as a drama in which honor was displayed at its best because the stakes were so extremely high. This is not to say that Montenegrins enjoyed the taking of blood or that they welcomed a feud. Indeed, it was potentially very difficult to kill a total stranger who happened to belong to an enemy clan. But they considered this ultimate kind of vengeance to be a moral necessity.

Therefore, given their total view of the world, feuding was not at all impractical. This viewpoint, however, did not make it easy to make all the decisions faced in the course of a feud. For example, there could be a sharp conflict between the requirements of practicality and the demands of honor, as when a smallish clan faced a feud with a clan that was considerably larger. Or there could be an ambiguous decision in which several different moral rules came into conflict. This we saw in the example from Marko Miljanov, when Tomo decided not to kill Luka's last remaining son, even though vengeance not only was culturally appropriate but was, in the opinion of his clan brothers, mandatory.

In such cases it was possible to make highly creative decisions in which some of the specific rules of feuding were broken in order to fulfill other practical or moral requirements, including those taught formally by the Eastern Orthodox Church. But a great majority of decisions about feuding had the appearance of being highly routinized, which in fact they were. This is exactly how a cultural tradition is maintained, as a series of similar but by no means identical actions that are intuitively decided upon by native actors. Obviously, this is not done by rote. Rather, the decision-making pattern becomes stabilized through careful weighing of antici-pated consequences in a series of similar problem situations, in the light of the belief system and of the values specific to the culture.

DECISION MAKERS AS REFORMERS
OF CULTURAL TRADITION

By looking at blood feuds as a series of routinized yet always creative decisions, we have seen that this violent activity by no means consisted of uncontrolled outbursts of homicidal rage. Otherwise, women would have been killed, or total war would have been declared upon one clan by another. Nor, for all its patterned regularity once it was under way, was a feud simply a blind, mechanical enactment of a cultural pattern known to the individuals involved in it. Indeed, we have seen that while Montenegrin decisions at the five decision-making points were quite carefully calculated in terms of the demands of honor, more-practical considerations also could enter in.

From a broader perspective, the very moral rules that both limited and channeled the process of feuding were constantly and thoughtfully revised by the Courts of Good Men. As leaders or as responsible older citizens, the kmets were wise enough to succeed in most of their attempts to arbitrate feuds, because they also kept a watchful eye upon the overall operation of the tribal social system in which they lived. Using these insights, they reformed the basic rules of feuding as they went along, in terms of their own sophisticated conceptions of what a tribal society required in order to function. Thus, in working as a Court of Good Men, they not only put precedent to creative use, but in their active approach they necessarily modified precedent itself as they went along.

This process of modification took place whenever an innovative decision was made. If generally approved, that decision was relied upon, of course, as a precedent for building future decisions. For this to take place, it was necessary that the tribesmen be willing to follow the rules of feuding and that their leaders in the decision-making process be compe-tent to understand the entire system of feuding with considerable sociological and psychological sophistication.

Being familiar with violence and accustomed to paying a high price for their honor, these wise men did not hope to stamp out all homicide within their tribal territory. Such an idea was not only foreign to their world view; in many kinds of situations it very obviously would have involved their people in dishonor. Indeed, when their bishops would insist that the tribal confederation set up judicial groups empowered to prohibit feuds by force, the tribesmen and their tribal leaders were not interested. This disinterest in coercive intervention did not come from a love of violence, however, but from a supreme distaste for any form of political coercion within the tribe or of political interference from without. Both went against their most basic values, as did the idea of denying a warrior the traditional right to guard his honor, as custom demanded.

The tribesmen's own solution to the problem of violence in their midst was to keep its level down to tolerable limits, so that total warfare between clans within a tribe or between neighboring tribes would not erupt frequently or for any length of time. They relied upon their political leaders and elders who sat on the Court of Good Men to keep this rather efficient system running and well tuned. And in feuds that were ripe for settlement but were unusually difficult to pacify, they readily accepted the services of their bishop, so that his wisdom and the force of his supernatural threats and prestige might help the disputants to set aside honor and come to a compromise. But this was undertaken only on the condition that there was no hint of applying physical force to stop the bloodshed.

By Montenegrin standards, the tribesmen generally did an excellent job on their own. Although the historical documents do not by any means cover the majority of feuds that have taken place, their contents suggest that many feuds were pacified immediately after the first homicide rather than after a long and destructive middle game. For this feat of social engineering we must pay tribute to the Montenegrin kmets and particularly to their leaders as sophisticated social theorists. In addition we must take off our hats to the ordinary tribesmen as being astute practical decision makers.

The blood-feud system described in this book is an eloquent testimonial to their abilities in these theoretical and applied fields of social policy making. In making that system work, they appear to have satisfied their own moral standards. But simultaneously they kept their social life reasonably tranquil much of the time and kept their tribes viable for survival in a very dangerous political environment.

9

Making Further Sense of the Feud

In the preceding chapter we drew very close to decisions involving honor and lethal retaliation, so as to see what it was like to be an individual Montenegrin carefully navigating the troubled waters of a feuding society. Here I shall try to make some overall sense of feuding as a way of dealing with conflict. In building a more integrated picture, I shall explore and try to clarify some questions that the excellent but limited ethnohistorical materials themselves do not directly resolve.

Some aspects of feuding in traditional Montenegro are perfectly apparent. For example, it was chiefly closer agnates of the victims who retaliated mainly upon the closer agnates of the killers, with a preference for the actual killer or for a good man who was closely related to him. It is also clear that scorekeeping was exact and public and that only the clansmen with the lower score went hunting, even though their intended victims might be vigorous and aggressive in protecting themselves, as Kečo was. As an idealized pattern, this provided a basis for the containment of violence between groups: by following the rules for taking turns, killings were kept isolated both in space and in time. On the other hand, as long as the two clans had males to carry on the feud, it could continue indefinitely. But feuds were always susceptible to resolution if both parties were willing.

Some data suggest that this predominant and obvious pattern does not encompass all the conflicts that called for retaliatory homicide. For one thing, there were numerous cases of individuals or smaller clans who relocated "because of blood" *(zbog krvi)*. Although the data do not make this pattern entirely clear, houses and property were sometimes destroyed in the preliminary phase of a blood conflict, during which it appears that the defending clan either had to hold out for several days or else flee the tribe if the clan did not wish to perish in the siege.

In an ethnohistorical context that cannot be complete, one way to deal with all these facts might be to isolate the subsequent pattern of killing back and forth and to set this aside as a most basic pattern to be labeled as "feuding"; but this pattern itself has many facets. Furthermore, I believe that both the killing back and forth and the fleeing of killers from the tribe can be understood as expressions of the same pattern, if the nature of segmentary tribal politics is considered carefully as the context in which feuding takes place.

SEGMENTARY POLITICS AND THE BALANCE OF POWER

When a segmentary tribal structure exists in a habitat offering resources that are marginal in comparison with population size, there will be competition for scarce resources. In Montenegro there were inter-tribal conflicts over pastures, and there were even rare full-scale tribal wars with the taking of heads between competing tribes (Vlahović 1939). Indeed, only a reasonable balance between the fighting strengths of different tribes could keep the division of territory stable.

In the absence of any forceful centralized or external political regulation, weaker tribes had to rely on alliances in order to resist the territorial designs of very large tribes, or else they would simply have to consolidate permanently into larger tribes. This balance-of-power model holds for political relations between tribes; but within the tribe, political affairs were quite different. For two reasons the tribe was defined as a peace group within which conflict was carefully managed. First, there was the peaceful quality of social life within the group that Montenegrins deeply valued. But also there was the question of increased vulnerability of the tribe to external predators, which serious divisiveness produced.

Furthermore, within the tribe it was individual households, rather than clans, that owned real estate at winter sites, while the entire tribe owned its summer pastures in common. Thus, clans were not very likely to compete for territory within the tribe, even though interclan rivalry is mentioned frequently in historical accounts. Such status rivalry was still quite prominent in the 1960s, but during traditional times, more than the clan's heroic standing was at stake, since leadership roles in the tribe tended to be determined by clan dominance. Very large clans or clans that were militarily very distinguished usually provided the tribe with its chieftain, and such clans had their special effect on tribal political policy (see Boehm 1983) even though the egalitarian nature of the society set rather strict limits on the dominance that they could develop.

CLAN COMPETITION WITHIN THE POLITICAL SYSTEM

We may now compare the situation of tribes that were competing with other tribes and the situation of clans that were competing within a tribe. Between neighboring tribes there was always the latent struggle for territory, which was kept in equilibrium by careful balancing of power but without any coercive mechanism to control conflicts. Among the clans there reigned also a generally competitive situation, but in the absence of territorial stakes, careful balancing of power was not necessary. Members of small and large clans were equally members of the tribal community, and external warfare provided an arena in which all of the clans could simultaneously cooperate and vie for heroic status. Thus, while the larger or more heroic clans were more influential in determining tribal policies, every clan had a right to exist peaceably within the tribal moral community.

This meant that there was little need for clans to form alliances with respect to warfare within the tribe, since the idea of such warfare went against everything the tribe stood for. But if conflicts did arise within the tribe, this absence of alliances left the two clans pretty much on their own in resolving the conflict. This put smaller clans at a marked disadvantage, because a man who belonged to a very small clan could be driven from the tribe if he killed or seriously insulted a member of a much larger clan. If the initial retaliation involved his entire clan as target, then the entire clan might have to emigrate. Such actions are poorly documented, because obviously no written pacifications took place. But many feuds took this direction; this is apparent from the very large number of refugee clans in Montenegro and from the large number of Montenegrins who had to settle elsewhere "because of blood."

In historical descriptions of longer-lasting feuds the issue of the relative size of clans is never raised, but this important aspect must not be overlooked. I believe that the feuding system was founded on the unstated assumption that whenever the two groups involved were sufficiently at parity so that use of coercive force could not resolve the issue without all but destroying both groups, then it was time for the complex of rules pertaining to the middle game to go into effect. Thus, it was necessary that some minimal degree of parity in clan strength and psychological motivation exist, before the alternating-homicide rules of middle-game feuding could be applied as a solution to the problem of internal conflict.

VARIATIONS ON THE FEUDING THEME

This means that feuding, with its elaborate oral legal code, must not be equated with a modern legal system, in which, in theory at least, the rules apply to everyone. In Montenegro it appears that the rules that caused homicidal attacks to alternate applied chiefly to cases in which clan strength was balanced in such a way that the threat of a very costly escalating conflict became obvious. These rules were not created by a convention of political theorists who were intent upon designing a fair system of government. They were developed by tribesmen who were adept at predicting the causes of conflicts of various types and were astute enough politically to develop forms of conflict that were more restrictive than all-out warfare. These rules stayed in place because of a combination of practical self-interest, including concern for honor as a form of community approval, and direct pressure from uninvolved parties.

There were really two modes for resolving homicidal disputes in such a way that the tribe was not weakened too seriously. In the first mode a larger clan simply drove out the killer from a smaller clan along with those of his clansmen who had helped in his defense, or else the killer's group anticipated the attack and left as soon as the homicide had been committed. In such cases, might made right. In the second mode the two clans either assumed or discovered (through a brief siege) that they were too evenly matched to permit an inexpensive victory and therefore turned to tribal tradition (i.e., to the rules of feuding) to govern their conflict in such a way that escalation to mutual clan suicide could be averted.

The many recorded pacification sentences that give evidence of longstanding feuds in which the rules for one killing at a time were followed prove that such balanced conflicts were numerous. On the other hand, the extremely large number of clans in Montenegro and in surrounding territories whose founders had fled to a different area "because of blood" attests to the fact that smaller clans often could not back their members well enough to establish the kind of initial parity that was needed in order to stay in the tribe and benefit from the rules of feuding. This interpretation fits well with the available facts.

To understand the Montenegrin blood feud, then, one must not view it as a set event, or even as a general process governed strictly by a set of rules that was followed to the letter. Rather, feuding consisted of a number of different problem solutions all of which were predicated on a single basic thought: if they are to maintain their honor and be safe from further attacks, men or clans cannot respond passively to a homicide. In a sense, this is a simple matter of social dominance—as is the case in the behavior of monkeys and apes—in which a dominant individual senses that he or she must stand up to a challenger or else be dominated. This analogy is a partial but significant one that will be treated in a later chapter.

What emerges for Montenegro is obviously a complicated picture for which some of the precise data are lacking. For example, we do not know how much discrepancy in the size of clans was necessary before members of a small killer clan would simply flee rather than try to defend themselves against a siege. Nor do we know how much discrepancy in size was involved when members of a victimized clan postponed taking revenge because they were afraid to retaliate against a far-stronger killer clan, which they knew would then go on the offensive.

The matter of size, by itself, surely was not all that predictive. Indeed, a small clan such as the Djilasi struggled valiantly and recklessly against the new Montenegrin government itself, virtually to the point of committing clan suicide; many other clans, facing less fearsome odds, emigrated or held their fire. As we have seen in the case of the Djilas clan, individual personalities and particular situations, or both in combination, affected the course of the conflict. Surely this was equally true for other small clans when they made their difficult decisions.

Obviously, blood conflicts were very much played by ear, and the definition of honorable conduct was judged according to the situation. If a member of a small clan killed a member of a very powerful clan, immediate emigration was not really viewed as being dishonorable (Djilas 1958). Conversely, when a member of a small clan was killed by a member of a much larger clan, this might simply result in inaction by the small clan, because the large clan could defend its members so well and, when its turn came, could take vengeance much more effectively. In spite of this predicament, a small clan that was theoretically on the offensive at least did not need to relocate, and there was an understanding of its weak position when the tribe reckoned its moral reputation. But when they had to bide their time, members of these small clans were always highly uncomfortable over the fact that blood was owed and not collected.[1]

This further analysis does not invalidate the earlier treatment of feuding and its rules. However, it does suggest that certain forms of conflict have become better known than others due to the nature of what was recorded as ethnohistorical data. The formal pacification documents treat two types of quarrels: (1) those in which a local community pressured closely adjoining clans to settle up quickly and (2) long-term feuds that had entered the middle game.

With the first type, it seems likely that often a small killer clan might be saved from its emigration dilemma by community pressure to pacify immediately, assuming that the larger victim clan could be quickly persuaded to accept first a truce and then blood money, instead of mounting an attack. Alternatively, if the smaller clan had suffered the homicide as victim, immediate blood payment would redeem its honor if the community's efforts at pacification were successful. Thus, it is logical that small clans were at a much greater disadvantage if they became homicidally involved with large clans outside their own immediate locality but within the same tribe, so that a siege was practicable.

With the second, protracted type of homicidal quarrel, it seems likely that the clans were usually balanced in size—or at least that neither was so small that a cheap initial victory seemed inviting. More-recent data from Albania (Hasluck 1954) suggest that the picture in traditional Montenegro could have been complicated by the building of alliances, since smaller clans in Albania sometimes formed expedient alliances so as to build up their strength during a feud. But the early attacks and destruction of property appear to have varied sharply in these two regions. For example, it is known that the Albanians took such destructive attacks to be a normal feature of feuding and did not require compensation for the damages upon pacification. By contrast, the Montenegrins had to pay for such depredations if the opposing clan survived to continue the feud and if pacification then took place (Jelić 1926). Thus, in this particular matter, it would be a mistake to extrapolate too much from the situation in Albania during the early 1900s to that in Montenegro a century earlier. Indeed, this fragmentary evidence suggests that sieges of smaller clans by larger ones in Montenegro may have been disapproved of by the tribal moral community at large.

In summary, the Montenegrin style of enacting blood conflicts seems to have encompassed far more than a series of standard operating procedures set in motion by a homicide. I have just discussed one factor that was of predictable importance—namely, the relative sizes of the two clans. But other factors surely entered in as well.

For example, a tribal community that was already extremely beset by internal feuds might well have failed to mount enough pressure to nip its newer conflicts in the bud. Since it is known that Bishop Petar Petrović at times was trying to resolve dozens of feuds within the same tribe (Jovanović 1948), it seems likely that such conditions could prevail. Thus, while I have praised the kmets' ability to solve political problems, not every tribe remained well enough unified that it could effectively exert pressure on feuding parties to pacify.

In addition, there was clan reputation as this affected the clan's determinedness to maintain honor: a clan that already had a very good reputation had the greater investment to protect. Individual personalities might also deviate from tribal norms, and accidents might turn cowards into heroes or make more-aggressive men hesitate or show mercy. There were also options that allowed women to take vengeance if they chose to do so. In such cases, inequalities in clan size became irrelevant, unless the woman normally bore arms and therefore was counted as a man. In that case, retaliation could follow the normal channels. There were also networks of alliance based on factors other than male blood. These deserve separate treatment because of their predictable importance.

ALLIANCES AND THE ESCALATION OF FEUDS

The fact that immigrant clans were not immediately integrated into larger clans of the same tribe on the basis of patron-client relationships or of fictitious kinship may seem surprising, given the prevalence of such behavior in the tribal world and given the need that a newly emigrated clan had for such support in Montenegro. But usually such people had to rely upon the usual bonds of alliance that were available to all Montenegrins: *kumstvo* (godfatherhood), *prijateljstvo* (the in-law relationship), and *pobratimstvo* (blood brotherhood). While Jelić (1926) includes such allies in the force that was available to an Albanian clan when vengeance was at issue, I believe this does not hold true for Montenegro, where the participants in feuds always seem to have been two sets of true agnates. This makes some sense in terms of needs for tribal unity: Montenegrin tribes often were under far-greater external political pressure than Albanian tribes, and if clans within a Montenegrin tribe had set up alliances for feuding, this would have seriously escalated intratribal conflicts and therefore would have increased vulnerability to external predation.

An area that remains generally unclear for Montenegro is the predictability about how a blood conflict would escalate beyond the targeting of the actual killer and his immediate agnates. While it was proper to hold the entire killer clan responsible, there was a clear prejudice in favor of killing the killer himself, if he was a worthy man. The data to unravel this mystery definitively are lacking, since a great many factors must have entered in. These included whether the killer had fled or remained fairly accessible; where and by whom he had been given sanctuary; the personal reputations of the killer, his closest agnates, and other clan members, because this determined their appropriateness as targets; the readiness of the avengers to kill a better person and so to escalate the feud; the willingness of the avengers to wait for the actual killer to return; and so forth. Two things are clear from the available data. One is that killing often remained restricted to close agnates. The other is that feuds could move to the clan level and that feuds between clans of different tribes could escalate to include the entire tribes, even though this was rare in Montenegro.

Given what is known of limited conflicts between groups in other feuding cultures, a major factor that probably curtailed escalation to the level of entire clans or tribes was the network of marriage alliances and other alliances through kumstvo or pobratimstvo that bound the head of each household to a rather large number of nonagnates. In addition, he had ties to kinsmen on his mother's side, particularly those who were known personally by him. Where strong ties happened to link the household of the killer with the household of the victim, it seems likely that early pacification would have been sought. Where the ties linked other households in the killer's clan with households in the victim's clan, it seems likely that escalation to the clan level would have been seriously inhibited. Since there was considerable intermarriage between tribes (Ehrich 1946), similar considerations could have arisen to inhibit escalation of intertribal feuding as well.

DECISIONS IN REGARD TO FEUDING

If the decisions analyzed in chapter 8 produced the main pattern of a blood feud through individual actions geared to the social context and the rules of feuding, it is clear also that there were other options on the periphery of the main pattern that often made decision making very complicated. Men of small clans sometimes could duck their feuding obligations and survive morally; but in situations that were more ambiguous they might also be branded as cowards. Alternatively, we have seen that if they played their cards right, men could tender mercy to their enemies in certain contexts and thus enhance their own reputations even more than if they had committed the normally required homicide.

Decisions to retaliate surely were sometimes very ambivalent ones, where in-laws or godfathers or close maternal relatives were involved in homicidal targeting or where members of small killer clans had to make difficult decisions between relocating or staying to fight at steep odds. Thus, Montenegrin decisions about feuding were still more complicated than they were portrayed as being in the previous chapter, if all of these probable factors are taken into account.

SOME GENERALIZATIONS ABOUT FEUDING

Feuding in Montenegro was a means of cultural problem solving. Anthropologists have labeled feuding as legal "self-help" (e.g., Middleton and Tait 1958), and this characterization is accurate as far as it goes; but it does not go far enough. It is perfectly true that the victimized group retaliated in a way that was independent of any formal legal control. But this took place on a public stage, with honor at stake and with rules to be followed. Thus, the problem solving involved not only the two groups that were in conflict but also a greater community, which included people who helped to pacify feuds and therefore continually reinvented the rules as they interpreted them in application.

Feuding had two basic goals. The first was always readily articulated to outsiders by warriors who were concerned with their honor. This was to retaliate for a homicide so that personal and clan respect would be maintained or enhanced. The second goal was not heroic and was not asserted publicly by the feuding parties, but it was obvious to Montenegrins. This was to keep the conflict within limits, so that a single homicide would not get out of hand and turn into an all-out war between people in the same community or between people in adjacent communities.

It was for both of these reasons that Montenegrins who feuded, with the help of their surrounding communities, developed the elaborate rules that governed their conflicts. Given the well-documented volatility of Montenegrin warriors, these rules allowed for the expression of homicidal retaliation, which, given the nature of the culture, was probably inevitable. But they also limited the escalation of internal conflicts to a degree that enabled the tribesmen to survive for several centuries as a thorn in the side of the powerful Ottoman Empire.

10

Feuding and Ecology: The Question of Costs and Gains

I now adopt more of a bird's-eye view of Montenegro, focusing upon the total refuge-area adaptation to see how feuding complemented or hindered such a precarious political adaptation. This chapter builds upon the discussion of natural and political ecology in chapter 3, but I shall introduce as well some vital data from tribal Albania to substitute for data that are lacking for Montenegro. I justify applying Albanian data to the Montenegrin case because these tribal feuding societies were culturally very similar, had almost identical modes of subsistence, and were located in similar geographic settings.

BIOLOGICAL LOSSES BECAUSE OF FEUDING

One of the most basic aspects of any population's adaptation to its natural environment is its size in relation to the amount of food that the environment can provide in a substandard year. A similar problem existed in both Montenegro and Northern Albania. Available land was already being intensively exploited, and the birth rate resulted in significant population growth while the Ottoman Empire prevented any appreciable expansion outside of existing tribal lands. If an area suffers from continual population increase but lacks the environmental resources to sustain that increased population, then something has to give. One possibility is that a portion of the population cyclically faces starvation or, in hard times, is severely victimized by diseases that accompany malnutrition. This happened but rarely in these tribal areas. Another is that individuals perceive the disadvantages of food scarcity and therefore decide to emigrate. This did take place in both areas, but only to a limited extent, because free tribesmen were very reluctant to do this. Another is to invent new technologies that will increase subsistence productivity. This did not happen in this area within the historically known period, although the importation of the potato from Russia in the eighteenth century may have provided temporary relief. Another solution is for hungry people to conduct more than their share of raids, in which they take away other people's food. Raiding did significantly ease the "overpopulation problem" in Montenegro; this was demonstrated graphically when, after the peace of 1878, Turkey recognized Montenegro's sovereignty. The new Montenegrin state under Prince Nicholas was obliged to prohibit raiding from that time forward, and the result was dramatic: literally tens of thousands of hungry Montenegrins immediately emigrated elsewhere in the Balkans or to North or South America (Boehm 1983).

Another solution is to limit fertility, either through conscious practices aimed at this or, more often, through various customs that reduce fertility as a side effect that remains indigenously unperceived. Montenegro and Albania had fewer customs involving infanticide or prohibition of sexual intercourse than many other overpopulated societies, and the age of marriage for women was quite young, which of course increased the rate of reproduction. However, warfare, and especially feuding, did serve as population controls.

Large-scale warfare sporadically helped to limit population growth through the killing of male warriors, through losses of noncombatants who were captured and sold into slavery, and also through the famines and epidemics that followed serious defeats and killed women and children as well as men. The feuding pattern also was developed to such a point that a considerable and much-steadier reduction of population resulted; but with long-term feuding, the population reduction was solely among males. However, when a smaller group fled to avoid being attacked by a large clan, this often involved several brothers and their entire families. If population pressure happened to be great in their community, it seems likely that they would not have been replaced by immigrants, so that the local population (i.e., that of the tribe in question) would have been adjusted downwards.

For nonliterate people the estimation of population size, mortality rates, and causes of mortality is always very difficult. No reliable figures exist for the traditional Montenegrins, aside from some estimates of the sizes of the tribes and the number of men at arms that they could put into the field (Vialla de Sommières 1820). However, for the northern Albanians, figures do exist that will help in making estimates for traditional Montenegro. The Albanians in today's Kosmet region of Yugoslavia number over nine hundred thousand persons, and about one hundred deaths due to feuding were reported in 1972, the year in which the *New York Times* article was written. This means that for every ten thousand people, there was about one death as the result of feuding, which would be slightly more than one-half of one percent of the annual deaths from all causes. Such a small loss could scarcely play a major part in the overall ecological adaptation, since the deaths were of males rather than of females and since remarriage was practiced.

However, in a technical monograph on the physical features of the Albanian tribesmen, the anthropologist Carleton Coon provides some fascinating data relevant to the traditional period there, which complicate this picture. Coon (1950) refers to the Catholic Church's estimates for the period 1901 to 1905, when the percentage of deaths due to violent causes in northern Albania averaged around 25 percent. The figures given by church officials do not specify how much of the mortality due to violence was caused by feuding, as opposed to warfare, raiding, or other killing that did not call for vengeance. But we may assume, since this was a time of little warfare in the Balkans, that between 10 and 20 percent of all the northern Albanians who died met their deaths because of feuding and that the deaths were of males. Coon also reports that 160 males were born for every 100 females. In terms of population dynamics, these patterns surely had a significant role in the overall ecological adaptation.

For traditional Montenegro, it seems likely that a similar adaptive mechanism was in operation. Vialla de Sommière's (1820) estimate for the proportion of the Montenegrin population that could be counted upon as men-at-arms to fight in the tribal army suggests that a higher proportion of Montenegrins were males of fighting age than was the case elsewhere in Europe. He states that normally 20 percent of a population could be counted upon as soldiers, but in Montenegro the figure was 25 percent. If Montenegro had the same unusual birth rate as Albania, and then if a fair number of the excess males were killed off in feuding, such a figure would be appropriate.

Because in the traditional period only a fraction of all the settlements of blood feuds were written down and because no record was kept otherwise of people's deaths and how they died, there is no other Montenegrin data that may be used to verify this estimate. But if male births greatly exceeded female births, losses due to feuding would not have lowered reproductive rates very much, unless widows had failed to remarry, which was not the case. Indeed, the strongest effect that feuding had on population size may have come through the loss of smaller clans that had to flee from the tribe, because these included females. Since such feuding was never recorded at the level of pacification, the effects cannot be estimated very well. But they were considerable.

It is also very difficult to estimate the effects of warfare on the death rates for males and females.[1] But it seems certain that during several periods when Turkish attacks were overwhelming, the population of about fifty thousand free tribesmen and women was reduced by thousands of souls, who either were killed in battle or were captured and sold into slavery or died afterwards as the result of famine and pestilence. Unfortunately, reports in Turkish archives, which could provide relatively definitive data, have not yet been sought out by researchers who are able to translate these materials.

Even without knowing the exact figures, it is still worthwhile to consider how warfare and feuding may have acted as adaptive—or maladaptive—devices that were sensitive to ecological problems. For example, where a particular tribe badly needed additional pasture in order to survive, it was likely to encroach on the territory of neighbors. This, in turn, would lead to quarrels over pastures, which could easily turn into feuds. Once the two tribes were feuding, this would increase the likelihood that the hungrier tribe, or else the larger tribe, might try by force to expropriate the other tribe's pastures. If stiff resistance were met, such a move could result in active warfare between the tribes, replete with headhunting (Vlahović 1939). One consequence of such protracted feuds and of this very rare intertribal warfare was that some of the surplus male population, which had created the problem, would be killed off. This would reduce population pressure for a time. Similarly, when overpopulation would cause intensified raiding, then the Turks eventually might become aroused to the point of attacking the unruly tribe. If the Montenegrins lost, this could result not only in population losses but also in reduced nutrition because of Turkish taxes.

For the overall tribal system, the beauty of these mechanisms was that clans and tribes that were overpopulated and hungry were most likely to begin feuds or to incur the wrath of the Turks. This meant that the increase in death rate was targeted where it would "do the most good" for the balance between natural resources and territorial groups. But from the perspective of a single tribe as a territorial survival unit, one danger of such mechanisms was that losses from feuding, combined with warfare, might be excessive. As a result, a tribe might suddenly find itself too weak, in spite of alliances, to resist other tribal predators or to maintain its refuge-area adaptation against Ottoman pressure. One reason that this did not happen was that Montenegro for centuries served as a haven for people from surrounding territories who wished to escape from feuds or Turkish oppression. When a particular tribe or settlement sustained very serious losses, there were likely to be refugees ready to snap up any land that would momentarily become surplus. The other was that a weakened tribe could try to shore up its position by further alliance building.

In the absence of definitive data, I shall try to generalize at this point. The population of the tribal refuge area would remain close to the maximum that natural subsistence activities plus raiding could sustain, but it would constantly go through cycles. In traditional times, when the population would rise above this carrying capacity, a few Montenegrins would emigrate. But the vast majority would stay at home to compete for scarce resources and would increase their raiding. Because of severe crowding, feuding and warfare would then become intensified, and excess male population, in particular, would be reduced. This would provide short-term relief. Once the population had fallen below this carrying capacity, then warfare would become less frequent and feuding would decrease as well, insofar as the causes were economic. While natural increases in population eventually would have led to serious overpopulation again, immigration would make this happen much more rapidly. Thus a low point in fighting strength would soon be compensated for; but it also helped the next overpopulation crisis to come along more quickly.

If feuding is assessed solely for its biological effects, it clearly reduced the male population—especially the portion that was involved in sexual reproduction—because boys and old men were not such honorable targets. The male birth rate in Montenegro may well have paralleled that in Albania; and given the probably great length of time during which feuding existed in the Mediterranean coastal area, it seems possible that such mechanisms could have developed at the biological level, though probably with considerable help from cultural practices such as a differential in the neglect of female children, which seems especially likely in Montenegro.[2]

Because wherever remarriage is practiced extensively the number of females, rather than the number of males, chiefly determines birth rates over the longer run, feuding may have played a far less important role in regulating population than did warfare, the epidemics that warfare brought, and occasional famines (see Boehm 1983), all of which directly affected females of reproductive age. But feuding did continually drain away males; it did slow down population increase when entire households or clans were obliged to flee the tribe; and it did cause severe and prolonged psychological stress and possibly malnutrition for entire households. Furthermore, feuding had pervasive effects upon other aspects of the traditional adaptation.

THE DIRECT EFFECTS OF FEUDING ON SUBSISTENCE ACTIVITIES

Feuding did more than to help somewhat in reducing the surplus population of Montenegro. There can be little doubt that feuding interfered seriously with household subsistence activities. Indeed, feuding households or clans virtually lost all use of their male workers except in regard to herding, where a man could work with his rifle at the ready and could stay under cover. Women were able to fill in some of this gap with the exception of heavy work (Jelić 1926). But based on my own experience in Montenegro, I know that at certain times of the year, notably during the summer and early fall, a household's potential economic resources were maximized only if all of its members could work out of doors constantly whenever it was daylight. This means that feuding must have done extensive economic damage, particularly to the households that were on the defensive.[3]

It is likely that raiding alleviated this problem substantially. The same men who would carefully remain under cover when at home were very apt to be out raiding during the six months' season when Montenegrins sallied forth on these profitable expeditions. Since raiders traveled surreptitiously, going on such expeditions did not greatly increase a man's chances of being killed by a blood enemy. When he returned home with his profits, these would go into the economy of his household. In this way, raiding surely compensated for some of the economic losses sustained as the result of feuding.

THE EFFECTS OF FEUDING ON SOCIAL LIFE

Within the same tribe, feuding could place serious stresses upon normal social relations, particularly when a feud had entered the "middle game" phase. Married women would sometimes find their husband's clan at feud with their father's clan, and, I was told, they sometimes suffered extreme ambivalence in their personal loyalties (see Vrčević 1890). Strain was felt by males and females alike, with respect to the constant threat of losing key male members of the family and economic group. Normal social acts, such as visiting or attendance at religious and secular social events, could become impossible for households or clans on the defensive, and in the absence of truces, feuding also reduced participation in the *moba,* where large groups of people would assist individuals who needed help in harvesting their hay or in putting a roof on a house.

It appears that most of the intratribal feuds were relatively short-lived in traditional Montenegro. With such feuds, the total disruption for the tribal community was not so great, because only a few households would become involved in middle-game killing and further escalation would be controlled. And even with escalation, people never killed beyond the clan of their blood enemy; and because clan membership was unambiguous, the feud would still be well contained.

I have emphasized that Montenegrins were keenly aware of the disturbances caused by feuding for primary groups such as households, clans, and tribes and that they developed their own sets of rules and problem-solving devices to resolve or limit feuds. By applying these rules intelligently the tribesmen seem to have been careful to limit feuding most sharply just where these conflicts would do them the most damage if they were not controlled. For conflicts within the household and the clan, the suppression of blood vengeance was all but total. Within the tribe, not all feuds could be resolved immediately; but early resolution of conflicts that were close to home nevertheless was usually effective. Indeed, as we have seen, the documents on pacification of feuds within the tribe suggest that very many were resolved early, at decision point three rather than at decision point five. This may be attributed directly to an indigenous awareness of the social and economic damages that these conflicts caused.

When a feud would prevail between two clans of different tribes, then the social disruption would be far less for two reasons. First, the much-greater distance between feuders would make the conflict less intense in its psychological effects, since punitive expeditions would be relatively infrequent. But second, there would be less at stake socially and economically, because the clans that were involved would have had little interaction in these areas. The main problem was that with intertribal feuds the conflict could more easily spread beyond the original households because there were fewer ties of godfatherhood or marriage alliance to slow down the escalation of a feud. When rarely a feud did escalate to include both tribes, the socially disruptive effects could be very serious indeed. Then you would have groups several thousand strong that were seriously at odds with each other, and this would terminate all friendly relations between the two tribes except when they were under truce. There even existed the remote possibility of intertribal warfare, a fearsome prospect given the enormous fighting power of two Montenegrin tribes.

FEUDING AND SOCIAL COHESION

Various anthropologists have argued that while feuds are disruptive, they constitute a cohesive force as well. Such functionalist arguments acknowledge that feuds put large social units into relations of mutual hostility and tension but suggest that each group, as a result, develops a much-greater degree of internal harmony and cooperation, simply because the external danger is perceived and an ethnocentric response results (see LeVine and Campbell 1972). This general argument has been made strongly by Black-Michaud (1975) in a book dealing with the feuding societies of the Mediterranean and the Middle East. He relies heavily upon the excellent sources for Albania and for the Bedouins, but he is not able to say very much about the Montenegrins because so many sources are in the Serbo-Croatian language.

I would agree that feuding—or even the prospect of having to feud—intensifies cohesiveness within feuding groups. But it is very difficult to gauge the costs and benefits of such an institution. In the case of Montenegro, tribal territorial rivalry and clan rivalry for political dominance within the tribe surely helped to shape the segmentary tribal system that made it possible to resist Turkish domination. But this segmentation into clans and tribes could conceivably have been maintained solely by the threat of external predation, without feuding. If we need a functional justification for feuding in terms of some distinctive and useful service that it provided, then I believe we will find in Montenegro that this came not so much in its operation as a cohesive force as in its operation as a possible major mechanism for population reduction and, more importantly, as a latent social sanction.

THE FEUD AS SOCIAL SANCTION

In my opinion, the positive social effects of feuding in Montenegro belonged primarily to the domain of latent moral sanctioning, a function emphasized by Evans-Pritchard (1940) and discussed in a previous chapter. While Montenegrins may have been largely or totally unaware of this overall function, they certainly were wary about indulging impulses that tended to start feuds, such as offering an insult gratuitously, committing adultery, dishonoring a virtuous maiden, violating a property boundary, or killing another Montenegrin. I have shown that either consciously or intuitively, individuals took such risks into account when making decisions and that they frequently exercised self-restraint. But even though individuals may have known consciously that they were modifying their behavior because of the risk of starting a feud, Montenegrins did not necessarily add up all the facts and come to the general conclusion that feuding was socially useful as a strong sanction. There is no good evidence from the traditional period that they had such a complete understanding. But then, feuding was a "given" in their lives; functionalist explanations are more for anthropologists who are trying to compensate for their own biases against feuding.

Whatever the level of tribal consciousness in this respect, I believe that the effects of feuding as a social sanction were highly significant for this very aggressive people, who deliberately chose to live their lives with the near absence of any coercive authority in human form. What I am suggesting is that feuding served as a substitute for such authority, in that the probability of lethal retaliation and then a costly feud sharply curtailed certain socially disruptive behaviors. The question remains, however, whether feuds created more disruption than they controlled.

Overall, the quality of Montenegrin social life was frequently disrupted by feuds. If we add up the social damage caused when old friends and neighbors were drawn into feuds that they did not even start, the psychological stresses of feuding, the economic losses and their effects, and the agony and dislocation resulting from loss of loved ones or from entire households or clans being uprooted, then the costs were very large. But as we have seen, Montenegrins were able to predict such consequences, and they made efforts to keep the costs within bounds. This was done, first, by arbitrating disputes before they became homicidal and, second, by pressing hardest for early pacification of feuds in which the costs were certain to be highest.

THE POLITICAL COSTS AND GAINS OF FEUDING

The external political adaptation of the Montenegrins was complicated, in that the tribe as a decision-making unit had to deal with an external enemy that sometimes was powerful enough to pose a potentially genocidal threat but that at other times was relatively quite weak. In a different book (Boehm 1983) I have discussed at length the way in which Montenegrin tribes collectively came to the crucial political and military decisions that they had to make. I reached the conclusion that the usual foreign stereotype of the traditional Montenegrins was incorrect, in that

Montenegrins were portrayed as recklessly defiant Christian crusaders who almost suicidally attacked the mighty Ottoman Empire.

This viewpoint seriously misrepresents Montenegrin political behavior. At times when the local Turks were most powerful, an aggressive policy would in fact have been suicidal for the tribes, particularly for tribes that were more vulnerable to external attack. For this reason, probably the most important political skill that the tribesmen possessed was that of negotiating limited political submission with the Turks (Boehm 1983). This was done by making it clear that the tribe would take to the hills and fight to the death whenever the Turks tried to take away its local autonomy beyond forcing it to pay taxes or tried to make its warriors fight in the Turkish army like Christian subjects of the empire. The tribesmen always viewed the payment of taxes as a temporary measure and as one that would leave their internal political autonomy intact.

Feuding played an interesting role in this curious relation between the several dozen autonomous tribes and the powerful political representatives of one of the largest and most permanent empires in history. I am not certain that the Montenegrins were clearly aware of this pattern, but the most severe threats to their free way of life and to their very biological existence came throughout the eighteenth century. This was the period in which their central leaders first began to have significant success in aggressively pacifying the stubborn long-term feuds that raged between clans of different tribes. These feuds had made widespread military alliances among the tribes unreliable at best. But if the feuds were pacified, then there would go into effect the natural tendency toward alliance building which was always present in Montenegro, and a powerful military confederation would begin to form.

Because of this predictable tendency, the bishops knew that if they could pacify the intertribal feuds, then a large tribal confederation would come into being almost automatically. They actively helped this to happen by aggressively intervening to pacify intertribal feuds prematurely. Then, if successful, they would promote an aggressive Christian policy against the Moslem enemy, in the hope of receiving financial or military support from European powers that were opposed to Turkey (see Jovanović 1948; Boehm 1983). If the sultan was not preoccupied with more-serious problems and if his Balkan lords were under his firm control, the usual Turkish response was to mount a genocidal expedition. This, if successful, at least would wreak economic havoc on Montenegro. In some of these infrequent defeats, a large number of the male tribesmen were killed, and many noncombatants were carried away into slavery, while much livestock was captured or killed and crops and houses were destroyed. Immediately afterwards, famines and epidemics would add to the damage (see Jovanović 1948).

What such efforts on the parts of Bishop Danilo Petrović, Bishop Vasilije Petrović, Stephen the Small, and Bishop Petar Petrović accomplished throughout the eighteenth century was occasionally to unite the tribes well enough to pose a serious threat to the Ottoman Empire's Balkan dominion. As Otterbein (1974) points out, an advanced state of military preparedness can invite a preemptive strike from the enemy. This confederation formed and then was shattered nearly half a dozen times before it finally became permanent in the period after 1800. In at least two cases, the entire population of Montenegro came close to genocidal extermination. Thus, the aggressive pursuit of Montenegro's possibilities for total and permanent independence entailed the taking of very large risks and resulted in losses that went far beyond the ecologically "benign" reduction of excess population, which was discussed earlier.

If we look carefully at the role of feuding in all of this, we see that during the traditional period, feuding helped to keep the Montenegrin tribes divided among themselves so that they never posed enough of a threat to be more than a nuisance to a large empire, even though they could form alliances effectively enough on a temporary basis to defend themselves fairly well. It was also feuding (and the threat of feuds) that helped to keep larger units in the segmentary system—namely, the clan and the tribe—in a state of internal cohesion and perpetual readiness to fight. This, of course, is a variant of the "cohesive force" theme. From this standpoint, feuding meshed nicely into the overall refuge-area adaptation, which was based on the fact that cohesive tribal groups were always prepared to defend their territory and autonomy.

To summarize, feuding was a well-integrated part of a very effective ecological adjustment that the Montenegrins made both to their mountains and to their external enemies. Feuding intensified the segmentary nature of the tribal society, but feuding also kept the segmentary system from unifying to a degree that might invite extinction at the hands of the Turks. While feuding often made tribes vulnerable to Turkish taxation, the Turks could not push this advantage to the point of total domination, because truce making made it possible to form alliances instantly when an ultimate threat was recognized.

The fact that Montenegrins understood their own tribal social system quite well and that they also appreciated the dangers inherent in their feuding enabled them to keep these conflicts reasonably under control. Thus, the traditional segmentary tribal system definitely was not destroying itself from within, even though most contemporary "civilized" observers implied that it was: the overall result was actually a rather stable adjustment to an external political predator that potentially presented extreme dangers. The curious point that I must emphasize here is that while feuding made individual tribes vulnerable to the temporary and partial loss of autonomy, the elimination of feuding was what led to the real danger of genocidal extinction for all of the tribes.

I cannot be certain whether traditional Montenegrins would have clearly identified any of these larger adaptive implications of feuding, as I have been able to discern them with the advantages of hindsight and some training in the science of cultural ecology. There is no ethnohistorical evidence that they resisted having their feuds pacified because they feared that the resulting stronger confederation would antagonize the Turks and thus jeopardize their entire ecological adaptation. Indeed, when a strong bishop used his influence to pacify feuds early, the tribesmen seem to have appreciated this assistance as long as there was no hint of coercion. They also seem to have appreciated the advantages of building a strong confederation, without fearing very much the disadvantages of antagonizing the Ottomans.

It was only when their central leader attempted to institutionalize forcible means of controlling feuds that the tribesmen stood firm in their right to follow their ancient traditions. This was because they perceived in such interference a threat to their basic political autonomy as it existed at the tribal level. The tribesmen were quite correct in the perception that coercive means of controlling feuding constituted a serious threat to the local autonomy that they prized and fought for (Boehm 1983).

AMBIVALENCE OVER THE ECOLOGICAL COSTS OF FEUDING

When the traditional period was near its end in 1840, Bishop Rade Petrović (also called Njegoš or Vladika Petar II) had slowly gathered enough coercive force around him so that his bodyguards, who tended to be closer to seven than to six feet tall, were able to suppress many of the feuds in the tribes that he controlled best (Djilas 1966). This application of force meant that many of the tribesmen had found themselves being executed by men from outside the tribe, or else they had experienced incarceration—a loss of freedom that previously they had known only in Turkish dungeons.

Resistance to this interference was stubborn until ten years later, when Daniel Petrović became prince. Daniel quickly broke the backbone of the tribal political system and soon acquired the power to suppress feuding far more ruthlessly than Bishop Rade Petrović had ever been able to do. But even the despot Daniel and his successor, Prince Nicholas, could not entirely stamp out feuding, as we have seen in the case of the headstrong and valiant Djilas clan.

Just before these two very busy decades, there is little doubt in my mind as to what the answer of the traditional tribesmen would have been, had I been able to go back as an anthropologist to ask them why they preferred to keep on feuding when their bishops had set up special courts and made special laws to help them become free of this "menace." I would predict an answer like this: "The cost of this 'improvement' would be that Montenegrins no longer would be free tribesmen who answered only to their own equals in clan or tribe, or directly to their God." Or perhaps the answer would have been the usual one, saved for impertinent foreigners who ethnocentrically tried to ask the Montenegrins embarrassing questions about why they did things the way they did: "Za to što, to nam je adet" (Durham 1928). Translated, this means: "Because it is our custom!" This typical, rather flat, and apparently unreflective verbal response would have concealed a very good intuitive understanding that Montenegrins possessed about the workings of their own feuding system and many of its costs and gains as well.

To traditional Montenegrins, it was perfectly reasonable that blood feuds should exist. But we must not assume that their respect for their own way of doing things signaled an absence of ambivalence. For them, their obviously disruptive blood feuds made perfectly good sense only because feuds provided a focus for the very finest things in a warrior way of life and because they knew that they usually were able to limit the extent of the heartbreak and stress and the economic, social, and political damage that feuds caused. From their perspective, the good and honorable warrior, as a moral actor on the tribal stage, was seen at his very best when he responded aggressively and well to the very difficult and costly obligation to seek blood. This was because both the enactment of krvna osveta and its pacification, as well, were ultimate moral necessities in this society of most honorable warriors. Morally speaking, feuding was the measure of what honor really was worth, while pacification was the measure of an equally moral concern for social harmony and for political viability.

AN ANALOGY FOR AMERICANS

If the reader is still unconvinced that an intelligent group of people could knowingly sustain such a "menace" in their own midst, it might be useful to think of the way in which we Americans handle our own "automobile menace" as an ecological problem. These vehicles kill approximately fifty thousand Americans each year, or one person in every five thousand annually, and they seriously injure many more. Another way to look at it is that during the average American's lifetime, cars kill over 3 million people. These losses by far outstrip our total losses in all wars. A question arises, since we are a scientifically minded people, supposedly committed to enlightened public policy, and are possessed of a centralized government that has fairly strong coercive sanctions: How is it that we have allowed this to take place as casually as we have?

I do not believe that the answer is that "democracy does not work" or that no one has really added up the entire problem or—certainly—that we recognize automotive fatalities as a needed means of population control. We are conscious both of the high human costs of running our automobiles and of the much lower cost (in human lives) of virtually any other form of transportation. Yet we also are aware, perhaps more on an intuitive level, of the gains that we derive from our beloved cars. They provide us with freedom to go where we please and to live where we please; and for many they serve as a basic expression of aesthetic taste, of social status, and, frequently, of personal potency in general. In short, for Americans the "killer-automobile" is closely tied to many of the things that we value most in life. We do regulate its potential destructive power by creating and sanctioning rules that apply to its use, but we never consider outlawing it or seriously restricting its ownership and use. And while the damage is considerable, at least it is fairly predictable. If we are prepared to accept the losses, then we can go about life believing that we have the situation under control, which we do.

In my opinion, Americans as a nation of car lovers have collectively made the decision, if quite intuitively, that the losses in human life and the resulting psychological and social disruptions are acceptable, if not welcome. They are acceptable to us as citizens because we are a practical but also a romantic people, who are concerned with personal autonomy, mobility, beauty, power, and status; and the automobile has helped most of us to express ourselves in at least several of these ways. We accept the large losses rather calmly, but only because we do control the situation pretty much to our own satisfaction. The same is true of other modern nations, some of which have far-higher automobile fatality rates per mile driven than we do.

If we compare just the costs in human life, blood feuds in contemporary Albanian Kosmet kill proportionately only one-half as much of the population annually as automobiles do in the United States.

For Montenegro, using my rough estimate for the biological cost of feuding during the tribal period, the proportionate losses obviously were much higher than they are in Albania today. But these warriors were better prepared to accept a high rate of violent death than we are, while their commitment to an egalitarian way of life, which favored feuding as a form of self-help, was probably much deeper than ours is to our cars.

One must keep in mind, in dealing with this analogy, that neither tribal Montenegrins nor modern Americans can be said to have ignored the costs of feuding or driving cars. In both cases, elaborate rules regulate the behaviors so as to reduce the costs, and special bodies make decisions on policies that improve this regulation—the drive to curb alcohol-impaired driving is a current manifestation. The point is that basically what seems to be a very high annual loss of life apparently is accepted, at the same time that efforts are being made to keep this rate as low as is feasible.

The case I have made is that Montenegrins had a pretty good overall grasp of their feuding problem, just as we do of our automobile problem. In spite of the obvious carnage, they felt that they had the situation adequately under control most of the time, and on a practical basis, they were willing to accept the costs rather than coercively to curtail the individual's freedom to feud.

This took place not because feuding itself was viewed as intrinsically useful. Indeed, the Montenegrins never gave any obvious sign that they believed in the "cohesive force" theory or that they valued feuding as a latent social sanction or as an activity that kept them in training for warfare or as a population control or as a mechanism that kept the tribal confederation from threatening the Turks. It is possible that, traditionally, a few wiser men and women in the tribes were intuitively aware that the threat of a potential feud contributed to the moral order, in that it pressured people to follow their own moral code's proscriptions in areas such as sexual conduct, the maintenance of territorial boundaries, and the committing of homicide. But I believe that the essential view of feuding and its functions was that it was socially disruptive but morally and politically necessary.

Clearly, feuding served as a focal point for many of the Montenegrins' most important values. I also believe that individual Montenegrins were able to appreciate consciously and positively the heroic glory that feuding enabled them to attain, when revenge was well executed. This is evident from the story of Kečo, recorded by Wyon and Prance, and from the account, given by Djilas, of the spreading fame of his own tiny clan as its vicious and heroic "feud" progressed with the prince of Montenegro and his agents.

THE MONTENEGRINS' CONTRIBUTION TO
THEIR OWN ADAPTATION

In this chapter, I have shown the place of feuding in the overall adaptation of Montenegrins to their environment. I also have suggested that the Montenegrins had a reasonably good understanding of their own adaptation and of the dangers posed by feuding to this adaptation. However, I do not believe that their understanding was the same as mine as an outside analyst.

I cannot predict how a particularly wise traditional Montenegrin would have reacted if I had tried to present him or her with my ecological model in which feuding serves to reduce population pressure, acts as a latent moral sanction, and usefully inhibits tribal confederation. But the Montenegrins did not have to look around for hidden positive social functions in order to justify the existence of feuds. In terms of their warrior mentality, feuding was morally necessary; and that was that.

Feuding was one of the givens of life, and the tribesmen themselves took on the job of keeping this potentially very dangerous activity under control, so that it would not ultimately jeopardize their community life or their adaptation for survival. This they were able to do by creating and sanctioning rules for feuding, by helping pacification to take place, and by using truces to discontinue feuds temporarily when obvious external threats arose.

I have emphasized that Montenegrins believed strongly in the moral necessity of revenge killing but also that they saw plainly the practical damage that feuds could do. Being well accustomed to taking risks where violent death was a possible outcome, they controlled feuds as much as they saw the need to do so, just as we do with our automobiles. They tolerated this steady source of disruption not only because they believed in killing over honor but also because they believed that there were precious few grounds for tribal interference in individual affairs. Here, the parallel with political implications of trying legally to regulate the driving rights of motorists in the United States is suggestive.

Accepting these disruptions, the Montenegrins went about their personal lives taking the risks that befitted a proud, free, and highly moral warrior people. At the same time, as members of their tribal moral communities, they consciously and cautiously helped to shape their own feuding tradition. There can be little doubt that if the Montenegrins had ceased trying to control the feuds in their midst, they soon would have been fighting as soldiers in the Ottoman army. But they kept the potential violence within bounds in such a way that their special refuge-area ecological adaptation was never destroyed, in spite of an ever-present external predator.

11

Feuding in the Nonliterate World

It is now time to look outward from Montenegro. In this chapter, I shall design a definition of feuding to apply to any nonliterate society having a culturally well-elaborated pattern of vengeance killing. I shall then test this definition against well-described systems of retaliatory killing from North America, South America, New Guinea, the Middle East, and Africa. In setting up and testing this definition, I shall disagree sharply with a central thesis of Black-Michaud (1975), who holds that feuds by definition are "interminable." I shall also expand upon my own interpretations, developed in the last several chapters, that feuding behavior involves substantial indigenous insight into the system of feuding itself.

In trying to explain feuding in the world at large, I shall rely heavily upon earlier anthropological interpretations of blood revenge. However, I shall not limit discussion to the political, legal, and ecological functions of feuding systems that are regularly emphasized. I want to emphasize that in this chapter I shall go beyond the mechanics of functional explanation in order to make the point that feuding systems grow out of deliberate processes of problem solving and must be defined in such terms.[1] Then, in chapter 12, I shall discuss some underlying aspects of human nature that make feuding a likely if by no means inevitable manifestation of the human spirit.

Before I define feuding formally, it will be useful to consider the range of homicidal patterns found in the nonliterate world and to examine briefly certain problems with the making of anthropological definitions. I shall illustrate this discussion with examples from Montenegro, since the reader is now familiar with that culture.

TYPES OF HOMICIDAL CONFLICT

Humans who live in families, bands, tribes, and chiefdoms exhibit an imaginatively wide range of homicidal modes. Witches may be executed by a local community, as may moral deviates or people who are aggressively insane. In some cultures, infants or older people may be selectively eliminated. Men may slay other men in order to take their wives or property, and entire groups often operate similarly against other groups or individuals. In addition, people may kill individuals or attack other groups from motives of revenge, because their honor will be affected if they fail to do so, to acquire plunder or captives, or to put a competing group politically off balance. And larger groups may attack other large groups with broader political objectives in mind, such as permanent territorial conquest or domination and exploitation.

Some kind of typology is needed to enable us to compare such behaviors from one society to the next, since these behaviors express a most important aspect of human nature and activity. However, no two anthropologists are likely to agree exactly as to what the most basic types are and where the boundaries lie between them. Given the problems that the world still has with homicidal violence and given the incompleteness of our understanding of such behavior, this problem of cross-cultural classification is by no means one of mere quibbling about semantics.

If we turn to the dictionary, we can find very general definitions of warfare, raiding, and feuding. Of course, these definitions reflect Western cultural biases. Furthermore, their extreme generality often makes it impossible to decide whether a particular homicidal activity that is practiced in a small-scale society fits into one or another of our own categories. On the other hand, we can look to the terminologies of nonliterate people. Not infrequently these terminologies differentiate between large-scale "warlike" campaigns that are too intensive to be sustained for a long time and less intensive but potentially much more durable "feudlike" conflicts, and they differentiate between both of the above and small-scale surprise "raids" aimed at escaping with desirable commodities. So, our modern definitions would appear to have some limited general validity.

Theoretically, if one could list all the indigenous terms in the world and all of the actual behaviors that, in a given society, were included under each term, then ethnographically valid universal definitions might be arrived at. However, even if some obvious central tendencies should emerge, there would be problems as to where the semantic boundaries fell. Even within a single culture its own labeling system can be far from precise when it is applied to actual practice. For example, in Montenegro there is *rat,* a noun signifying that tribal armies have been mobilized so as to be able to attack one another with full force, taking heads as trophies and seeking the advantage of definitive political domination or victory. In rat, territorial acquisition or some other kind of decisive political domination is usually at issue. Then there is četovanje, in which small groups of fifteen to thirty men stealthily move into enemy territory in order to seize movable property, usually women or livestock, and quickly escape before numerically superior enemy forces can be mobilized. Next comes krvna osveta, in which individuals, kin groups, and sometimes entire clans or even tribes act out conflicts by perpetrating one killing at a time for revenge against the other side. Then there is the dvoboj, which is conceived of as a fight to the death on a one-against-one basis. And finally there are *streljenje,* execution by the tribe or local community, and *ubistvo,* which translates as either "killing" or "murder."

What can be seen in these definitions are fairly close equivalents to what we call warfare, raiding, feuding, dueling, execution, and homicide in English. However, even in using this Montenegrin typology to categorize behavior strictly for Montenegro, there are serious problems. For example, an intertribal feud can quickly or gradually escalate to warfare. One very old informant in Kuči tribe told me about a blood feud involving the killing of a tribal leader, which at one point saw both tribes line up ready for warfare. He emphasized that this was rat, even though large-scale fighting was averted and only some isolated vengeance killings took place. Or a surprise attack by what normally would be called a četa (raiding party) could be mounted purely for purposes of retaliation for previous killing by the other group, with no concern for plunder. Likewise, a killing that was perpetrated in a feuding context might also involve the taking of plunder, while a very-large-scale raid might be rather difficult to distinguish from warfare (see Boehm 1983). Furthermore, a dvoboj, or duel, could easily turn into a military free-for-all between the two clans backing the duelers.

A few arbitrary types can be very useful within a single society, when it comes to labeling complex and varied behavior in contexts that make the use of labels clear. However, in building a grand typology for many societies, the problem is no longer restricted to one of fuzzy boundaries within a single system of meaning. The word that we would classify as "war" in one society may mean an all-out genocidal attack between two large groups, as it does for Montenegro. But elsewhere it may mean that two groups line up, insult one another, and hurl spears until someone is killed or injured (Radcliffe-Brown 1952). Then they all go home until the next "war."

The job of making viable universal definitions cannot realistically be passed along to the indigenous peoples of the world; nor is it appropriate to rely on dictionaries that exhibit biases that are appropriate to a complex society. Rather, anthropologists must carefully examine the world range of homicidal-conflict behaviors and pick out arbitrary features that will provide the most-useful points of comparison (e.g., Otterbein 1970).

A typology intended to be useful for universal application might be set up as follows:

1. *Duel:* A conflict between two parties, terminating in one episode of combat that resolves the conflict permanently.

2. *Raid:* A single sortie by a small party, aimed at inflicting homicide or expropriating valuable commodities, followed by rapid escape from enemy territory.

3. *Feud:* Deliberately limited and carefully counted killing in revenge for a previous homicide, which takes place between two groups on the basis of specific rules for killing, pacification, and compensation.

4. *War:* Active confrontation between hostile groups that are fully mobilized for large-scale combat.

I provide this very general set of categories to orient the reader in a preliminary way to the discussion of feuding and its definition, which follows.

SOME COMMON-SENSE IMPRESSIONS ABOUT FEUDING

When one looks beyond feuding in Montenegro, it becomes apparent that a similar phenomenon has arisen independently in many parts of the world. Wherever homicidal retaliation has become a culturally elaborated pattern, there is always reported a serious concern on the parts of males that they be esteemed for their bravery and self-assertiveness, while undue submissiveness is valued negatively. After a homicide, concerns for honorable retaliation generalize from the individuals who are directly affected to their groups, and homicides are exchanged between groups. Such exchanges provide a culturally defined channel for expressing hostilities, but the conflicts are controlled very well. Thus, while they are potentially very durable, they seldom escalate into all-out warfare aimed at decisive victory; the cultural theme would seem to be one of "nonpeaceful coexistence." Other obvious and widely reported aspects of feuding are the intervention of third parties, who are not directly involved, in favor of resolving the conflict and the use of truces and material compensation as a means of interrupting or pacifying the feud. Very often, all of these general features seem to fit together as a package, although in matters of detail there may be considerable variation from one society to another.

In small-scale societies that lack centralized political control and therefore lack special organs of government that punish homicide, such a feuding pattern is far from inevitable. But its considerable frequency of occurrence and its very wide distribution do raise an interesting question. Why is it that on every continent, humans rather frequently tend to feud; whereas in many other ways, cultural differences from one part of the world to another are so pervasive and striking? I shall suggest some answers to this question in the next chapter, but first it is necessary to take up the technical anthropological definition of feuding in the nonliterate world. In building a more technical definition of feuding as one important form of institutionalized violence, I shall first discuss some prominent anthropological viewpoints on feuding and then compare the Montenegrin feuding system, which the reader now knows very well, with several systems of retaliatory violence from other parts of the world.

EARLIER DEFINITIONS OF FEUDING

Feuding, because of its many rules and regulations, is rather suggestive of modern law, even though, with feuding, coercive sanctioning by a central government is absent. Radcliffe-Brown, in defining "primitive law" for the *Encyclopaedia of the Social Sciences* in 1933, states that

> an action which constitutes an infringement of the rights of a person or group of persons may lead to retaliation on the part of the injured against the person or group responsible for the injury. When such acts of retaliation are recognized by custom as justifiable and are subject to a customary regulation of procedure, various forms of retaliatory sanctions may be said to prevail. In preliterate society generally warfare has such a sanction; the waging of war is in some communities, as among the Australian hordes, normally an act of retaliation carried out by one group against another that is held responsible for an injury suffered, and the procedure is regulated by a recognized body of customs which is equivalent to the international law of modern

nations. The institution of organized and regulated vengeance is another example of a retaliatory sanction. The killing of a man, whether intentional or accidental, constitutes an injury to his clan, local community or kindred, for which satisfaction is required. The injured group is regarded as justified in seeking vengeance and there is frequently an obligation on the members of the group to avenge the death. The retaliatory action is regulated by custom; the *lex talionis* requires that the damage inflicted shall be equivalent to the damage suffered and the principle of collective solidarity permits the avengers to kill a person other than the actual murderer, for example, his brother or in some instances any member of his clan. When the institution is completely organized, custom requires the group responsible for the first death to accept the killing of one of their number as an act of justice and to make no further retaliation. . . . In all instances of retaliatory sanction there is a customary procedure for satisfying the injured person or group whereby resentment may be expressed, frequently by inflicting hurt upon the person or group responsible for the injury. . . . In many societies retaliation is replaced more or less by a system of indemnities; persons or groups having injured other persons or groups provide satisfaction to the latter by handing over certain valuables.

This general definition of "organized and regulated vengeance" is very much in accord with the common-sense characterization given above, although Radcliffe-Brown is primarily concerned with "legal" aspects of feuding.[2]

A more specific reference point for anthropologists who study feuding is Evans-Pritchard's (1940) much-discussed study of political organization among the Nuer people in North Africa. Evans-Pritchard discusses the "lengthy mutual hostility" between various political communities or segments as being a "feud," but he feels that this term involves a "broad and slightly vague usage" (1940:150). He then speaks of a blood feud as being a "more specific relation between the kin on both sides in a situation of homicide." Among the Nuer, a blood feud necessarily is within the tribe, since it depends upon some breach of law being recognized and upon arbitration within the same jural community. As such, the threat of a feud serves as a sanction that protects life and property. Between tribes, however, homicidal retaliation results in war, because there is no institution for arbitration at this level.

Although there are differences, there are strikingly specific parallels between Nuer and Montenegrin blood feuds. Both patterns of feuding express direct concerns of agnatic kinsmen for whom a warrior's honor is paramount, although their entire local communities become affected as well. In both cultures, feuding is precluded within the most closely cooperating groups, and potential feuds are settled quickly when they occur close to home. However, they go on much longer between tribal segments that are geographically close enough to make the necessary attacks, but are distant enough in terms of social ties and cooperation to remain hostile without incurring any prohibitive social, economic, or political costs. Because feuds do not activate segmentary alliances, they do not tend to escalate to additional groups of agnates, and blood feuds do not often lead to open warfare. In both cultures, tribal elder statesmen intervene to help settle feuds, and their persuasions and curses help the embroiled warriors to set aside honor and to accept compensation rather than to take new blood, as honor otherwise demands. As with Montenegro, Nuer pacification is noncoercive and depends upon effective arbitration, while in both cultures, oath taking is sometimes used to screen the evidence and to arrive at a solution that will be acceptable to both sides.

Gluckman (1959), another eminent British social anthropologist, reanalyzes the Nuer to elaborate Evans-Pritchard's point that there is peace in feuding. He emphasizes that although feuding pits agnates against each other and that their entire groups tend to be drawn in, there exist many kinds of cross-cutting ties that produce serious conflicts of loyalty in such a situation. Gluckman believes that "if there are sufficient conflicts of loyalties at work, settlement will be achieved and law and social order maintained" (1959:17). In emphasizing Evans-Pritchard's point that the closer a conflict is to home, the less likely it is to become homicidal or durable, Gluckman comes to the conclusion that homicidal retaliation, if combined with pacification and compensation mechanisms, actually enhances peace close to home. However, with more-distant groups, similar conflicts may be expressed over a very long period of time.

These functionally oriented definitions and discussions go far beyond an obvious common-sense characterization of feuding and emphasize ways in which feuding functions as a sanction against disruptive behavior. Emphasized as well is the welcome fact that homicidal violence is more closely controlled the closer it is to home. I now turn to several more-recent discussions of feuding that relate to the same culture area as Montenegro and Albania, the region around the Mediterranean Sea.

BLACK-MICHAUD'S ASSESSMENT OF FEUDING

In his book *Cohesive Force,* Black-Michaud (1975) treats the feuds of Bedouins, Albanians, Moroccans and other North African tribesmen, and other tribal peoples in the Mediterranean area and the Middle East. He builds upon Peters's (1967) analysis of conflicts among the Bedouins to provide an anthropologically useful definition of feuding. To begin with, Black-Michaud agrees with Peters's major point that in practice the feuding behavior of Bedouins is "interminable," a point upon which I must immediately disagree. Black-Michaud highlights as well the game aspect of feuding as a relationship between two groups, with the emphasis on feuding as a means of one group's establishing political dominance over another. He builds upon Nadel's (1947) views on the collective nature of feuding among the North African Nuba, both in the taking of vengeance and in the delimitation of liability to vengeance, a feature that is also emphasized by Moore (1972). But Black-Michaud does not deal with Nadel's (1947) equally important point that feuding is guided by the notion either of parity in blood or of monetary compensation as a means of composing the conflict. In differentiating feuding from warfare among the Nuba, Black-Michaud holds that warfare is "collective but not selective" (1975:28), a distinction that agrees with the general typology provided at the beginning of this chapter. Black-Michaud also adds the notion of a rough equality in the targeting of victims. Taken all together, these features define the feud, for him, as a practice that arises when people view their resources as being in very scarce supply.

Following Peters, Black-Michaud treats what he calls a vendetta as separate from feuding. The vendetta form of conflict, as exemplified in villages in Lebanon, consists of a single retaliatory killing, which by cultural definition definitively terminates the conflict. In Black-Michaud's view, vendettas are between individuals, not between groups, and are finite; by contrast, feuds are between collectivities and provide no means for the cessation of hostilities. He sees raiding as being similar to feuding insofar as distinct groups interact using rules that minimize loss of life; but he sees raiding and feuding as being different, because raiders do not keep exact scores. Obviously, this typology differs from the general one proposed at the beginning of this chapter. While Black-Michaud's distinction between raiding and feuding might work for the Middle East, where Bedouin raiders are known to be particularly careful to avoid homicide (e.g., Sweet 1970), it would scarcely apply to Jivaro headhunting raids, in which the intention is to butcher an entire household and to escape with their heads as ritual objects (see Harner 1973).

Black-Michaud's definition of warfare is more consonant with my own. Warfare, for him, is collective; but it is not selective in the way that feuding is in the pinpointing of human targets. However, a major point of disagreement remains in his definition of feuding as being "interminable," a point that has serious ramifications for the definition and further study of feuding. To explore that disagreement, I shall turn to the original definition that inspired Black-Michaud, one based on retaliatory homicidal practices of the Bedouin herdsmen of Cyrenaica.

A BEDOUIN-BASED DEFINITION OF FEUDING

Peters (1967) discusses an interesting relationship between feuding and ecology for the Arab tribesmen of Cyrenaica. These Bedouins live in rather large territorial groups (tribal sections) which normally feud as entire units, even though each group is composed of different and sometimes unrelated clans. These conflicts are similar to Montenegrin feuds, but only after the latter have escalated to the level of involving entire tribes. Of course, this is the exception in Montenegro, where feuds normally are confined to pairs of households or clans.

The Bedouins live in a region that has great microecological variability from year to year, in that availability of rainfall for watering stock and raising grain is unpredictably different in locations that are only ten to thirty miles distant from one another. About half of the time, the families in these large territorial groups marry their daughters to members of other households in their own group. But the remaining women are married into just a few of the surrounding groups, perhaps a third of them. This sets up a pattern by which a given group has half a dozen allied groups within a thirty-mile radius, and it is these groups that help one another when rainfall is scarce in one zone but plentiful in another.

As a result, within each very large tribal unit there are various scattered coalitions, made up of tribal sections that cooperate within the coalition. However, between these coalitions there is an absence of cooperation, coupled with a strong potential for competition. For example, a particularly powerful tribal section, with the help of a few individuals from allied sections within its coalition, may take away a strategic well from a weaker section by armed force if this can be done easily. Thus, there can be fierce territorial competition (but never warfare) between the different coalitions that make up a large tribe composed of many sections.

In the light of these political arrangements, what happens with respect to feuding makes good sense. Initial homicides between cooperating sections are pacified quickly by the initiation of a long series of payments, although a revenge killing sometimes takes place after the payments have been started. In the Bedouin mind, such a killing resolves the imbalance better than payments can, since it evens the score with blood instead of money, and this better satisfies honor. But such retaliation takes place, nevertheless, in the context of trying to preserve an advantageous, cooperative relationship between two sections in the same coalition. Peters does not include such quickly pacified homicidal incidents within his definition of feuding.

When two sections are not allied economically through marriage alliances, then in the minds of the tribesmen, there is no sufficient reason to try to resolve a blood conflict definitively. For this reason, once a homicide occurs, the chain of retaliation appears to be endless. Members of feuding sections shoot at one another on sight; they also try to usurp one another's territory if it is adjacent to their own, although this aggression falls far short of warfare. Presumably, such disruptive relationships can be tolerated with only a few immediately neighboring sections but can be managed more easily with noncontiguous groups. Peters allows that in any given case of homicide, the mechanism for effecting a compromise does exist. But if the sections are competitors, then they themselves take the position that the feud is "interminable."

Peters believes that the Bedouin situation is ripe for feuding at the section level, as opposed to the clan level, for three reasons. First, the Bedouins live in highly discrete territories that are communally owned; so section territories are unambiguous when the killing starts. Second, because a particular man is a member of one and only one such group, in any feud it is clear, down to the last man, who are enemies and who are friends. The third reason is that marriage alliances are negotiated only with those neighboring tribal sections that form the same coalition, not with the remainder. This pattern effectively segregates groups that may "feud" from similar groups that cooperate economically and try to keep the peace.

Thus, there is a clear association of territorial competition with feuding and with localization into territorial groups, and there is an association of these groups in allied clusters, which are referred to as coalitions. The result is a relatively stable distribution of groups into territories; and these groups compete with some neighboring groups but cooperate with others. A similar situation prevails in Montenegro. Each tribe (similarly composed of mostly unrelated clans) has certain neighboring tribes that are friends and others that are territorial competitors. It is between two clans from competing tribes that there are liable to be the most-prolonged feuds, and these feuds sometimes (if rarely, in Montenegro) escalate to the tribal level. With both the Bedouins and the

Montenegrins, a tribal section generally avoids warfare with the same hostile neighbors with whom it tends to feud.

Peters makes it clear that Bedouin decisions about how to conduct a conflict contribute to these patterns. The basis for a decision to pacify rather than to fight for honor is that an alliance would be disrupted. Otherwise, they see no pressing need to pacify and to preserve the peace. Indeed, in the absence of an alliance, it may well be useful to continue the conflict if the group's members think that they might be able in this way to acquire some territory from their enemy. Thus, a feud intensifies territorial competition; but at the same time, a feud is likely to arise from such competition in the first place: disputes over grazing or water rights are likely to lead to homicide, and from homicide to an "interminable" feud. Feuding and competition go hand in hand, a point that is emphasized still more heavily by Black-Michaud (1975).

Taking his cue from the Bedouins' own statements, Peters has defined blood feuds as existing "forever," with no possibility of resolution. There arc several problems with this definition. The first simply has to do with facts and their interpretation. I believe that in arriving at such a restricted definition, Peters may have taken indigenous ideology and rhetoric too literally, in the absence of opportunities to observe "interminable" feuds directly and over the very long period of time that is needed in order to certify their great durability. The feud, according to Peters's definition, means that any member of either very large group may kill any member of the opposing group, without regard to kinship connections between previous killers and victims. This simply goes on forever, while Peters excludes from his definition of feuding the quickly controlled retaliatory killings that take place within the localized tribal section or within a coalition of cooperating sections. Peters also contrasts "feuding" with a "vendetta," which, by his definition, involves only the killing of the original killer and the washing away of the original victim's blood with the blood of the killer in a public place. The vendettas that he discusses take place in Lebanon and are carried out by the victim's son or nearest male relative. This is the same definition used by Black-Michaud.

If one thinks back upon the Montenegrin way of feuding, it is clear that for them, all of the above would have been called krvna osveta. Osveta could begin with a limited conflict, with only the victim's brother going after the actual killer, or involving only very close kinsmen on either side. But it could escalate to include two entire clans in the same tribe or in different tribes, and in the latter case, it could even come to involve two entire tribes.

FEUDING AS LIMITATION OF CONFLICT

Like the large tribal sections among the Bedouins, Montenegrin tribes were composed of a number of unrelated clans, so that when a feud rose to this level, anyone in the enemy tribe could be shot, regardless of kinship ties. But in Montenegro, this was simply a more durable and more generalized expression of the krvna osveta that was either headed off or enacted between clans. I believe that this indigenous mode of classification from Montenegro may be of use to anthropologists in thinking about feuding elsewhere in the world.

According to my view, all of these types of behavior involve feuding, as this activity is most effectively defined for anthropological purposes of comparing patterns of retaliatory homicide across different cultures. This wider definition of feuding contrasts sharply with the one suggested by Black-Michaud.

To justify such a broad scope, I must emphasize the parts that ideology and rational decisions play in feuding as a carefully controlled form of conflict between groups. Households, clans, villages, and tribes frequently make collective decisions about whether to initiate or continue a homicidal conflict. When they decide not to kill, the threat of a protracted conflict and its attendant disadvantages is what leads them to set aside needs for revenge and honor. This decision to compromise may come almost automatically and immediately, as in the case of a killing within the immediate local community in Montenegro or as in the case of a killing within the basic territorial section or within a cooperating coalition of such sections among Peters's Bedouins. Thus, while the ideology of honor and group dominance spurs people to retaliate, rational decision making keeps them from ruining the quality of life—or possibly their very adaptive viability—in the process of trying to maintain respect. It is indigenous common sense that limits escalation in these volatile conflicts.

It also is evident that retaliatory homicide is at least *conceived* of even within very closely cooperating kin groups, since specific cultural rules or definitions have been set up in both of these cultures, and in many others as well, to anticipate and deny or to sharply limit this possibility. Between neighbors whose cooperation is somewhat less intense, forebearance may be less automatic, but pacification will nevertheless come quite surely and in a short time. However, as the predictable social disruption and loss of cooperation decreases, native actors who are responsible for weighing these effects will more readily decide to initiate or continue a feud.

There exists, then, a continuum of decision-making patterns. At one extreme lies the all-but-instantaneous decision that retaliatory homicide is untenable within the most-primary social groups. At the other end lies the easy decision to continue a conflict with a previously competitive group that lives some distance away but not to escalate that conflict from feuding to warfare. Thus, as I define it, feuding is best understood as a pair of indigenous ideas: (1) *homicide calls for lethal retaliation,* and (2) *such retaliation may call for further retaliation, so that a chain of such incidents becomes predictable.* Given these premises, a careful weighing of costs and benefits results in making decisions about whether to activate a potential feud in the first place and about how far to let it develop. It is because of such decision making that the basic concept of blood revenge finds so many expressions within a single culture.

Two kinds of fear move decision makers to conclude an early compromise regarding a potentially long-term feud. The more obvious fear comes simply through anticipation of prolonged homicidal conflict. While far more restricted than warfare, this killing back and forth will slowly drain away lives and energies and will seriously damage the potential for cooperation and social interaction between the groups. This motive for compromise is frequently reported by ethnographers who write about feuding societies. However, if the feud is between people who live close by, live in large corporate units, and also practice intensive warfare, then a second fear motivates them to pacify their feuds quickly. A feud at close quarters is particularly dangerous, because the feuding groups both are extremely vulnerable to each other and are easily able to assemble rapidly at a mutual frontier. This exacerbates the possibility that an episode of a supposedly limited homicidal retaliation might quickly escalate to warfare and then become extremely destructive.

This fear of escalation may not necessarily be obvious to an anthropologist, because frequently the feared effects are controlled so routinely that it is taken for granted indigenously that they will not occur. But an average-sized Montenegrin clan, for example, has a truly fearsome potential military force by either local or outside standards; and full-scale warfare Montenegrin-style would be extremely disruptive and destructive at close quarters. I believe that the Montenegrins themselves were aware of this possibility, since they seem to have sharply limited the optional short period of clan warfare at the beginning of feuds. As we have seen, this custom allowed two neighboring households or even two neighboring clans to fight it out for several days at the house of the original killer, with one side on offense and the other on defense. But after that, by local rules, they had to slow down and limited themselves to isolated killings, one at a time.

It was with good reason, then, that the tribesmen created and maintained these rules to limit clan warfare within the tribe, wherever parity in clan size did not forbid such an attack in the first place. Three factors kept such conflicts from turning into all-out warfare. One was the time limitation. Another was the fact that one side was on defense, and if it held out for several days, the feud would automatically de-escalate. The third was that other clans in the tribe would remain aloof, rather than join in as allies on one side or the other. Such limitations usually kept the tribe from being seriously damaged by internal warfare.

Thus, I propose the hypothesis that in any society that practices both feuding and warfare, one important function of feuding, as a highly rule-bound activity, will be to control the potential for expression of the warfare pattern within the local group or between closely cooperating groups. I do not know of any ethnographer who has suggested that native actors deliberately use feuding in this way. But feuding is a routinized form of cultural problem solving, and after routinization sets in, indigenous actors very often fail to tell anthropologists things that are perfectly obvious to themselves. Thus, while my assumption about the avoidance of warfare is inferential, it is susceptible of testing where ethnographic materials are very rich.

More generally, what I am proposing is that feuding involves the making of political decisions about both the expression of homicidal conflict and its limitations as well. Some of these decisions are essentially based on morals—for example, in most cultures that feud, women are excluded by making them dishonorable as homicidal targets at the same time that males are considered to be legitimate prey. Others are based mainly on practicality, as when a large Montenegrin clan that is feuding with another large clan within the same tribe skips the initial siege, presumably because its members know that neither side will win such a limited ''war,'' or as when a potential feud is resolved quickly because the two groups are close cooperators. In both cases, anthropologists tend to speak of rules, but it is important to distinguish that while some of the patterning of feuds derives from well-routinized rules backed by pressure of public opinion, some of it comes directly out of carefully calculated practical self-interest. In either case, however, decisions are made in favor of alternatives that will keep the conflict within reasonable bounds.

Of course, recognizing the moral legitimacy of homicidal conflict itself may seem impractical to a Western observer. But in small-scale societies that have no coercive means of controlling the homicidal inclinations of individuals, it is, in fact, logical to assume that a certain amount of homicide is inevitable. Realistically, this problem often is better solved by mitigation than by unrealistic attempts at strict suppression.

Given this interpretation, it is logical to look at a potential feud that is culturally proscribed, a feud that has been nipped in the bud, a protracted feud, or an apparently "interminable" feud—all as manifestations of the same underlying indigenous assumptions: (1) that one must either kill in retaliation for a homicide or else accept the adverse psychological, social, and political consequences of behavior that is viewed as being submissive in the local warrior community; (2) that the initiative for killing will depend on which group has the lower score; and (3) that every feud can be compromised if the will to do so arises. In any culture, different enactments of feuding vary predictably according to different contexts that hasten or delay the process of compromise or pacification. This means that in contrast to Peters and Black-Michaud, I hold that pacification is an intrinsic and important part of feuding as this is conceived of indigenously.

In my own mind, there remains the question of whether some feuds actually do go on "forever." This implies either a permanent absence of adequate motivation to pacify or else the absence of a mechanism for doing so. In Montenegro, at least, I think that the art of resolving conflicts was flexible enough to resolve any feud as long as the motivation to do so was present. In the one case when a feud that was more than a century old had to be resolved by relying upon the oldest man in the village to help count up the score, the two social units at feud had no obvious reason to cooperate, since one was in the tribal zone and the other was on Venetian territory, and after more than a century of exchanging homicides, they were no longer keeping the score accurately. But I would guess that in this case, community pressure combined with weariness eventually overcame demands of honor; this is consistent with other reports from Montenegro of stubborn feuds having finally yielded.

In other parts of the world, as with the Bedouins described by Peters, groups that compete (but never cooperate) may, in fact, feud "interminably," at least as long as this relationship of competition persists. But since mechanisms do exist to contain or resolve the expression of feuding closer to home, these mechanisms should be applicable to all limited conflicts, either through simple extension or through further cultural invention. Therefore, I would suggest that even the most-enduring feuds are only potentially interminable, not necessarily so. I believe that this is true even when natives themselves speak of feuds as though they never ended. Peters (1967) himself indicates that the coalitions of cooperating and competing groups shifted at times. Given sufficient historical information, I suspect it would be discovered that when such alliances realigned, the newly cooperating groups somehow were able to resolve their "interminable" feuds if this was in their self-interest.

Since Peters does not mention whether the Bedouins were capable of "counting up the score" in their long-lasting feuds, it is difficult to classify such violent activities as to whether they were closer to feuding or to low-key warfare. But he reports that open warfare between the localized tribal sections that we are speaking of was totally avoided. In any event, Peters had very little written data for the Bedouins in the earlier times, when they were freer from outside influence, and he was obliged to rely heavily upon oral tradition. It may well be that Bedouins, surely as gifted in poetic exaggeration as Montenegrins, have exaggerated the "endlessness" of their past feuds.

While I believe that Peters and Black-Michaud have overinterpreted indigenous "factual" statements about the interminable nature of feuds between competing tribal sections, this indigenous notion nevertheless is an important one to consider. I suspect that it is precisely a recognition of the potentially interminable nature of feuding that drives parties in a feud to pacify, in spite of the fact that for both sides it is usually more honorable to continue the feud. This certainly is true in Montenegro, where in compromising, humiliation for the side with the lower score is extreme, but even the "winner" generally ends up feeling quite humiliated. Thus, if pacification takes place and particularly if the blood score is even, this can amount to what might be called a "less-than-zero-sum game." By its nature this game of reputation and domination requires that both parties must lose, because it is always less honorable for true warriors to compromise once the blood of their group has been shed.

It is through realistic appraisal of a feud's stubborn nature that indigenous problem solvers arrive at routinized modes of handling the potential feuds in their midst. And it is this idea of a well controlled but potentially interminable conflict that defines the nature of feuding. Black-Michaud's mistake, in my opinion, was to generalize from Peters's reliance on indigenous verbal characterizations of the maximal behavioral expression of the idea of feuding among Bedouins. He followed Peters in defining as "feuding" only behavior that matched that extreme expression and then applied this quite-restricted definition to a very large culture area. While such an anthropological definition is perfectly legitimate, it will have limited use in guiding the study of feuding in the nonliterate world as a whole, or even in the Mediterranean and the Middle East. I believe that my alternative conception of feuding effectively sets that activity apart from raiding and warfare at the same time that it places a special emphasis on the hypothesis that feuding—in all its manifestations—is a form of cultural problem solving that is aimed at containing or channeling homicidal violence.

VENGEANCE IN THREE NON-MEDITERRANEAN CULTURES

While so far this chapter has dealt primarily with blood feuds around the Mediterranean area, I have also emphasized that feuding is widespread in the world. Presently I shall set up a more detailed model to explain feuding not only in Montenegro but also elsewhere in the world. First, however, to broaden the reader's perspective, I shall describe briefly three other cultures and their homicidal retaliatory practices, to serve as points of comparison with Montenegro and the Bedouins. These cultures were chosen to illustrate the great variety of feuding patterns in the non-Western world.

REVENGE KILLING AMONG NETSILIK ESKIMOS

Compared with Montenegrins, the Netsilik Eskimos engaged in a rather different form of blood revenge. The Netsilik lived in the Central Eskimo area within the Arctic Circle (Balikci 1970), and a Netsilik local community consisted of various people who were connected by blood through either the male or the female line, with people tracing kinship equally through their mothers and their fathers—that is, bilaterally. Thus, every individual had his or her own personal kindred, but obviously there could be no unilineal clans. Homicide among the Eskimos was sometimes occasioned by grudges or by what appeared to be trivial conflicts; but often it was motivated by the desire to take someone else's wife, since there was a scarcity of women.

The local community took an active part in trying to control internal conflicts before they would become homicidal, and pairs of men who had grudges would publicly be made to sing derisive dueling songs against each other, which would resolve the conflict, or else they would take turns pounding one another with their fists until one party would back off and the conflict would be terminated. Thus, community action saw to it that many potential homicides were nipped in the bud.

Balikci (1970) reports that parties were formed to avenge a member of a local group who had been killed by a member of another group and that such conflicts involved having the victim's and the killer's kindred line up to duel after a messenger had announced that the revenge party was coming. Personal opponents would be chosen, and all the men of the two groups would fight with bows and arrows, although a man who was very closely related to members of the opposing group could remove himself from the fight. This meant that eligible members of a local group would back its member and would retaliate against the opposing small community as a liability group. In theory, and apparently in practice as well, this very controlled attack would settle the affair. In affording the protection of the kindred to any man who traveled away from his group with his wife, which often was necessary, this counteracted the tendency for people from other groups to kill him so as to take his woman.

These two modes of handling homicidal conflict or potential homicide were designed to express hostilities in a context that defined such expression as final and susceptible of resolution. Lacking was any manifestation of further killing back and forth or any payment of material goods for human lives in lieu of taking revenge.

In traditional cases of homicide taking place within the local group, nothing at all seems to have been done in the way of revenge. Balikci (1970) feels that this was because the Netsilik knew that this would reduce the number of hunters supporting the group. But revenge may also have been inhibited by the fact that the respective kindreds of the victims and the killer would have overlapped too much to allow for a conflict between these subgroups to take place, as was possible between distant groups.

BLOOD FEUDS AMONG JIVARO HEADHUNTERS
OF SOUTH AMERICA

A second and more complicated system of retaliation was that of the Jivaro Indians, who still live in the interior of Ecuador and Peru and who, like the Montenegrins, were able to collect their various tribes into a large and cohesive, if temporary, confederation in order to guard their local autonomy. The Jivaro apparently were unique in South America, insofar as they had thrown off the Spanish yoke very early (Harner 1973) and for several centuries had remained entirely autonomous locally, living like the Montenegrins in refuge-area tribes of perhaps a thousand or so, which until very recently resisted subsequent attempts at external control.

The Jivaro were hunters who also practiced horticulture. Like the Eskimo, they lived in small groups—usually either in one or two fortified households isolated from other such households or in small clusters of households. Each household was composed of a man, one or two wives, and their children. A household relocated every five to nine years, as local game became exhausted. When the daughters married, they and their husbands tended to settle near the house of the woman's father, and the households helped each other out in self-defense. Thus, in contrast to Montenegro, a Jivaro relied mainly upon his daughters' husbands as close allies, rather than upon his brothers and other agnates.

The Jivaro had a very elaborate system by which certain males built up their reputations as warriors, partly through complicated supernatural methods involved in headhunting, which was limited to foreign tribes as targets, and partly through revenge killing on their own behalf or on the behalf of allies, which took place within the tribe. On headhunting expeditions, the Jivaro attacked entire households and tried to kill everyone in a household except for the women, whom they carried away, so as to take a goodly number of heads which, once they had been ritually shrunk, provided a supernaturally based source of strength and protection. These attacks on members of other tribes could be motivated by revenge as well as by warrior needs, but they stood in stark contrast to revenge killing within the tribe, which was limited to the single assassinations of males, without any thought of headhunting.

Relations among agnates did not automatically imply solidarity in conflict, for trading partnerships were the most important bond between men aside from the son-in-law relationship; indeed, "Brothers, fathers, and sons can and often do fight with one another, but it seems to be unthinkable for a man to fight with his 'friend' " (Harner 1973:131). A "friend" here means a trading partner, and a friend who was killed while visiting to trade would be avenged by his host. Of course, if a close agnate should become a trading friend, then a particularly strong bond would be developed.

With respect to revenge killings, Jivaro vengeance groups were formed very differently from those in Montenegro. But as in Montenegro and as with the Netsilik, there was nothing like governmental control of homicide. And as in Montenegro, within the tribe it was considered wrong for a Jivaro to kill anyone unless this was done to punish a similar act with "precise equivalence in retribution" (Harner 1973:172). The primary corporate group involved in retaliation was the household of the killer, including his wife or child and sometimes his brother. Preference went strongly toward killing an adult male, and "great pains are usually taken to kill only one person in retaliation for one murder" (Harner 1973:172). The Jivaro also dealt in blood compensation. If vengeance was not taken after several years, the killer's group could send a shotgun to the victim's eldest relative in the same household, who would then tell his relatives that if they took vengeance, he would kill them (Harner 1973).

Lethal revenge was directed not only at killers but also at men who stole other men's wives, while a mere adulterer would only have his scalp slashed by the husband. If the adulterer should flee, the husband could then kill the adulterer's father, if he was alive, or else his brother or any male cousin. Another breach of custom that was sanctioned by lethal retaliation occurred when someone would marry a widow without paying a shotgun to her deceased husband's brother or cousin.

While feuds among the Jivaro were susceptible of resolution by blood wealth, they tended to be of long duration. As in Montenegro, feuding activities dominated the Jivaros' social life. Harner sums this up nicely, also making an important point about selective perception and the nature of feuding: "Feuding is a state of mind as much as a pattern of overt behavior. Both of the parties concerned feel that the other family has not been properly punished for past wrong-doings. These feelings are evident from the daily conversations in which individuals continually remind their families of the wrongs committed against them or their close relatives" (1973:180).

Whenever retaliation was not for a lethal physical attack, the Jivaro would formally announce their feuds. Thus, if a wife had been stolen or a poisoning or witchcraft was suspected, a message would be sent: "Let us fight with guns . . ." (Harner 1973:181), an invitation that would be formally acknowledged. However, from this time it would usually be a matter of years before the attack would take place, by surprise. This mode of enacting disputes within the tribe tended to turn every household into a fortress and to confine people closely by night—an embattled state of conditions that closely paralleled those in Montenegro.

There were three bases for ending feuds. Sometimes, when each side had drawn blood once, the final killers would state that all had been paid, and the other side would agree. In some feuds, the killings would stop when one side had lost its senior male. This would mean that the other side had "won." Feuds also were ended through payment of a pig or a shotgun, if the last killing was not recent and if the victim's relatives had become willing to settle for compensation instead of killing again. The payment would go to the victim's oldest male close relative, who would be given the pig or the shotgun by his counterpart in the opposing family. These men would then see to it that other men who had been involved in the feud would desist from committing further homicides.

In spite of this complicated network of feuds between households, when attacked by external enemies, the Jivaro could rally effectively to fight as raiding groups, as entire tribes, or as a large tribal confederation, depending on the target. The truce system was partially trusted, but in cooperating with their blood enemies, people tried to remain very close to their trusted allies so as to avoid assassination.

I have relied so far exclusively on Harner (1973), who studied Jivaro in the interior areas where feuding had continued unregulated until shortly before he made his field study. Karsten's (1935) earlier report makes several additional features clear. Where a single homicide was committed in retaliation for a prior homicide, the potentially long-term feud tended to end at that point. However, if the cause for retaliation was ambiguous in how it was viewed, then the killing could go back and forth, since the two sides had varying definitions of the situation and neither tended to be satisfied.

When a homicide took place within the family, Karsten is explicit in showing that while retaliatory tendencies were to be expected, the family members would not wish to see another member lost and therefore would pardon the killer. This parallels Montenegro both in practice and in rationalization.

Karsten also points out that when a retaliating group issued its warning to the killer group, the latter could either prepare its defense or run away to a remote area and so would avoid the conflict. This provided an option similar to that of a small Montenegrin clan, which, when an attack was coming from a larger clan, could either defend itself or flee to avoid the feud.

TERRITORIAL CONFLICT AND REVENGE IN THE NEW GUINEA HIGHLANDS

The Mae Enga of the central New Guinea highlands are the subject of a very thorough descrption of armed combat by Meggitt (1977), who chooses the label "warfare" even though he sees similarities between certain warlike behaviors and what is called feuding in the African literature.

Before recent governmental regulation, the Mae Enga lived in tribes (Meggitt calls them phratries),[3] consisting of a half dozen or more adjacent territorial clans all of which were descended from a single male ancestor. Each clan was divided into territorial subclans which ideally were not supposed to fight (but sometimes did) over land. Subclans within the clan made their territorial adjustments by brawling; so these conflicts among very close male kinsmen were sharply limited by use of nonlethal weapons. However, when a clan was ready to divide into two separate clans, then certain more-serious modes of warfare could be employed. If one clan was much larger, it might try to surprise the smaller one with an all-out attack and then drive it away completely rather than merely take a portion of its land. But even so, women and children were supposed to be spared, and personal property was not to be damaged too extensively. In such cases, other related or allied clans in the phratry would try to pacify the conflict since it would weaken an entire network of alliances based on kinship, in-law relations, and trading.

Contiguous clans of the same tribe would sometimes go to war; the problem usually stemmed from the growth of one clan to the point that it viewed its neighbor as having too much land. As with intraclan conflicts, the hostile groups were "brothers," and ideally, brothers were not to fight. When they did, surprise attacks were not used; rather, a fair warning would be given. This would permit careful preparation and the enlisting of individuals of other clans as allies. Because of these preparations, such wars frequently would become costly stalemates. However, if a large clan that had perhaps three hundred warriors of its own to start with and also had many allies were to go after a small clan that had only sixty warriors plus a few allies, territory could quickly change hands among these "brothers."

Normally, then, such warfare between fraternal clans did not permit the use of surprise attacks and total destruction of property, which might lead to a complete rout. This was especially true because there was a time limit of one day for finishing such conflicts before negotiation would take over. However, where perceived land scarcity was particularly sharp, interclan attacks within the same tribe could escalate to include ambushes and the burning of houses and goods with the intention of territorial dispossession, as opposed to merely making a political point about clan strength and dominance.

Fights between a clan and one or another of its contiguous neighbors were likely to be fairly frequent. Such fights occurred just as frequently between related clans of the same tribe as between clans from adjacent tribes. However, with the latter, warfare became far less restricted: surprise attacks, total destruction of property, failure to recognize noncombatant status (which was actually very rare), mutilation of fallen enemies, and refusal to listen to arguments for peace—all were condoned practices. Meggitt (1977) found that while 86 percent of such disputes were over land or possessions, 14 percent were to avenge deaths.

In addition, there were "great fights" between entire tribes, which served chiefly as oportunities for all of the clans on either side to demonstrate their military prowess. These one-day fights were highly rule-bound and were carefully contained so that they would not escalate into serious warfare. They began and ended with individual duels, but in the middle of the day, bows and arrows were used by both sides. Thus, the Mae Enga seem to have placed strict limits on fights within the clan, while the very rare fights between two entire tribes were also quite carefully controlled. It was mainly clans of different tribes that served as the most unrestrained, aggressive instruments of territorial adjustment.

Two salient features of serious warfare among these densely packed people were that their conflicts remained limited in duration and that a generally acknowledged relationship always persisted between the primary adversaries, who were viewed as the "owners of the quarrel." After a fight, one "owner clan" was supposed to compensate its own allies and also the opposing "owner clan" for any deaths, using a set number of pigs as the payment.

In actuality, such compensation was always played by ear. To a certain extent, the payment depended upon which group was at an immediate political disadvantage or advantage in terms of other conflicts and upon what the state of alliances was for each group. It also depended on how many pigs a group had on hand or could collect quickly. But the ground rules pertaining to ownership of quarrels provided an important structural context for resolving conflicts, even though compensation was rather flexibly improvised.

Fights of the Mae Enga were not genocidal in effect. Conflicts within a tribe averaged about three deaths per fight, while between clans of different tribes the average was closer to four persons killed. The fact that precious territory changed hands with so few fatalities can be attributed to the Engas' obviously very developed political sense, insofar as they knew when to accept military defeat and to turn to compensation payments or to other kids of nonviolent bargaining mechanisms. It is here that their warfare begins to show similarity to Montenegrin feuding.

The essential rules of compensation for homicides were quite clear and precise: the owners of the quarrel had to compensate their enemy and their own allies with forty pigs for each man slain. However, we have seen that a Mae Enga clan always had so many transactions afoot that compensation of pigs for homicides often was being renegotiated, stalled, or avoided, rather than being paid in full promptly. This was partly because frequently a clan had to collect outstanding debts in order to pay the ones it owed and partly because there was a flexible element of political self-interest in deciding whom to pay. Thus, compensation was given most readily when valuable trading alliances might be damaged or when a group that had been driven off its land hoped to get some of it back or when the group that had a payment due was becoming very aggressive about demanding it.

The ceremony of payment thematically was one of clan rivalry: the donor clan would praise itself for killing a good man and for being generous in payment; while the other clan would praise its own warlike prowess. The victim's clan could indicate that it was satisfied and that peace was assured, or it could accept the offered pigs only as an interim payment. To this the killer's clan could either agree (usually hoping to avoid further payment) or else state that the payment was final; in either case, further trouble was likely.

The sanctions behind such payments varied. There was, of course, the threat of retaliation in kind. But further homicide was not entirely predictable because other political contingencies competed strongly with the demands of honorable retaliation. The threat of losing valuable trading partners or political allies tempered inclinations toward lethal retaliation. Furthermore, a clan that was impatient for full payment after having received a paltry interim payment could, if it resorted to force, give its debtor an excuse for never completing the compensation. For the Mae Enga, decisions always seemed to be complicated and highly contingent. This was their style of doing political business.

In spite of all the evasiveness and compromise, 75 percent of all compensations due were, in fact, paid. Meggitt sums up the function of compensation as follows:

> I believe that this emphasis on meeting commitments correlates with the high density of the Central Enga population and with the frequency of military provocations, which arise not only from the constant confrontations over relatively scarce land but also over the deaths occurring in these conflicts. Given that with their traditional fund of knowledge the Mae can do little about population density, their concern to define a way of discharging more or less peacefully their obligations to indemnify killings does relieve to some extent the bereaved's pressing need for retaliatory violence. Otherwise, life would be an even more grueling round of ambush and raiding, and to that extent it would become well-nigh intolerable. [1977:142]

While Meggitt prefers to call the entire Enga pattern of organized violence "warfare," by my earlier definitions the system seems to be a close blend of warfare and feuding.

A BRIEF COMPARISON

In applying the preliminary conception of feuding that was developed by comparing Montenegrins and Bedouins to these three far-flung cultures, it is obvious that the Eskimos developd the notion of homicidal retaliation to only a limited state of cultural elaboration. Within the closely cooperating local group where kin ties were also strong, retaliation simply was avoided; outside, group retaliation was carried out by the victim's kindred against the killer or his kindred, as a signal to other people to respect the lives (and wives) of group members who traveled alone. Among the Netsilik Eskimos, it appears that all potentially serious quarrels were culturally defined as being susceptible to final resolution through either sorcery or a contest. Within the local group there was the chest-pounding duel or the song contest, while between groups there was the collective dueling described above. Thus, a protracted pattern of killing back and forth remained unexpressed behaviorally because, as Balikci puts it, "the community could not passively watch a murder followed by a revenge which in turn could provoke a third homicide and lead to a chain reaction" (1970:182). Among the Netsilik, one-time-only homicidal retaliation did take place in a highly rule-bound manner, while the notion of blood compensation as a substitute for homicide remained absent. Given these facts, on the surface the Eskimo mode of retaliation appears to resemble a Montenegrin dvoboj (duel) or a "great fight" between two Mae Enga tribes almost as much as it resembles feuding. However, it closely resembles feuding in the indigenous conception of a *potential* chain of killings, in the avoidance of retaliation close to home, and in the collective nature of retaliation as a means of gaining respect for the local group against outsiders.

Of these three societies, the Jivaro came the closest to engaging in feuding as I have tentatively defined it. Retaliation and targeting could extend to the group level of responsibility and liability, and killing could go back and forth beyond the inital act of retaliation. Furthermore, compensation could be substituted for lethal retaliation, which meant that precise accounting took place. One result of this accounting, which was similar to that used in Montenegro, was that each side viewed itself as being vulnerable in its warrior standing if the feud should stop. Naturally, this tended to perpetuate the chain of killings.

The Enga case is far more complicated. Like the Montenegrins but unlike the Jivaro, the Enga population was crowded in respect to available land; therefore, scarcity existed (see Black-Michaud 1975). However, while Montenegrin territorial boundaries were stabilized by the fact that an entire tribe and its allies were willing to fight on an all-out basis in defense of territory, the Enga developed a different pattern. With them, when the territorial greed of a clan that had grown beyond its resources was strengthened by seeing that there was unused land nearby, the clan would attack its neighbor. But entire tribes would not be mobilized, even though individuals would enter in on both sides as allies. It appears that such attacks were set up by accidents of demography, when one group would grow beyond its resources or its neighbor would diminish in size.

Territorial fights between Enga clans fit very well with the definition of warfare, insofar as they were aimed at a specific kind of victory rather than at controlled retaliation through back-and-forth killing. However, they differ from intensive warfare insofar as casualties were limited, and they differ from all warfare insofar as those few casualties were subject to careful scorekeeping and compensation regardless of who came out victorious.

This feudlike system of compensation means that carefully controlled and counted chains of revenge killings could take place as a secondary effect of territorial conflicts. Because revenge for homicide accounts for 14 percent of Mae Enga fights, it seems that retaliation was not necesarily on a one-for-one basis but that it might escalate to a fight between entire groups, with one as the attacker and the other as the defender. But since the average number of fatalities per fight was only three to four men, the proportions are still consistent with feuding as a highly controlled form of conflict. In certain circumstances, the Mae Enga did indulge in behavior that was much closer to blood feuding as I have defined it. When an individual had a grievance against a noncontiguous group and when his group could not cross hostile territory to make an attack, single retaliatory killings might be consummated by individuals or small parties. Meggitt (1977), using African feuding patterns as a model, hesitates to label this as feuding. But many of the features specified in my definition are present, and certain similarities to the system in Montenegro are marked. For example, after making a retaliatory ambush, the killers would announce their deed publicly; and if the specific victim who was targeted took refuge elsewhere, one of his clansmen would do as the target or—unlike in Montenegro—the clansman's wife would do, as well. Also, a host assumed responsibility to avenge his guest, just as in Montenegro.

What we have in New Guinea in the case of Mae Enga is a rather thorough blending of ''feuding'' and ''warfare'' as I have defined them in this chapter. The Mae Enga version of warfare obviously was a restrained one, in that in case of a stalemate, the two clans had enough sense not to fight it out; and when a rout took place, genocidal extermination was seldom practiced. Furthermore, hostilities between two entire tribes were expressed largely through symbolic means. This deliberate limitation of escalation, combined with a system of compensation that keeps the participants involved in a web of ongoing bargaining relationships, controls warfare rather effectively so that it erupts mainly as a result of imbalances in population. It is not surprising, therefore, that such a brand of warfare manifests features similar to those of feuding.

Even from this obviously limited cross-cultural survey it is apparent that, however one chooses to define "feuding," one will encounter many partial or mixed examples. Thus, the Eskimo case may be deemed to be partial because compensation is absent, and it might make sense to set up "revenge killing" as a frequently encountered subtype of "feuding" in which the first retaliation settles the matter in a final manner. But since the Eskimos settle their retaliatory conflicts in such a definitive way precisely because they envisage the possibility of an endless chain of homicidal attacks, their behavior still fits rather closely with the more general definition.

With the Jivaro, there is considerable correspondence with Montenegrin, Albanian, Bedouin, and Nuer patterns of feuding, in spite of a rather different situation with respect to how kinship is involved in feuding. Such similarities include a rather clear distinction between patterns of feuding and patterns of warfare or raiding in all these cultures. With the Enga, by contrast, we have seen a rather close blending of patterns of feuding and of warfare. I suspect that this blending is facilitated by the fact that the Enga practice warfare at very close quarters. Such "wars" require a great deal of control if life is to go on and is to remain reasonably predictable.

In terms of my hypothesis that feuding can be a relatively safe substitute for warfare insofar as the rules of feuding control escalation, it is of interest that the pattern of feuding is most elaborated and most separated from warfare just where the expression of warfare is most intensive. Thus, both with the Montenegrins, who fought intensively and took heads of combatants and sometimes of other captives, and also with the Jivaro, whose raiding attacks were genocidal and amounted to small-scale but totally intensive warfare, this was very much the case.

By contrast, with the Mae Enga a very complicated network of alliances and debts tended to limit conflicts, as did the necessity of paying compensation to both enemies and allies. Because warfare generally was kept under control, even when serious territorial adjustments became necessary, perhaps the specter of all-out warfare did not stimulate a distinct alternative pattern of conflict. However, just as in the other three cultures, the Enga limited the expression of homicidal retaliation more, the closer it was to home.

While there are many possible definitions of feuding, I believe that the one tested here has the special merit of taking into account indigenous intentions in that it treats feuding as a routinized form of social engineering. The merits and disadvantages of such a definition can best be discerned by further testing it against a sample of world societies. These societies must exhibit some pattern of homicidal retaliation, and the ethnographic materials must be rich enough to demonstrate not only the general patterns of retaliatory behavior but also the motives that guide such behavior. It is these motives which produce the mechanisms that control the escalation of homicidal violence.

A MORE-DETAILED DEFINITON OF FEUDING

The reader now is familiar with half a dozen manifestations of "feuding" in the nonliterate world. Keeping in mind both the variation and the common elements, I shall now make more precise the preliminary definition arrived at earlier. To start with, I believe that Evans-Pritchard (1940) makes a sensible point in separating the more-general term "feuding" from "blood feud," or vengeance exchanged by groups constituted of kinsmen. I also believe that "revenge killing" is a suitable label for single killings that permanently resolve a homicidal incident. To most people, by contrast, "vendetta" signifies a protracted conflict involving multiple killings and is best reserved as a synonym for "feuding."

In building on the important notions developed by Radcliffe-Brown, Evans-Pritchard, Middleton and Tait, Moore, Peters, and Black-Michaud, my own position on the nature of "feuding" can be reduced to a list of distinctive features:

1. Feuding involves the indigenous assumption that retaliatory homicide is a righteous act and that one homicide legitimately deserves another.

2. Regulation of feuding comes through established rules, which are understood by both sides. This implies a mutual relationship between the feuding parties.

3. Feuding involves the idea of scorekeeping.

4. Feuding most often is alternating, in that the two sides take turns at offense and defense. This alternating status is determined by a score that is known by both sides.

5. Some means is available for permanently or temporarily stopping the conflict. This is done either automatically, by reaching parity, by truce, or by payment of material wealth for blood, and is based on precise scorekeeping.

6. Feuding is motivated and rationalized in terms of need for manly esteem or "honor," but more fundamentally it has to do with dominance relations.

7. Feuding involves notions of dominance between groups as well as between individuals: a homicide that is accepted passively invites further aggression toward both the person and the group that fails to retaliate. This is the practical disadvantage that accompanies "dishonor."

8. Feuding, in essence, involves the notion of controlled retaliation, which is directed at an aggressor and/or at his close associates. The degree of control is determined by how much the particular groups stand to lose by being at feud.

    a. Within a very closely cooperating group, feuding is generally outlawed by definition: the group cannot exact blood from itself; therefore, potential feuds are precluded.

    b. With groups that are separate but cooperate usefully, a potential feud is tightly controlled and is resolved with dispatch because of practical concern for loss of benefits. In such cases, strong community pressure helps to outweigh the demands of honor.

    c. When feuding groups do not ordinarily cooperate and are not part of the same cohesive community, then termination of feuding becomes problematical, although conformity to the general pattern of feuding does limit escalation of the conflict.

9. Feuding is retarded to the degree that the hostile groups are connected by cross-cutting social ties such as marriage alliances or economic relationships.

10. Feuding can be used as a means of avoiding warfare, because feuding allows people to retaliate for homicide in a controlled way such that the conflict is not likely to escalate to warfare.

11. Feuds tend to be very difficult to resolve, because the game tends to be one with a less-than-zero sum insofar as honor is concerned. Thus, feuds, in fact, can be long-lasting or all but "interminable" unless some strong force militates for pacification.

12. From an evolutionary standpoint, feuding seems to correlate with a high-enough population density relative to natural resources so that avoidance mechanisms become politically unfeasible or economically too costly as a means of controlling serious conflicts.

The most-basic things about feuding would seem to be that retaliation is homicidal but measured and that retaliation legitimately can be extended to people who are close to the killer so that responsibility for homicide becomes collective. My use of the word "legitimately" suggests necessarily a relation between the two sides and some agreement as to the rules of the game. Feuding sometimes takes place within the same face-to-face moral community, where community pressure sees to it that everyone plays by the same rules; but it can also prevail between far-more-distant groups for which such sanctions are lacking. In that case, rules may be followed partly out of morally based concerns for personal or clan reputation, but they will also be reinforced by a desire to avoid impractical escalation that is not necessary to the preservation of honor.

In short, the indigenous conception of feuding is one of measured and pacifiable alternating retaliatory homicide, with scorekeeping. Usually this is performed and targeted mainly with respect to certain individuals in each group, but always with potential collective involvement on both sides. Behaviorally this idea is expressed variously within a single culture, depending upon the social and spatial distance between assailants. Within the group, retaliation is defined as illogical or immoral; between groups, in certain other contexts, it is routinely pacified in a hurry, while in others it can be expressed for a long time or, in theory, "interminably." But these different patterns of behavioral expression all revolve around the same notion of a morally necessary measured retaliation by one side at a time.

"INTERMINABILITY" REEXAMINED

What about the view that feuding is "interminable"? By indigenous theory—and in terms of concrete possibility—a feud potentially can go on forever. But by my definition, feuding involves scorekeeping and reciprocating offense and defense, with the possibility of pacification. There are two reasons to keep score: one is to know which side is on the offensive, and the other is to have a basis for eventually settling the conflict. According to this definition, feuding can go on for a long time for a variety of reasons. For example, the score may become very lopsided, both feuding parties may be exceptionally committed to honor, or there may be no external pressure or other practical reason to resolve a less-than-zero-sum game that makes it difficult for both parties to stop when they have a perceived deficit in honor. Thus, "interminable" feuds are actually most likely to occur where the feuding parties are at long range, have no perceived need to cooperate, and receive little pressure to pacify. In such cases, as was the case in the century-long feud between Montenegrin tribesmen and fellow Serbs living in a Venetian protectorate, a very careful score was not kept, and I suspect that attacks were continual by both sides, rather than alternating, just as with the Bedouin.

Yet, apparently the conflict did not ever erupt into warfare. Peters (1967) and Black-Michaud (1975) have chosen to view this as a classic feud, while I view it as a minimally controlled and peripheral manifestation of feuding. Thus, I agree with Black-Michaud that feuding is a relationship. But I am far from agreeing with him and Peters that feuding is "interminable," even though very-long-term feuds on the peripheries of the system may help to keep people aware of the high costs of failure to pacify.

If one draws up a continuum starting with the feud that is otherwise likely but is impossible by definition, and extending to the feud that can go on forever, the question arises: Which point on the continuum constitutes a real, classical feud? My answer is that this is the wrong question and that a wrong question has led Peters (and after him, Black-Michaud) astray. Only by taking the statements of informants too literally and by fragmenting what is an organic system of symbols and behavior can one characterize feuding, in its concrete expression, as conflict without end.

FEUDING VERSUS WARFARE

Feuding is quite different from all-out warfare for several reasons: feuding is limited to one or a few killings at a time; only one side takes the offensive at a time; and there is no necessary political objective beyond the maintenance of honor. In this respect, even the early house attacks in Montenegro involve a clear separation of offensive and defensive roles. Feuding might also be differentiated from all-out warfare because warfare is episodic and is aimed at a triumph, whereas feuding usually ends with a compromise or with a stalemate. However, when a small Montenegrin clan is driven out of the tribe, there is a similarity to warfare, even though alliances are not activated.

Where warfare become merely symbolic—in the sense that the sides line up as though for warfare but merely make warlike gestures and settle for just one or a few killings and then go home until the next time— "warfare" may become very similar to "feuding." And as we have seen with the Mae Enga, certain manifestations of homicidal violence can be genuinely ambiguous. But such overlapping of categories is to be expected with any typology. Indeed, I selected the Enga as an example precisely so as to make that point.

DANGERS OF A BALKAN BIAS IN DEFINING FEUDING

This assessment of the nature of feuding is not based on a careful qualitative survey of all reported nonliterate cultures that engage in feuding. Indeed, it is typical of much typology building in anthropology. Like Peters and Black-Michaud, I have used the people and the area I am familiar with in order to set up a type that, to be validated, must be tested against world ethnography.

Having admitted that I am, in effect, trying to set up a global type on the basis of Montenegro, I owe it to the reader to say something more about this Balkan bias. Along with the better-studied northern Albanians, the Montenegrins appear to have one of the most highly specified and rule-bound systems of feuding in the world. In addition, they have lived for millennia in densely packed tribal territories that have chronic problems of overpopulation, and for thousands of years have been in contact with centralized state systems that have writing and written law. This is true of most of the feuding peoples in the Mediterranean and Middle Eastern areas.

Two kinds of special influence are likely to affect the feuding patterns of such refuge-area warriors. For one thing, pressure from external predators will be taken into account in developing rules for feuding. One obvious example is that effective means of making truces may be developed so that feuds do not cripple the defensive system of making alliances. A second influence is a cultural one. When tribesmen become aware of empires that have formal legal codes and formal court systems, it is possible that either specific institutions or laws may be borrowed or that through stimulus diffusion (Kroeber 1948), externally observed legal institutions may be put to some different use by means of cultural creativity. The fact that Albanian and Montenegrin feuds are so highly rule-bound and that formal courts have been developed may derive in part from such influences, although similar rules and institutions may be found with nonliterate peoples on continents that are more removed from state civilizations.

Thus, my model of feuding may need refinement. But I propose that feuding is best viewed as a pattern of homicidal conflict that simultaneously involves the ideas of scorekeeping and alternating retaliation and that is theoretically interminable but generally is pacifiable through the payment of compensation for blood. I offer this hypothesis for further testing with regard to feuding in the nonliterate world.

The fact that feuding seems to be very similar between the Montenegrins in Balkan Europe and the Jivaro Indians of South America, and between both of these groups and the Nuer in Africa, suggests that at some point in history or prehistory, feuding either diffused all over the world or that it arose independently in many places in spite of other social and cultural differences. Here the Otterbeins' (1965) notion of fraternal interest groups, which will be discussed in the next section of this chapter, provides a possible key to the theory of independent development, although feuding groups do develop sometimes without a strongly agnatic flavor.

THE TYPICAL FEUDING SOCIETY

Given the perspective that I have developed, it is important to emphasize that systems of feuding do not arise simply through some kind of blind process of cultural selection. They are the result of moral, social, economic, and political problem solving practiced both by the particular parties or groups at feud and, frequently, by the members of the larger communities that become involved. This weakens the hypothesis that feuding might have developed once—say, in the Upper Paleolithic or, more likely, in the Neolithic—and then have diffused all over the world. Rather, it would seem that people in many parts of the world have faced similar problems, because of similar features of social structure, social attitudes, and behavior, and that they also have tended to define and solve these problems in a similar fashion.

In their article "An Eye for an Eye, a Tooth for a Tooth," the Otterbeins define feuding simply as "blood revenge following a homicide" (1965:1470). They make no distinctions based on whether a feud is conducted on an individual or a group basis, and a feud, according to their definition, may end in compensation and pacification. Looking at a sample including fifty-one prestate-level societies, they found that feuding very seldom occurs in societies that practice matrilocal residence (this means that a man moves to his wife's parents' house at marriage). In such societies, localized clans are based upon the inheritance of house and land through the female line; so the local group consists of a cluster of closely related females plus males from various other matriclans who marry into the female lineage. On the other hand, where patrilocal groups exist, it is a cluster of closely related male kinsmen who stay together to control the real estate, while women from various other groups marry into the group of "brothers." Many societies that have this patrilocal pattern of postmarital residence also have feuding.

The Otterbeins characterize this patrilocal type of society as having "fraternal interest groups," because male kinsmen tend to stay put for life and develop extremely close relations with one another. For this reason, they tend to be quite aggressive in looking out for one another's interests, in contrast to matrilocal groups, in which the males "marry in" from various other lineages and therefore never develop such a degree of closeness. In both types of society, of course, it is the males who are directly responsible for violent activities such as warfare, raiding, and feuding. For this reason, it is logical that revenge killing more readily develops in patrilocal societies.

Another finding is that in patrilocal egalitarian societies in which central political authority and power are severely limited, as is the case with Montenegrins or Bedouins, feuding may take place whether a pattern of warfare exists or not. Somehow, the politically divisive effects of feuding are tolerated, even though they often impair the capacity to wage war by making alliances between certain clans or tribes impossible or unpredictable. By contrast, in strong chiefdoms and kingdoms in which warfare is frequent, feuding is generally absent, because in spite of the existence of quarrelsome fraternal interest groups, there is enough coercive force in the hands of political leaders so that they can effectively suppress the tendency to feud. But where such politically centralized societies do not go to war, then feuding does tend to take place. I would presume that this is because, in the absence of warfare, the disruptive effects of feuding are not especially dangerous in the eyes of powerful leaders who are decision makers. Such strong leaders were nonexistent in Montenegro until just after 1850. With political centralization, feuding was finally suppressed, as Montenegro became still more active in its desperate external struggle with the Ottoman Empire.

The large sample analysis made by the Otterbeins on a world-wide basis jibes nicely with the in-depth analysis made in this book, because Montenegro most decidedly is organized on the basis of fraternal interest groups. Throughout the world, such groups concentrate together the males whose role it is to commit whatever homicidal violence is appropriate, and such concentration increases the likelihood that retaliation will come at the group level. I emphasize, however, that males can find other bases for strong political community aside from the patrilocal basis that is correctly emphasized by the Otterbeins; as their sample shows, societies that have different systems of descent and residence also may develop feuding. For example, Schlegel (1970) describes the violent feuding of the Tiruray people in the Philippines, whose system of descent is bilateral and whose feuds are conducted by kindreds.

HOW CAN FEUDING AND WARFARE COEXIST?

The Otterbeins (1965) have suggested that logically one might expect feuding to be absent when a society practices warfare. This is because feuding is internally disruptive, and the resulting divisiveness makes a group that practices warfare highly vulnerable to external attack. However, in examining a world ethnographic sample, they discovered the opposite to be true. Feuding and warfare were positively correlated, at least in small-scale politically uncentralized societies such as Montenegro. On the other hand they found that when politically well centralized societies practiced warfare, they showed an absence of feuding.

Common sense would suggest that when people practice warfare, the warrior attitudes that they develop will make them highly prone to retaliate for homicides that are suffered intrasocietally. Thus, feuding becomes very likely wherever warfare is present, regardless of social scale or degree of centralization. In the centralized political systems mentioned above, powerful leaders realize that tendencies toward feuding are detrimental to the war effort, and therefore they either eradicate feuding or control it very tightly. This is an instance of rational problem solving in action, made possible by the centralization of political power. But what about small-scale societies that lack such centralization? How do they manage to survive, given the divisive effects of feuding?

In tribal societies, to judge from Montenegro, the tribesmen realize perfectly well that internal conflict weakens a group's potential for waging war. However, unlike a king presiding over his kingdom, they have no absolute or very strong means of regulating their internal political life. As will be emphasized in the next chapter, their egalitarian beliefs would not permit such means to develop. Thus, they are unable to eradicate feuding definitively, and in any event they probably would be unwilling to do so, even if they could, since they consider feuding to be a legitimate and honorable activity. What they do manage to do is to identify the more-problematical manifestations of feuding and to control many of the conflicts that are most likely to do serious damage to tribal unity.

Thus, in tribal societies the principal reason that feuding can coexist with warfare is that tribesmen and their leaders are adept at solving political problems. They are able to assign priorities to their problem solving in terms of the severity of the anticipated consequences, and their political sophistication is such that they can see a clear relationship between strategically controlling certain feuds and maintaining the group's effectiveness in external warfare. This is one major reason that feuding (by my definition) includes the idea and practice of permanent pacification. It is also a major reason for the prominence of more expedient, temporary truce making among those tribesmen who feud and who also practice warfare.

Refuge-area warriors like the Montenegrins are obliged to practice warfare, and therefore it is predictable that they will feud. It is these problem-solving practices that very strategically adjust a system of feuding to the exigencies of external warfare and that enable such warriors to hold out against major empires if tribal military sophistication (see Otterbein 1970) is up to the job. For tribesmen who live in refuge areas and who challenge the domination of highly centralized societies, the danger of extinction can be immediate; yet, people like the Montenegrins, the traditional northern-Albanian Catholic tribes, and the Berber tribesmen of Morocco have all engaged in feuding during their sometimes desperate careers as refuge-area warriors who are obliged to practice intensive defensive warfare. My argument is that they could afford to do so because they knew how to regulate their own feuding and did so precisely where feuding was most likely to interfere with their effectiveness in waging external warfare.

THE NATURE OF FEUDING

To summarize the major points made in this chapter, functional explanations such as those of Radcliffe-Brown (1952), Evans-Pritchard (1940), and Black-Michaud (1975) are highly useful for describing systems of feuding; but the functionalist perspective itself tends to obscure the analyst's perception of active strategizing on the parts of indigenous actors. In explaining systemic aspects of feuding in Montenegro as an enactment of cultural rules, I have also emphasized the relevance of individual decisions to feuding, following a tradition stimulated by Firth (1951) and applied elsewhere to vengeance killing by Kiefer (1970). However, I have carried this emphasis beyond the interpretation of individual actions, to suggest that the communities in which feuds take place collectively arrive at sophisticated insights and positions concerning the expression of homicidal violence. My most radical suggestion is that both the parties at feud and also their larger tribal communities realize that their own rules for feuding are what protect them both from intratribal war and from war at such close quarters that the consequences could be disastrous. I believe that this hypothesis deserves further testing with ethnographic data that is rich enough to allow more-definitive conclusions to be drawn (e.g., Turton 1977).

Given this perspective, I have defined feuding as a manifestation of the human capacity to solve internal social problems on a rational basis (see Boehm 1978). I also have distinguished feuding from war. The definition that I have arrived at has obligated me to disagree very sharply with Black-Michaud's (1975) definition of the feud as "interminable," although I have not denied that some feuds potentially may be without end. Rather, in characterizing the feud as a case of carefully controlled, alternating conflict that is susceptible of resolution, I have extended the definition to include a much-wider range of behaviors and outcomes. What these have in common is that all are intended to prevent escalation of serious individual conflicts to the level of intensive group conflict at close quarters.

In this chapter I have discussed many aspects of feuding in an attempt to set up a useful model of how feuding systems operate. The most general finding is that feuding is a form of active problem solving. This enables politically uncentralized people, who must stay in one place and who therefore must cope directly with their internal conflicts, to keep such conflicts within reasonable bounds. Specifically, this is done by limiting the conflict to certain pairs of groups, by having one group go on the offensive while the other goes on the defensive, by limiting the scale and duration of homicidal attacks, by providing a substitute for killing in the form of material compensation, and by providing agencies for compromise and pacification.

Since I have tested this model chiefly on the same society that inspired it, the model must be considered to be preliminary. But I hope that this characterization of feuding will prove to be useful by giving a more complete definition to one of the most-fascinating behaviors that humans are likely to develop.

12

An Ethological Perspective on Feuding

HOW DO FEUDING SOCIETIES DEVELOP?

In spite of the disruptive effects of feuding, this type of violent activity obviously can be compatible with a successful overall adaptation. Indeed, fraternal interest groups that feud would appear to be well set up for predation upon neighbors who are organized on some other basis (see Sahlins 1961). I emphasize that such an evolutionary development has not come about entirely by chance. On the contrary, systems of feuding have developed and survived with substantial assistance from human reason and problem-solving ability, even though clearly it is nature that sets the basic limits for possible human adaptations.

Because human beings are reasonably good social engineers, their apparent tendency to retaliate in kind for homicides is not allowed to flourish unrestricted. Rather, revenge killing is controlled as carefully as possible, given the particular views of native actors as to what is or is not feasible from a practical standpoint. The effectiveness of this control depends also upon the kinds of political and ideological mechanisms that native actors are able to invent and routinize, over time, in attempting to manage their own propensity for violence.

What has been neglected in so many ethnographic treatments of feuding is the fact that indigenous actors not only accept feuding as morally necessary but also understand their own feuding systems and purposefully modify them as they go along. My argument here must not be misunderstood. Feuding systems are not consciously constructed from the ground up by omniscient native social engineers. But they are, in fact, routinized modes of behavior that keep conflicts under control as long as indigenous problem solving continues to be reasonably enlightened and inventive.

That this creative input is present is borne out by the fact that feuding involves rules, scorekeeping, and customary means of pacification and that these controls are applied most vigorously where the primary functions of groups are threatened. Thus, the human capacity to foresee and avert severe and dangerous social disruption functions as a deliberate mechanism of selection (Boehm 1978). This mechanism should reduce the chances of extinction for a given group, if the group does a superior job of anticipating and solving its problems. To take an obvious example, a group that is well integrated internally may be better able to cooperate and survive during a famine, or it may be better able to defend itself from external enemies who plan to wipe it out and take over its territory.

We must assume that certain groups of humans have failed to control effectively their own propensity for violent conflict within the group and therefore have perished through internal warfare or by fragmenting and falling prey to other groups that keep their political house in better order. I say this to make an evolutionary point: when fraternal interest groups develop and when blood vengeance therefore becomes very likely, those groups that develop a more effective means of controlling retaliatory homicide will have the better chance of surviving biologically and of continuing the same form of social organization.

In defining feuding in the nonliterate world as a form of cultural problem solving that arises where homicidal retaliation becomes culturally predictable, I am suggesting that feuding develops as a result of the political sophistication of human beings. In this sense, violent as they may be, feuding societies remain as a tribute to human political intelligence. In the present chapter, I shall expand this evolutionary outlook to consider feuding not only as an exercise in adaptive problem solving but also as an expression of what might be called our basic human nature. This discussion builds upon the earlier treatment of the balancing of power; but here an ethological perspective is introduced, to provide an overview that helps to explain feuding in Montenegro and elsewhere in the world.

SOCIAL DOMINANCE IN OTHER SPECIES

If one wishes to place the feuding of Montenegrins and similar peoples in a much-broader perspective, that of natural history, then one useful way of looking at the feud is to consider its relation to social-dominance behavior in general. In many social species, a dominance hierarchy provides a predictable and stable social system (see Lorenz 1966; Gauthreaux 1978) based on the fact that all of the different individuals have tested out their fighting power on one another without destroying one another. This testing takes place as follows: a conflict over access to food occurs between two individual animals, A and B, in which B eventually (or sometimes very quickly) decides it is not going to win and therefore exhibits submissive gestures in such a way that cessation of aggression is triggered in A. This becomes a learning experience for both parties. From then on, B submits to A by habit, and no dangerous conflict takes place over food, preferred places to sit, mating opportunities, and so forth. On precisely this basis, an entire chicken yard becomes an orderly society (Schjelderup-Ebbe 1935) and one that is highly predictable to its members.

A linear hierarchy, such as is found among certain monkeys, is one in which the alpha male is deferred to by every other male, then the next highest ranking male is deferred to by all males but the alpha male, and so on down the line. This very orderly system makes it easy for an alpha male to dominate as the group leader. Among many primates, dominance hierarchies are less linear and are complicated by the formation of coalitions. But dominance hierarchies do result in leadership functions and in social regulation of individual impulses.

CULTURAL USES OF DOMINANCE

In other species, genetically well prepared mechanisms set up animals to exert dominance or to exhibit submissive signals. They also prepare a dominating animal to cease its attack when it receives a submissive signal. The strength of such preparations varies according to the species. Among all humans, and therefore in human groups that feud, dominance tendencies also may be assumed to be present among individuals; but these tendencies are set up by a combination of far-less genetic preparation for behavior, far-more individual learning, and a strong influence from cultural beliefs in the form of a shared tradition that effectively shapes role behavior.

Thus, cultural insights and practices of human beings very strongly mediate any genetically disposed tendencies toward dominance in interpersonal relations, while submissive behavior seems to be far less visible as a check on human dominance than it is in related species such as monkeys and apes (see Boehm 1982). In small-scale human groups, tendencies to dominate are controlled in part by individual predictive ability as to who will retaliate how much; but they also are controlled by sensitivity to cultural norms, by third-party intervention resulting in mediation, and by avoidance mechanisms by which one party to a quarrel simply leaves the group.

EGALITARIANISM AS A "CURE" FOR INDIVIDUAL TENDENCIES TO DOMINATE

One cultural control over the tendencies of certain adult individuals to dominate others is a moral view that humans in small-scale societies always seem to develop on the subject of one person's right to forcefully control another—namely, an egalitarian ethos. Every band or tribe has a similarly egalitarian ethos—that is, a collectively believed-in focal value, which holds that every adult (more often, every adult male) is equal as a politically autonomous person.

Such an egalitarian ethos has two marked effects. The first is to guarantee that one man may not easily dominate another permanently, if the pair have cause for conflict. When a particularly strong or aggressive individual begins to throw his weight around, the group, as a collectivity, sets limits on how much of this it will accept and sanctions him accordingly by becoming moralistically aggressive. Thus, while other individuals may not always dare to challenge him individually, group social pressure sees to it that his dominance of others does not exceed certain reasonably well defined limits of "equality." This enables humans to live an orderly, predictable social life without having a hierarchy in which every individual either dominates or submits to every other individual in a predictable manner. In effect, human beings have come to understand their own varying tendencies toward dominance and have done something about it: they have decided that everyone has the right to control his own personal destiny as long as he remains reasonably loyal to the group and follows its egalitarian norms to a reasonable degree.

The second signal effect of egalitarian cultural orientations is that leadership that is based on a bald coercive force, such as that exerted by a powerful alpha-male rhesus monkey over a few dozen other monkeys, is precluded in human groups of comparably small scale. It is precluded precisely for the reasons discussed above. People sense the tendencies of certain leaders or very assertive individuals to convert their influence into power, and therefore they set up rules to constrain such behavior. This is possible because human beings dwell in moral communities that exert public opinion as a sanction to which all community members, including leaders, are very sensitive. If the general force of public opinion fails to work with a leader who would like to take on too much power, then he can be ostracized, expelled from the group, or physically attacked by everyone. While very strong individuals may be obviously useful as leaders, such groups nevertheless make their decisions by consensus, and the leaders mainly facilitate the decisions made by their groups. This is a universal tendency, and a very strong one, among small-scale societies (see Service 1962 and 1975).

The fact that egalitarian ideology and consensual decision making appear to be universal in small-scale societies requires further exploration by anthropologists. But enough is known at present to suggest that humans at this level of social scale have transcended the social-dominance hierarchy arrangements of other animals. This has not taken place through total loss of genetically controlled tendencies toward individual dominance. Rather, these tendencies have become flexible enough so that a group belief in the equality of adult males can channel them into a very different and far-less-hierarchical mode of social life.

Thus, human beings are the only animals in which entire collectivities arrive at rather definitive ideas about how they would like to arrange their political life and, to a considerable degree, are able to do so. The result, in our evolution up to the level of strong chiefdoms or kingdoms, has been a primary social group that behaves as a moral community and consensually takes stands about how much individual social dominance the members will tolerate. Individual behaviors are judged not only against an idealized egalitarian blueprint (e.g., "every adult is equal") but also against a far-more-realistic blueprint (e.g., "adults are superior to children"; "men are superior to women"; or "all men are equal insofar as no man may coerce another beyond a certain point for his own selfish purposes"). The widespread distribution of such blueprints throughout the world's smaller-scale societies poses a fascinating puzzle that anthropologists have not yet solved in its entirety.

DOMINANCE BETWEEN GROUPS

Let us now return to ethology, to make a brief examination of nonhuman primates and, more particularly, the higher primates that (1) exhibit strong social-dominance tendencies and live in cohesive groups; (2) tend to attach themselves to specific pieces of real estate; and (3) tend to defend from attacks by conspecific groups at least parts of the real estate that they use.

The best examples would seem to be rhesus monkeys and chimpanzees. Rhesus groups sometimes engage in bluffing behavior—and sometimes in rather serious skirmishing—when they meet along the peripheries where the ranges that both groups use overlap (Southwick et al. 1974). It seems likely that the use of territory is regulated by such behavior and by the anticipation of such conflicts. In a sense, this is a higher-level instance of social-dominance behavior, one that seems to establish at least crude boundaries between groups rather than individuals. It would appear that these boundaries sometimes remain in equilibrium but sometimes change, as a result of demographic changes that affect the relative size of groups or as a result of population pressure on available resources.

Among chimpanzees, Goodall (1979) has documented systematic behavior in which closely bonded males patrol the borders of the territory that their group uses. Where they meet with members of other groups, attacks may take place in which individuals may be severely wounded or killed and because of which one group may eventually take over the territory of another. Similar behavior is reported by Japanese ethologists studying chimpanzees elsewhere than at Gombe.[1]

One might build an idealized picture from this, to suggest that over the very long run in a large region inhabited by macaques or chimpanzees, there will be a constant shifting of group territories because of changing population pressure on available resources, based on such factors as changes in health conditions or predator pressures, changes in leadership that affect aggressive maintenance of territorial boundaries, the breaking up of larger groups into small ones, and so forth.

With respect to dominance among groups, something similar prevails in the tribal systems of human beings. But again there is an important difference which results from a combination of human cultural flexibility and our ability to size up and manipulate complex social and political situations. Tribal territorial segments do sometimes go to war, in a way that is far more concerted even than among chimpanzee groups. Indeed, in a single day, tribesmen may drive away an enemy group and take over its territory as a carefully planned activity (e.g., Meggitt 1977). But tribal boundaries often are highly stable, and even where natural resources are relatively scarce, as in Montenegro, such territorial conflict seems to take place quite infrequently. This is because the groups tend to balance power among themselves in such a way that attacks simply do not seem profitable.

This equilibrium among groups is different from the equilibrium that an egalitarian life style promotes among human individuals within the group: that is, it does not result from various tribal segments deciding that they should all be equal and then collectively sanctioning such an ideal. In this case it is not an egalitarian ethic in operation but a sophisticated practical human political capacity to balance power. This creates equilibrium in the face of strong tendencies favoring selfish dominance at the group level. The mechanism is simple: because tribesmen are able to anticipate the land grabbing of more powerful groups, this enables smaller groups to combine in defensive alliances. As a result, political power is balanced well enough to permit the stable division and use of territories by well-defined groups, in the absence of frequent territorial attacks.

Such an alliance may be between segments that see themselves as separate units, or it may involve the fusion of several originally different units into a single permanent unit. The latter obviously took place with the Kuči tribe in Montenegro, in which the majority of the tribesmen were Eastern Orthodox Serbs but in which a smaller segment was Albanian Catholic and one very small segment was Albanian Moslem (Erdeljanović 1926). On the other hand, in the Brda District, Upper Morača and Rovca habitually came to each other's defense, even though these two relatively small tribes always remained politically separate (Vlahović 1939).

Thus, the human capacity to grasp the larger dynamics of political life has enabled tribesmen to transcend the modes of regulating social dominance that have been arrived at by other animals, both at individual and at group levels. Indeed, I have shown that in the absence of forceful superordinate political control, such as that possessed by alpha-male rhesus monkeys or human kings, all people who live in small-scale societies have created very similar political-problem solutions that regulate dominant self-assertiveness among individuals and groups respectively. These systems of regulation are not "perfect" in terms of some idealized model of social harmony. In any group there are always individual conflicts and at least occasional homicides; and between competing groups there are sometimes homicidal attacks aimed at territorial dispossession. But even among the Mae Enga, where such attacks were quite frequent, their area remained very well populated because violence was carefully limited.

When it comes to serious attacks on other groups, small-scale societies sometimes seem to make little effort to control the effects of such warfare. However, within moral communities, some attempt to mediate conflicts is always made by third parties, particularly when one party to the conflict cannot readily solve the problem by removing to another locale. Many higher primates evidence similar third-party behavior in the form of interference in conflicts, and with some, it appears that a fairly high degree of sophistication in solving problems is operative (Boehm 1981). But other primates do not enter into long-term feuds between groups. Human beings are the ones who seem to have the long memories in matters of hostility.

This provides a broader social and political context in which systems of blood feuding have come into being in the smaller-scale societies in which they seem to flourish. Given our understanding of feuding in Montenegro, the fit with this larger perspective from natural history is not difficult to make, but it requires that we take a fresh look at the expression and limitation of conflict.

THE ROLE OF RULES IN REGULATING POLITICAL BEHAVIOR

I have shown that an ethological perspective can be useful in looking at human behavior if one keeps in mind the fact that individual human inclinations toward dominant self-assertion are relatively very flexible and that within the group, maladaptive effects of dominance behavior are far more often controlled by long-term avoidance or by cultural controls than by gestures of submission that defuse aggression. When conflicts arise between groups of human beings, there are two major differences from other, similar primates. First, humans can self-consciously organize expeditions for all-out genocidal attacks on other groups; but second, they also can defensively balance power against such attacks.

Thus, within the group, by allowing more-assertive individuals to act usefully as leaders, human beings have coped with problems arising out of tendencies of individuals to dominate; but simultaneously they have set sharp limits on the dominance of leaders and of other strong males over members of the group. This is essentially a solution of social control, arrived at by a moral community. On the other hand, when a problem of dominance arises between groups, this is handled by the balancing of power, a purely practical political solution that is not based on moral consensus among groups. It is a fascinating fact of political life in small-scale societies that such problem solving has taken the same direction so uniformly all over the world.

In kingdoms and states, of course, the picture is very different with respect to the regulation of dominance within the society. There, political centralization puts coercive force in the hands of leaders, and leaders are the ones who legitimately control (or permit) the expression of dominance among the rank and file by means of police officers and courts. This is the antithesis of band or tribal policies, where egalitarian reluctance to place such power in the hands of leaders prevails so strongly. However, when it comes to external relations between states or kingdoms and other states or kingdoms, the dependency upon balance-of-power equalization remains very similar to that occurring in small-scale societies.

DOMINANCE RELATIONS IN SEGMENTARY TRIBES

To understand how all of this relates to feuding in Montenegro, we must consider a rather special, intermediate type of society, labeled by Durkheim (1933) as "segmental" and by Evans-Pritchard (1940) and others (e.g., Bohannan 1954) as "segmentary." In such a society, there is not just a large group of totally separate territorial units, spread out on the ground and held in place by an alliance-based balance of power. Rather, there are large territorial groups and also sizable subgroups within these larger groups. In Montenegro the tribe was the largest permanently unified territorial unit, while a number of clans made up a tribe, and a number of households made up a clan. It was the clans, as we have seen, that were the important subgroups in feuding.

In one sense a traditional Montenegrin tribe was like a very large egalitarian band. Everyone tended to know everyone else, power in leadership was strictly limited, and the entire group looked after its territory collectively. But in another sense it was like a collection of different bands, all consolidated into one single political territorial unit, the tribe, because of the need for balancing power at that level against powerful external predators. These included not only large empires but also other collections of clans that had unified into territorial tribes. The question that remains is whether the different clans within a tribe would tend to fight one another, as different tribes did, and therefore would need to balance power to prevent this, or whether they would be morally regulated so that their tendencies toward dominance would remain in check and they would behave like members of the same community.

In quieter times, the clans in a Montenegrin tribe did tend to exist in an egalitarian mode because there was no serious basis for territorial conflict. The household, of course, owned the winter homestead, while the entire tribe owned the summer pastures. But the tribe, in any event, would not have permitted the cold-blooded grabbing of land by its constituent clans. Furthermore, there was the egalitarian ethic, which prevented the more-powerful clans from dominating political life beyond a certain point, even though they tended to supply the tribal leaders.

This means that there was no good reason for clans within a tribe to duplicate the very thorough balance-of-power arrangements for making alliances, which were arrived at by the various tribes. Instead, during quieter times, the clans would channel their tendencies to be dominant in the same way that individual males did: they competed for heroic prestige. However, in times of interclan conflict they behaved like the fraternal interest groups that they were: they backed their own members through thick and thin.

In a sense, the political solidarity of a tribe was precarious. The clans, especially the larger ones, were formidable fighting machines. In theory, they were all members of the same community and should never fight. For that reason, they were not arranged in a tight balance-of-power pattern. On the other hand, warriors like the Montenegrins who belonged to domination-conscious fraternal interest groups did not take kindly to having their members killed by rival groups. It was at this juncture that the feuding system came into play.

Given this perspective, feuding is tailored to the needs of the tribe as a self-consciously defensive territorial unit embedded in a potentially precarious balance-of-power political equilibrium. Montenegrin rules on feuding very directly reflected such concerns. For example, when an interclan killing would create conflict between a very powerful clan and a very weak one, it did the tribe no great harm for the weaker clan to be driven out, because the loss of manpower would be minimal and the conflict would be resolved instantly. Furthermore, even if the smaller clan should decide to resist an all-out attack, the outcome would be arrived at quickly and with little general disruption. In borderline cases where clan sizes were closer to equal, the time limit on such sieges would prevent the tribe from becoming vulnerable to external predators.

Where clan size approached being equal, and particularly if both clans were quite large, a clear danger existed that if there were an all-out conflict between them, many of the tribe's warriors might become casualties. That posed the obvious threat of weakening the tribe suddenly both in political unity and in fighting power. It was in such cases that an alternating "one homicide at a time" system worked very well, whenever third-party mediation, combined with strong community pressure, could not quickly resolve the issue. This alternation of offensive and defensive modes kept the conflict at a low-enough level that a truce usually could be employed to quickly reunify the tribe in case of external attack.

Feuding rules were developed intensively within the tribe to reduce unwanted social disruption and to keep the tribe in a good competitive position. But these rules also applied to homicidal conflicts between tribes, in which two tribes saw significant advantages in avoiding deeper conflicts. This means that feuding rules were not limited to conflicts within a single moral community. They also provided competing communities with a way of minimizing several kinds of damage that an intertribal homicide could create. One was the damage to an intertribal political alliance, if such existed. Another was the danger of becoming preoccupied with the conflict to the point that other groups might quickly move in and grab territory from both groups. Furthermore, tribal strength could be decimated if intensive fighting broke out, while even feuding would partially damage cooperation as well as siphon off energy. Warrior tribesmen do not necessarily thrive on conflict; on the contrary, they appreciate the lasting social and economic ties between tribes, which intensive warfare destroys but which often may coexist with feuding.

Thus, feuding within a tribe was very much controlled by closely sanctioned moral rules within the tribal moral community, and the same (or similar) rules could be applied to regulating homicidal conflicts between such communities as well. However, the more distant the two communities in terms of social or political bonding or economic reciprocation, the smaller was the role of community pressure and the greater was the role of political self-interest in motivating adherence to the same set of rules.

This means that as conflicts in Montenegro became more socially or spatially distant, two things changed. First, the predictable immediate disruption caused by the conflict diminished, and second, control of the conflict was determined less by moral pressure and more by practical considerations that inhibited escalation. It also appears that if the feuding parties were very far apart, they might follow the available rules less precisely: in some cases it appears that scores were not kept carefully, and possibly even that rules for alternating offense and defense were ignored.

CONCLUSIONS

To return to the social-equilibrium mechanisms that are found among other primates that are highly disposed toward expressing individual dominance, it appears that hierarchy and strong leadership are characteristic of such systems. It also would appear that among human beings, similar, but far less genetically precise, tendencies toward selfish self-assertion over others are put to uses that result in very different kinds of social arrangements, at least until the level of kingdoms and states is reached. (At that point, we sometimes come to resemble rather closely the macaque monkeys, with their very dominant leaders.)

Being by nature self-assertive in the face of competition and being quite capable of committing homicide, human beings fortunately are also capable of diagnosing their own social and political dynamics. The combination of all these factors is what has enabled our species to invent and to fine tune systems of feuding such as that of the traditional Montenegrins.

The behavior of clan members involved in a Montenegrin feud is interesting, if one considers two factors simultaneously. One is the strong urge to establish dominance over the other clan in a contest in which clan rivalry is played out on the ultimate public stage, that of tribal life. The other is the interest of the clan not only to avoid open warfare, assuming that both clans are large and therefore very powerful, but also to avoid escalation of the feud to a point that it becomes more costly than honor really demands. I believe it was precisely this kind of caution that prompted Marko Miljanov's thoughtful heroes to pass over a tribal leader and merely kill his brother or son.

As we have seen, feuds between clans within the tribe seem to exhibit simultaneously both the "egalitarian" and the "balance-of-power" modes of dealing with tendencies to dominate. Insofar as feuding is all about honor and social pressure, it depends very much on the moral community for its regulation, as does the egalitarian ethos. Insofar as feuding is about calculations of political consequences that have nothing to do with ethics, it is more like the balance-of-power realpolitik problem solving that takes place between tribes. Of course, when a feud involves two clans of different tribes, the motives for avoiding escalation rest more—or perhaps exclusively—with practicality.

Given the great range of feuding patterns in the world and given the uniformity of the background features I have outlined—innate human tendencies to dominate, egalitarian approaches to political life within the group, and balance-of-power approaches to solving external political problems—it is not illogical that feuding would tend to arise wherever groups regularly came into contact in situations where avoidance could not easily resolve intergroup conflicts. This is particularly the case where intensive warfare is present and where fraternal interest groups have arisen. Within such societies it is predictable that the closer the degree of friendship and cooperation and the tighter the moral community, the more thoroughly the tendencies to feud will be suppressed.

It is well known that human tendencies to self-assertion and social dominance rather easily result in warfare, and our species is sometimes judged harshly in this light. But we must also be judged for our capacity to control such proclivities. In this light, the Montenegrins and their confrères all over the world have managed very well in creating systems of feuding that prevent the very fabric of society from being torn apart.

13

A Final Word on the Blood Feud in Montenegro

When one chooses to think about systems in making a social analysis, a serious problem may arise. This is the natural tendency on the part of an analyst to see the mechanical systems that he has created in his own mind as being the agents that actually cause patterns of behavior. It is easy to all but forget about the individual actors on the social stage, whose insights and purposive actions contribute so much to the pattern of social life.

In this book, I have tried to give both people and systems their due, as causative agents and as explanatory devices. In the attempt, I have decided that the Montenegrins were capable of some rather-sophisticated systems-analysis of their own, in certain areas upon which they focused. In fact, their assessments have guided some of my own. This means that a significant portion of the analysis that I have written is based upon astute social appraisals, sometimes made intuitively and sometimes made very explicitly, by nonliterate Montenegrins living well over a century ago. By analyzing the group and individual decisions that contributed to the overall pattern of blood feuding, I have tried to make the thoughtful human contribution to this system of violent behavior more apparent to the reader.

For the benefit of those who are not trained in anthropology, I have emphasized the need to set aside views or prejudices held by ourselves as members of societies that do not permit feuding. My purpose has been to enhance a better appreciation of the fact that systems of feuding are really not so wild and uncontrolled as they may have appeared to people such as the foreign travelers who visited traditional Montenegro. However, setting aside one's cultural prejudices is only the first step. One must then strive actively to understand the phenomenon of feuding from the perspective of native actors. Once the indigenous perspective has been made clear, the anthropologist must try to make some broader sense of his or her data by comparison with other cultures or through explanations that use external theoretical interpretations. My intention is that this book be effective, in making it easier for the reader to reach this basic state of anthropological comprehension. In that state, one never really "becomes" a native; but one does consciously try to appreciate the natives' view of the world, in spite of a continuing personal awareness of deeply ingrained differences between one's own orientation and the exotic one.

I began by trying to portray feuding effectively as Montenegrins saw it: simultaneously honorable and morally necessary but socially and economically disruptive. Later, as an outside analyst, I took a different perspective, to maintain that feuding was, at one and the same time, socially disruptive but also socially integrative in several very important ways, particularly as a practical alternative to warfare at close quarters. As I have said already, there is no absolutely definitive evidence that Montenegrins perceived their feuding in these ways. Nor is there any proof that they did not recognize some of these functions, which may have been too obvious to them to deserve mention. Unfortunately, I cannot reverse the passage of time so that I can investigate these questions directly. But it is greatly to the credit of the abler tribesmen that they did understand their feuding system well enough to make it work under most dangerous circumstances and to reshape it as needed, so that they could continue to survive as free men and women in their refuge area.

The final judgment as to how well a social institution works lies neither with the natives nor with outside analysts who try to understand and explain native social life. Rather, this is decided in the grand arena of social and biological evolution. The Montenegrins seem to have survived very nicely, even during several centuries when the power of the Ottoman Empire was at its peak and tribal autonomy was most endangered. Other tribes in the same region gave up their religion, their economic independence, and sometimes even their tribal political and social organization itself in submitting to the Turks. All of these submissive groups continued to feud, but the divisive effects of feuding did not place them in any ultimate danger, because after the fifteenth century few of them ever antagonized a mighty empire to the point that genocidal military expeditions were mounted against them.

The Montenegrin tribesmen, sometimes along with a few of the Catholic Albanian tribes, consciously selected a different adaptive course for themselves. Knowing that they faced risks of biological decimation or even extinction, they time and time again chose not to submit. They accepted some very heavy losses, but they gloried in their own triumphs against a formidable and predatory enemy. This risky course was open to them only if they were able to keep their feuding reasonably well under control. When political and military unity became crucial to biological or political survival, apparently they were able to join forces and to fight together effectively against their enemies, the Turks, if that seemed to them to be the right decision.

As an excellent example of a tribal feuding society, the Montenegrins provide us with an understanding both of the stress that results from living under continual threat of homicide from ambush and of the code of honor that makes people accept such disruption as necessary. But also they have shown us how creative the human imagination can be and, in particular, how adept our species can be at solving its social and ecological problems. In choosing to coexist with blood vengeance rather than unrealistically trying to suppress it totally, the Montenegrins, over a long period of time, fashioned a truly intricate system of symbols, rules, sanctions, institutions, and rituals. These enabled them to maintain the predictability of social behavior that is necessary when large numbers of people must live at relatively close quarters. I have stressed the view that such a tradition is not merely a cultural "habit" to which people become passively conditioned, because anthropologists sometimes inadvertently create this impression when they reify systems of behavior that are governed by tradition in order to publish about them. Rather, Montenegrin feuding constituted an ongoing feat of social engineering. This problem-solving activity required almost as astute an understanding of the overall situation on the parts of those who continued to make it work as it had on the parts of the gifted problem solvers who had had a hand in its (surely) gradual development in the first place.

Anthropologists sincerely try to give to the nonliterate people whom they study the credit for thinking and making decisions. But I follow Firth (1951) in believing that the static structural nature of our descriptive and theoretical approaches often tends to make us blind to the force that decisions exert in maintaining and continually reshaping social life. In this book I have gone out of my way to share with the reader a concern that fuller credit be given to native actors as inventors of culture and as thoughtful contributors to its ongoing pattern.

In describing Montenegrin feuding, I have paid nearly as much attention to ideas as to concrete behaviors. In anthropology, cognitive approaches often are highly structural and static, but I have concentrated instead upon decisions and the processes in which they are embedded. One reason for taking such an approach is that I believe this will improve the state of ethnography. For this reason I have emphasized the cognitive side of feuding in offering a definition of this activity. But a second motive has been to highlight active contributions, made both by ordinary Montenegrins and by their tribal leaders, to the enterprise of maintaining and reshaping the moral rules that guided their social and political life.

My hope is that the moral probity, intelligence, and civility of the Montenegrins have shone forth in this book, just as they struck me personally when I first journeyed to live among this proud, fierce, and quite-unusual European tribal people. This favorable impression of present-day tribesmen was further reinforced later, when I delved deeply into their necessarily violent past. As traditional warriors determined to stay freer than any of their Christian neighbors, the Montenegrins accepted their own violent style of life, not with rejoicing, but with resignation, with dignity, and above all, with imagination.

EPILOGUE

As of 1984 the Montenegrins have lived without war for the unprecedented time span of thirty-eight years. For over a century they have lived all but free from feuding. In the absence of these violent activities, they have turned their aggressive energies to forms of accomplishment other than the ones that must preoccupy warriors. Indeed, Montenegrins, considering their relatively small number and their slim economic means, are surely the most accomplished people in Yugoslavia today. They have turned to higher education as a different arena in which to compete and succeed, and they are active not only in higher levels of government but also in the arts and sciences. Most Montenegrins, including many well-educated people who no longer live in tribes, still feel that blood feuding, motivated by honor, was an important and morally necessary part of their past. But they do not really expect other Europeans or Americans to understand this. My hope is that this book will make that noble, heroic, and highly moral past more comprehensible to a world that has never known the violence of feuding.

Notes

CHAPTER 1   INTRODUCTION

1. The gusle (f. pl.) is a single-stringed bowed instrument with a skin head, which is used to accompany the chanting of heroic-epic songs.

CHAPTER 2   DOING RESEARCH ON EUROPEAN TRIBESMEN

1. As I mentioned in the Note on the Serbo-Croatian Language, the official designation is Serbo-Croation, and this designation is followed by educated Yugoslavs. Insofar as this book deals with the period before the political unification of the Serbian and Croatian peoples, I have followed local rural usage as this persisted during the 1960s.

2. I follow Montenegrin local usage in referring to Balkan Moslems as Turks. The great majority of these people were either Serbs who had Islamized during the fifteenth century or Albanian tribesmen who had Islamized somewhat later, all of whom served as subjects of the Ottoman sultan in Istanbul. In this capacity they acted as administrators in Christian areas under Ottoman domination and, when needed, supplied units for Ottoman military campaigns. It was usually these soldiers, along with Christian conscripts, who mounted campaigns against Montenegrin tribes or against the Montenegrin tribal confederation.

CHAPTER 4   THE MEANING OF OSVETA

1. Dictionary definitions of feuding will be cited later in the book. A more-extensive definition is available in *The Encyclopaedia Britannica* under "Blood feud" (1971:803) and under "Vendetta" (1971:944–45). The latter definition is based in part on Otterbein and Otterbein (1965), a work that is also relied upon in the present book.

2. Recently, the issue of personal biases of anthropologists has received wide and largely unfavorable publicity, which is largely undeserved. While anthropologists are necessarily human beings who have biases, normal methods of fieldwork (participant observation) go far in correcting for such biases, particularly if the native language is mastered to the point that ordinary conversation can be understood. Elsewhere (Boehm 1972, 1980) I have discussed the use of natural or "folk" definitions as a means of reducing observers' biases beyond the levels normally attained in doing fieldwork.

3. In cases where subjects are deceased or are very obviously identifiable, I have used their actual names.

4. See also Bogišić (1874) and Jelić (1926).

CHAPTER 5   THE MORAL LEGITIMACY OF FEUDING

1. In *Montenegrin Social Organization and Values,* to provide a general ethnographic description, I have synthesized the historical sources in French and English for traditional Montenegro. Those include a chapter on military activities, which briefly treats feuding (see Boehm 1983).

CHAPTER 6   THE TRAJECTORY OF A FEUD

1. On a distant continent, the Jivaro Indians of Ecuador also practiced feuding, raiding, and warfare. Among them, as among Montenegrins, the taking of heads normally was reserved for warfare or raiding, while such an insult was avoided in blood feuds (Karsten 1935).

2. Jelić (1926) gives an example of how, it was hoped, such generalized attacks would be pacified by means of a ritual involving stones. This pacification procedure was much less elaborate than the one used to pacify feuds, and no strict scorekeeping or final settlement was involved.

3. I shall use the masculine pronoun when discussing the actors in feuds, because these actors almost always were men. The exceptions were women in a special status *(baša)* who became men in the sense that they adopted men's clothing and bore arms and were counted indigenously as men, and also, if rarely, other women who decided to take vengeance because the appropriate men were unavailable or, possibly, reluctant. See also Škerović (1929).

4. This account comes from Grbalj, a small coastal plain near Kotor, which was culturally Montenegrin but remained under Venetian and Austrian protectorates throughout the Ottoman period. For all practical purposes, the people of Grbalj may be likened to a Montenegrin tribe, insofar as they dealt with their own internal problems. However, the foreign authorities under whose jurisdiction they lived provided them with written pacification documents, in the hope of better resolving feuds.

5. Durham (1928) uses the term *"bratstvo,"* which is preferred in literary treatments, whereas I have used the indigenous equivalent—*"brastvo."*

6. While northern Albanian and Montenegrin feuding patterns are very similar, Jelić (1926) points out that when Montenegrins destroyed an enemy's house and other property at the beginning of a feud, this had to be paid for when the total material and blood damages were tallied up at the time of pacification. By contrast, Albanians had a free license to destroy such property if this was done at the proper time and in the proper manner.

7. I have not found anywhere a single definitive account of such attacks and their place in Montenegrin feuding. Jelić (1926) gives the best information, including an account of how women actively helped during nighttime sieges by carrying firebrands. The accounts for northern Albania are far more complete (see Hasluck 1954); but because this particular aspect of feuding was not uniform between the two regions (Jelić 1926), I have not relied very heavily on Hasluck's report. For other accounts of attacks made on property in the context of feuding, or of attacks made on one clan by another, see Dragičević (1935), Simić (1967), and Tomasić (1958). The first account by a foreigner of such behavior is that of the Austrian Colonel Paulich, who visited Montenegro in the latter part of the eighteenth century (see Djordjević 1912; Vuksan 1939, 1951).

8. In Albania, during a circumscribed period early in a feud, the avengers could kill anyone in the enemy clan if the feud was within the tribe, and anyone in the enemy tribe if the enemy clan was of another tribe (Jelić 1926).

9. Jovanović (1948) tells how two Brda tribes were at feud, and when the Turks came to attack both of them, they refused to cooperate. It was only after the victorious Turks had captured many women and children from both tribes and were leading them away to sell them into slavery that the two tribes agreed to a truce and set out to save their captured noncombatants.

10. At times, Jelić (1926) seems to disagree, portraying blood feud killings in certain contexts as duels in which the enemy is given a chance to defend himself. The available case histories indicate the contrary, although in oral tradition I have heard it said that the avenger may make a speech informing his victim who he is and why he is killing him. This usually happens when the victim does not know the avenger personally.

11. This account is based on Hasluck (1954), who devotes an entire chapter to the law of the dog. There is no definitive evidence that exactly the same rules prevailed in Montenegro.

12. With respect to this case, it is of interest that my friend had served his time in America, paying his debt to society for the killing. But his victim's brother did not take that into account as settling the personal debt. Jelić (1926) makes two interesting points that are relevant. One is that even execution of a killer by the Montenegrin government in its earlier days did not diminish the obligation to take personal vengeance. The second is that a judge who decreed execution could be held liable for krvna osveta.

13. Bishop Danilo used Russian foriegn aid, when he first received it very early in the eighteenth century, to set up courts composed of specialists who were to pacify feuds, as did his successor, Bishop Vasilije. The egalitarian tribesmen quite properly sensed that there were designs on their local autonomy and therefore resisted. Stephen the Small, as a charismatic leader who had special coercive powers that were not available to bishops, was able to make such a court work for the few years during the mid 1700s when his rule was effective. Bishop Petar, half a century later, created Old Montenegro's first laws (in 1796) and also the *"kuluk,"* a kind of blood-feud court. But both were virtually ignored (see Dragičević 1935; Jovanivić 1948), and it was only Bishop Rade, late in his career, who managed to interfere definitively with feuds in certain tribes (Djilas 1966). Jovanović (1948) has dealt with all of these developments in some detail. For a modern Yugoslav experiment that uses similar councils to control feuds among Albanians in Kosovo see Karan (1974).

14. Bishop Petar's missives are available in published form (Vuković 1971); but readers who are familiar with Serbo-Croatian should also consult Dragičević (1935), who discusses specifically this bishop's efforts to pacify krvna osveta.

CHAPTER 7   THE END GAME: MANAGEMENT OF CONFLICT

1. This expression was still current during the 1960s and was being used by Montenegrins of both sexes.

2. This theme is prominent in many of Bishop Petar Petrović's proclamations, in which he exhorts the tribesmen to settle their feuds (see Vuković 1971).

3. The document is available in Nikčević and Pavičević (1964:72).

4. Jelić (1926) has included a number of such documents in an appendix to his book.

CHAPTER 8   THE IMPORTANCE OF DECISIONS

1. There was also the need to placate the soul of the person who had been killed. Our information is so incomplete as to the precise nature and strength of this belief that I do not treat it as a major motive in homicidal retaliation. But its importance in motivating krvna osveta may have been greater than it would appear from this treatment.

2. In very bitter feuds, certain Albanian tribes seemed to condone the killing of women (Jelić 1926). In Montenegro, this was only possible if a woman had fully entered the male role as a baša.

3. In the Grbalj case, young Miloš obviously miscalculated his chances of being killed, or else he could have left the community for a time. Thus, it would appear that ruining someone's daughter was merely very risky, rather than being a certain cause for lethal retaliation.

4. As a sidelight to the feuding system, it is of interest that a clan sometimes repudiated one of its own members (Bogišić 1874; Rovinskii 1901). Such ostracism followed a pattern that is widespread in feuding societies (Moore 1972), in that wherever clans are corporately liable to homicidal retaliation for aggressive acts done by their members, a man who proves to be an incorrigible troublemaker often is either killed by fellow clansmen or else is repudiated by the clan so that if he is killed, the clan will not have to take vengeance. This status of ostracism, or being *odličen,* figures in pacifications documented in Jelić (1926).

5. I refer here to classic game theory in which a zero sum game is one that one player or the other must lose (see Rapoport 1964). My point is that since feuding is really about honor and dominance, both sides feel as though they are losing. One clan has the lower score, while the other clan must humiliate itself in the pacification ceremony and considers that, in any event, it is more honorable to continue the feud.

6. Kiefer (1970) has made good use of a decision-making approach in explaining what he calls "private warfare" among the Tausug. See also Meggitt (1977).

CHAPTER 9   MAKING FURTHER SENSE OF THE FEUD

1. In my field notes there are three cases of Montenegrins' taking revenge a century or more after the original unavenged killing. It is to be emphasized that these were cases in which smaller clans were forced to flee, not cases of feuds that had been pacified. I was told personally of one such case in which the members of the smaller clan had relocated in the early 1800s and felt so keenly the affront over being forced out of the tribe that in the late 1930s their few males, over a century later, attempted to kill every adult male in the much-larger clan with a single attack and did succeed in killing

seventeen of them. This story was recounted by the son of one of the attackers. I think that it is reliable factually, even though I had no opportunity to cross-check it because it did not happen in Morača. But such an incident cannot necessarily be generalized to the traditional period. It seems more like the attack made on the Djilasi by Prince Nicholas's agents, in which they tried to kill every male so as to preclude future feuding. The cultural premises, therefore, are quite different from feuding during the traditional period, even though the long-term preoccupation with vengeance is similar.

CHAPTER 10   FEUDING IN THE NONLITERATE WORLD

1. Obviously, if only males are killed and if widows generally remarry, rates of natural increase will be little affected. However, the effects of warfare upon nutrition and health affected all Montenegrins, while the Turks captured women for wives and took noncombatants generally as slaves.

2. Coon (1950), relying on verbal accounts of informants, reports that there were more than 50 percent more males than females born in northern Albania. Divale (1970) has discussed sex ratios and warfare for a large sample of tribal societies that practice warfare, and he demonstrates that young males tend to exceed young females quite substantially, while among adults this proportion is reduced, and sometimes there are fewer adult males than adult females. Divale believes that female infanticide and relative neglect of young females creates the initially lopsided ratios, while warfare brings them back into balance. He points out that infanticide is usually hidden from anthropologists, but he believes that this is what creates the strong male bias in birth ratios. Coon's (1950) data show that among the Albanians whom he surveyed, a strong male bias appears to operate at birth; and ethnographic evidence indicates that northern Albanians treasured female children because of the large price that a bride brought (Hasluck 1954), making female infanticide unlikely. In Montenegro, the only reports of infanticide are by unwed mothers trying to avoid shame. But given the strong Montenegrin bias in favor of sons over daughters (see Boehm 1983), Divale's (1970) hypothesis that traditionally, relative neglect of female children could have tended to even out the sex ratio after birth seems likely. However, an equally plausible hypothesis is that in both Albania (see Coon 1950) and Montenegro, it was a biological rather than a cultural mechanism that adjusted the male birth ratio upwards to fit with a pattern of feuding and warfare.

3. According to the *New York Times* report on feuding by Albanians, one man was killed when he sought to tend his vineyards. This may have meant that the besieged clan was suffering a general shortage of labor, or it may have meant that no one else had the particular expertise that was needed. In either case, however, one may assume that the feud was doing economic damage.

CHAPTER 11   FEUDING AND ECOLOGY: THE QUESTION OF
                COSTS AND GAINS

1. This idea has been shared previously with academic colleagues in unpublished form, first as a presentation in 1975 to the Chicago Anthropological Society ("The Place of Blood Feud in Moral Systems") and subsequently as a presentation in 1980 at the meetings of the Southwestern Anthropological Association in San Diego ("Blood Feud Interpreted in the Light of Decision Theory"). A similar interpretation has been proposed by Service (1975) with respect to feuds that are converted into duels.

2. Some other sources on blood revenge or its legal implications are: Bohannan (1977), Dozier (1966), Glasse (1959), Hallpike (1977), Hardy (1963), Hoebel (1972), Koch (1974), Kopytoff (1961), Moore (1972), Reid (1970), and Schlegel (1970).

3. I have relabeled Mae Enga phratries as "tribes" to assist the reader in comparing the Montenegrin and Enga segmentary systems in their operation. Strictly speaking, a few Montenegrin tribes profess themselves to be phratries, in that they claim that all members of their major clans are descended from founders who were brothers. The majority of the tribes, however, make no such claims and openly acknowledge their composite nature.

CHAPTER 12   AN ETHOLOGICAL PERSPECTIVE ON FEUDING

1. Jane Goodall (personal communication). My understanding of chimpanzee territorial aggression was augmented by participation in a seminar held by Dr. Goodall at Northern Kentucky University in April 1983.

Bibliography

Balikci, Asen.
    1970 *The Netsilik Eskimo.* Garden City, N.Y.: Natural History Press, for the American Museum of Natural History.
Black, Donald
    1983 "Crime as Social Control." *American Sociological Review* 48:34–45.
Black-Michaud, Jacob.
    1975 *Cohesive Force: Feud in the Mediterranean and the Middle East.* New York: St. Martin's.
Boehm, Christopher.
    1972 "Montenegrin Ethical Values: An Experiment in Anthropological Method." Ph.D. diss., Harvard University.
    1978 "Rational Preselection from Hamadryas to *Homo Sapiens:* The Place of Decisions in Adaptive Process." *American Anthropologist* 80:265–96.
    1980 "Exposing the Moral Self in Montenegro: The Use of Natural Definitions to Keep Ethnography Descriptive." *American Ethnologist* 7:1–26.
    1981 "Parasitic Selection and Group Selection: A Study of Conflict Interference in Rhesus and Japanese Macaque Monkeys." In *Primate Behavior and Sociobiology,* edited by A. B. Chiarelli and R. S. Corruccini, pp. 161–82. Berlin, Heidelberg, and New York: Springer-Verlag.
    1983 *Montenegrin Social Organization and Values: Political Ethnography of a Refuge Area Tribal Adaptation.* New York: AMS Press.
Bogišić, V.
    1874 *Gragja u Odgovorima iz Različnih Krajeva Slovenskoga Juga* (Data in the form of responses from various South Slavic regions). Zagreb: Župana.
Bohannan, Paul J.
    1954 "The Migration and Expansion of the Tiv." *Africa* 24:2–16.
    1977 "Anthropology and the Law." In *Horizons of Anthropology,* edited by Sol Tax and Leslie G. Freeman, pp. 290–99. 2d. ed. Chicago: Aldine.
Briggs, Jean L.
    1970 *Never in Anger: Portrait of an Eskimo Family.* Cambridge: Harvard University Press.

Colson, Elizabeth.
    1953 "Social Control and Vengeance in Plateau Tonga Society." *Africa*
        23:199–212.
Coon, Carleton.
    1950 *The Mountains of Giants: A Racial and Cultural Study of the North Albanian
        Mountain Ghegs.* Cambridge, Mass.: Peabody Museum Papers, vol. 23, no.
        3.
Denton, William.
    1877 *Montenegro: Its People and Their History.* London: Daldy Isbister.
Divale, William T.
    1970 "An Explanation for Primitive Warfare: Population Control and the Signifi-
        cance of Primitive Sex Ratios." *New Scholar* 2:173–92.
Djilas, Milovan.
    1958 *Land without Justice.* New York: Harcourt Brace.
    1966 *Njegoš: Poet, Prince, Bishop.* New York: Harcourt, Brace & World.
Djordjević, Vladan.
    1912 *Crna Gora i Austrija u XVIII Veku* (Montenegro and Austria in the eighteenth
        century). Belgrade: Državna Štamparija Kraljevine Srbije.
Djurdjev, Branislav.
    1953 *Turska Vlast u Crnoj Gori u XVI i XVII Veku: Prilog Nerešenom Pitanju iz
        Naše Istorije* (Turkish rule in Montenegro in the sixteenth and seventeenth
        centuries: Analysis of an unresolved question in our history). Sarajevo:
        Svjetlost.
Dragičević, Risto.
    1935 "Mitropolit Petar I i Mirenje Krvne Osvete" (Bishop Peter I and the
        pacification of blood feuds). *Zapisi* (Cetinje) 5:275–60, 327–35.
Durham, Mary E.
    1928 *Some Tribal Origins, Laws and Customs of the Balkans.* London: George
        Allen & Unwin.
Durkheim, Émile.
    1933 *The Division of Labor in Society.* Translated by George Simpson. Glencoe,
        Ill.: Free Press.
Ehrich, Robert W.
    1946 "A Racial Analysis of Montenegro." Ph.D. diss., Harvard University.
Erdeljanović, Jovan.
    1926 *Stara Crna Gora: Etničke Prošlost i Formiranje Crnogorskih Plemena* (Old
        Montenegro: Ethnic past and formation of the Montenegrin tribes). Belgrade:
        Rodoljub.
Evans-Pritchard, E. E.
    1940 *The Nuer: A Description of the Modes of Livelihood and Political Institutions
        of a Nilotic People.* Oxford: Clarendon Press.
Firth, Raymond W.
    1951 *Elements of Social Organization.* London: Watts.
Gauthreaux, Sidney A., Jr.
    1978 "The Ecological Significance of Behavioral Dominance." In *Perspectives in
        Ethology,* vol. 3: *Social Behavior,* edited by P. P. G. Bateson, pp. 17–54. New
        York: Plenum Press.
Glasse, R. M.
    1959 "Revenge and Redress among the Huli: A Preliminary Account." *Mankind*
        5:273–89.

Gluckman, Max.
   1955 "The Peace in the Feud." In *Custom and Conflict in Africa,* by Max
      Gluckman, pp. 1–26. Glencoe, Ill.: Free Press.
Goodall, Jane.
   1979 "Life and Death at Gombe." *National Geographic* 155:592–622.
Hallpike, Christopher Robert.
   1977 *Bloodshed and Vengeance in the Papuan Mountains: The Generation of
      Conflict in Tauade Society.* Oxford: Clarendon Press.
Hammel, Eugene A.
   1968 *Alternative Social Structures and Ritual Relations in the Balkans.* Englewood
      Cliffs, N.J.: Prentice-Hall.
Hardy, M. J. L.
   1963 *Blood Feuds and the Payment of Blood Money in the Middle East.* Leiden:
      Brill.
Harner, Michael J.
   1973 *The Jívaro: People of the Sacred Waterfalls.* Garden City, N.Y.: Doubleday,
      Natural History Press, for the American Museum of Natural History.
Hasluck, Margaret M.
   1954 *The Unwritten Law in Albania.* Edited by J. H. Hutton. Cambridge: Cam-
      bridge University Press.
Haviland, John Beard.
   1977 *Gossip, Reputation, and Knowledge in Zinacantan.* Chicago: University of
      Chicago Press.
Hoebel, E. Adamson.
   1972 "Feud: Concept, Reality and Method in the Study of Primitive Law." In
      Essays on Modernization of Underdeveloped Societies, edited by A. R. Desai,
      vol. 1, pp. 500–513. Bombay: Thacker.
Jelić, Ilija M.
   1926 *Krvna Osveta i Umir u Crnoj Gori i Severnoj Albaniji* (Blood revenge and its
      pacification in Montenegro and northern Albania). Belgrade.
Jovanović, Jagoš.
   1948 *Stvaranje Crnogorske Države i Razvoj Crnogorske Nacionalnosti: Istorija
      Crne Gore od Početka VIII Vijeka do 1918 Godine* (Creation of a government
      in Montenegro and the development of Montenegrin nationality: The history
      of Montenegro from the beginning of the eighth century to 1918). Cetinje:
      Narodna Knjiga.
Karadžić, Vuk Stefanović.
   1922 *Crna Gora i Boka Kotorska* (Montenegro and the Bay of Kotor). Belgrade:
      Zastava.
   1935 *Srpski Rječnik* (Serbian dictionary). Belgrade: Royal Yugoslav Press.
Karan, Milenko.
   1973 "Krvna Osveta: 'Patološko' ili 'Normalno' Ponašanje?" (Blood feud: "Patho-
      logical" or "normal" behavior?). *Sociologija* 15:117–36.
   1974 "Rugovska Povelja: Dokument Samopravnog Sužbijanja Krvne Osvete u
      Kosovskom Selu" (The Rugovska Charter: An example of self-management
      control of vendetta in a village in Kosovo). *Sociologija Sela* 12:28–36.
Karsten, Rafael.
   1935 *The Head-Hunters of Western Amazonas: The Life and Culture of Jibaro
      Indians of Eastern Ecuador and Peru.* Helsingfors.

Kiefer, Thomas M.
　　1970 "Modes of Social Action in Armed Combat: Affect, Tradition and Reason in
　　　　Tausug Private Warfare." *Man,* n.s., 5:586–96.
Koch, Klaus-Friedrich.
　　1974 *The Anthropology of Warfare.* Reading, Mass.: Addison Wesley.
Kopytoff, Igor.
　　1961 "Extension of Conflict as a Method of Conflict Resolution among the Suku of
　　　　the Congo." *Journal of Conflict Resolution* 5:61–69.
Kovaljevski, E. H.
　　1935 "Dvoboji i Krvna Osveta" (Duels and blood revenge). *Zapisi* (Cetinje)
　　　　14:214–17.
Kroeber, Alfred L.
　　1948 *Anthropology: Race, Language, Culture, Psychology, Prehistory.* New ed.,
　　　　rev. New York: Harcourt Brace.
LeVine, Robert A., and Donald T. Campbell.
　　1972 *Ethnocentrism: Theories of Conflict, Ethnic Attitudes, and Group Behavior.*
　　　　New York: Wiley.
Lorenz, Konrad.
　　1966 *On Aggression.* New York: Bantam.
Medaković, B. M. G.
　　1860 *Život i Običaj Crnogoraca* (Life and customs of the Montenegrins). Novi Sad:
　　　　Brzotiskom Episkopske Knjigopečatnje.
Meggitt, Mervyn.
　　1977 *Blood Is Their Argument: Warfare among the Mae Enga Tribesmen of the New
　　　　Guinea Highlands.* Palo Alto, Calif.: Mayfield.
Middleton, John, and David Tait, eds.
　　1958 *Tribes without Rulers: Studies in African Segmentary Systems.* London:
　　　　Routledge & Kegan Paul.
Miljanov, Marko.
　　1901 *Primjeri Čojstva i Junaštva* (Examples of manly virtue and heroism).
　　　　Belgrade.
Milović, Jevto M.
　　1956 *Zbornik Dokumenata iz Istorije Crne Gore (1685–1782)* (Source book on
　　　　Montenegrin documents [1685–1782]). Cetinje: Obod.
Moore, Sally F.
　　1972 "Legal Liability and Evolutionary Interpretation: Some Aspects of Strict
　　　　Liability, Self-Help and Collective Responsibility." In *The Allocation of
　　　　Responsibility,* edited by Max Gluckman, pp. 51–107. Manchester, Eng.:
　　　　Manchester University Press.
Nadel, Siegfried Frederick.
　　1947 *The Nuba: An Anthropological Study of the Hill Tribes in Kordofan.* London:
　　　　Oxford University Press.
Nikčević, Tomica, and Branko Pavičević, eds.
　　1964 *Crnogorske Isprave xvi–xix Vijeka* (Montenegrin documents from the sixteenth
　　　　to the nineteenth century). Cetinje: Obod.
Otterbein, Keith F.
　　1968 "Internal War: A Cross-Cultural Study." *American Anthropologist* 70:
　　　　277–89.
　　1970 *The Evolution of War: A Cross-Cultural Study.* [New Haven, Conn.]: HRAF
　　　　Press.

_____, and Charlotte Swanson Otterbein.
    1965 "An Eye for an Eye, a Tooth for a Tooth: A Cross-Cultural Study of Feuding." *American Anthropologist* 67:1470–82.
Péristiany, Jean G., ed.
    1966 *Honour and Shame: The Values of Mediterranean Society.* Chicago: University of Chicago Press.
Peters, E. L.
    1967 "Some Structural Aspects of the Feud among the Camel-Herding Bedouin of Cyrenaica." *Africa* 37:261–82.
Piers, Gerhart, and Milton B. Singer.
    1971 *Shame and Guilt: A Psychoanalytic and a Cultural Study.* New York: Norton.
Radcliffe-Brown, A. R.
    1952 *Structure and Function in Primitive Society: Essays and Addresses.* Glencoe, Ill.: Free Press.
Ranke, Leopold von.
    1853 *The History of Servia, and the Servian Revolution.* Translated by Mrs. Alexander Kerr. London: Henry Bohn.
Rapoport, Anatol.
    1964 "Three Modes of Conflict." In *The Making of Decisions: A Reader in Administrative Behavior,* edited by William J. Gore and J. W. Dyson, pp. 393–402. New York: Free Press of Glencoe.
Reid, John Phillip.
    1970 *A Law of Blood: The Primitive Law of the Cherokee Nation.* New York: New York University Press.
Rovinskii, Pavle.
    1901 *Chrnogoriia v eia proshlom i nastoiashchem* (Montenegro in its past and present). Vol. 2, pt. 2. St. Petersburg: Printing Office of the Imperial Academy of Sciences.
Sahlins, Marshall D.
    1961 "The Segmentary Lineage: An Organization of Predatory Expansion." *American Anthropologist* 63:322–45.
    1968 *Tribesmen.* Englewood Cliffs, N.J.: Prentice-Hall.
Schjelderup-Ebbe, Thorleif.
    1935 "Social Behavior of Birds." In *A Handbook of Social Psychology,* edited by Carl Murchison. Worcester, Mass.: Clark University Press.
Schlegel, Stuart A.
    1970 *Tiruray Justice: Traditional Tiruray Law and Morality.* Berkeley: University of California Press.
Service, Elman R.
    1962 *Primitive Social Organization: An Evolutionary Perspective.* New York: Random House.
    1975 *Origin of the State and Civilization: The Process of Cultural Evolution.* New York: Norton.
Simić, Andrei.
    1967 "The Blood Feud in Montenegro." In *Essays in Balkan Ethnology.* Kroeber Anthropological Society Special Publications no. 1, pp. 83–94. Berkeley, Calif.
Škerović, Nikola.
    1929 "Crnogorka" (The Montenegrin woman). *Zapisi* (Cetinje), vol. 4, no. 5.

Southwick, Charles H., M. F. Siddiqi, M. Y. Farooqui, and B. C. Pal.
1974 "Xenophobia among Free-Ranging Rhesus Groups in India." In *Primate Aggression, Territoriality, and Xenophobia: A Comparative Perspective,* edited by Ralph L. Holloway, pp. 185–209. New York and London: Academic Press.

Stanojević, Gligor.
1955 *Crna Gora u Doba Vladike Danila* (Montenegro in the epoch of Bishop Danilo). Cetinje: Obod.

Steward, Julian Haynes.
1955 *Theory of Culture Change: The Methodology of Multilinear Evolution.* Urbana: University of Illinois Press.

Sweet, Louise E.
1970 "Camel Raiding of North Arabian Bedouin: A Mechanism of Ecological Adaptation." In *Peoples and Cultures of the Middle East,* vol. 1: *Cultural Depth and Diversity,* edited by Louise E. Sweet, pp. 265–89. Garden City, N.Y.: Natural History Press, for the American Museum of Natural History.

Thurnher, Majda.
1956 *A Survey of Balkan Houses and Farm Buildings.* Kroeber Anthropological Society Papers no. 14. Berkeley, Calif.

Tomasic, Dinko.
1948 *Personality and Culture in Eastern European Politics.* New York: George W. Stewart.

Turton, David.
1979 "War, Peace and Mursi Identity." In *Warfare among East African Herders,* edited by Katsuyoshi Fukui and David Turton, pp. 179–211. Osaka: National Museum of Ethnology.

Vialla de Sommières, L.
1820 *Voyage historique et politique au Montenegro. . . .* Paris: Alexis Eymery.

Vlahović, Vl.
1939 "Medjuplemenski Odnosi u Brdima" (Intertribal relations among the hill tribes), *Zapisi* (Cetinje).

Vrčević, Vuk.
1890 *Narodne Pripovijesti i Presude iz Života po Boki Kotorskoj, Hercegovini i Crnoj Gori* (Oral traditions and judgments from life in the Bay of Kotor, Hercegovina, and Montenegro). Dubrovnik: Dragutin Pretner.

Vuković, Čedo, comp.
1971 *Nadvremenski Glasovi* (Voices from the past). Titograd: Grafički Zavod.

Vuksan, Dušan.
1939 "Crna Gora u Doba Mladosti Mitropolita Petra I" (Montenegro in the era of the youth of Bishop Petar I). *Zapisi* (Cetinje) 21:5–34.
1951 *Petar I Petrović Njegoš i Njegova Doba* (Petar I Petrović Njegoš and his era). Cetinje: Narodna Knjiga.

Wilkinson, Sir John Gardner.
1848 *Dalmatia and Montenegro.* Vol. 1. London: John Murray.

Wyon, Reginald, and Gerald Prance.
1903 *The Land of the Black Mountain: The Adventures of Two Englishmen in Montenegro.* London: Methuen.

Index